Endorse
The Art o
Storytelling

'Political storytelling is one of the most persuasive forms of communication with voters. What is most chilling, however, is that it works even if the story isn't true. In this updated edition of his brilliant work, *The Art of Political Storytelling*, Philip Seargeant's insights help us come to terms with the perplexing, frightening, damnable, heartbreaking juggernaut of events that was 2020 … and likely beyond.'

LEE MCINTYRE, Author of *Post-Truth* and Research
Fellow, Center for Philosophy and History
of Science, Boston University, USA

'A brilliant deconstruction of propaganda and how it co-opts dramatic and narrative technique, throwing into doubt truth, fact and identity.'

IRISH TIMES

'Interesting and readable, this survey of the political storyteller's toolbox goes a long way to account for the recent successes of provocative populist leaders around the world and makes an enlightening guide to our current political moment … 4 stars.'

THE HERALD

'Everybody with at least a fleeting interest in politics *must* read this book.'

LSE REVIEW OF BOOKS

'Enlightening and entertaining, this book reveals how we have become actors in politicians' stories and how we can take back control of our own destinies.'

PETER POMERANTSEV, Senior Fellow, Institute of Global
Affairs, London School of Economics, UK and Research
Fellow, Johns Hopkins University, USA

The Art of
Political
Storytelling

ALSO AVAILABLE FROM BLOOMSBURY

Linguistic Inquiries into Donald Trump's Language,
edited by Ulrike Schneider and Matthias Eitelmann
More Wordcrime, John Olsson
Political English, Thomas Docherty
Political Metaphor Analysis, Andreas Musolff
The Language of Brexit, Steve Buckledee
The Political Samaritan, Nick Spencer

The Art of Political Storytelling

Why Stories Win Votes in Post-truth Politics

Philip Seargeant

BLOOMSBURY ACADEMIC
LONDON • NEW YORK • OXFORD • NEW DELHI • SYDNEY

BLOOMSBURY ACADEMIC
Bloomsbury Publishing Plc
50 Bedford Square, London, WC1B 3DP, UK
1385 Broadway, New York, NY 10018, USA
29 Earlsfort Terrace, Dublin 2, Ireland

BLOOMSBURY, BLOOMSBURY ACADEMIC and the Diana logo are trademarks of
Bloomsbury Publishing Plc

First published in Great Britain 2020
Paperback edition published 2022

Cover design by Ben Anslow
Images: Donald Trump © Spencer Platt / Getty Images, Letter X © Milan M / Shutterstock

A catalogue record for this book is available from the British Library.

A catalog record for this book is available from the Library of Congress.

ISBN: HB: 978-1-3501-0738-0
PB: 978-1-3502-6614-8
ePDF: 978-1-3501-0741-0
eBook: 978-1-3501-0740-3

Typeset by Deanta Global Publishing Services, Chennai, India
Printed and bound in Great Britain

To find out more about our authors and books visit www.bloomsbury.com and
sign up for our newsletters.

For Denisa,
who loves a long story

Contents

Part Four Fiction and reality 175

Acknowledgements

Many thanks to Dan Berlinka, Selina Packard, Alexandra Georgakopoulou, Korina Giaxoglou, Guy Cook, Frank Monaghan and Mark Pack for various ideas, insights and suggestions that were of great help in the development and writing of the book. Much thanks also to Andrew Wardell and his colleagues at Bloomsbury, as well as my agent Sandra Sawicka, for all their help in supporting and guiding the book from initial idea through to finished product.

Earlier versions of a number of short sections from the book have previously been published in the following places: 'The world's words of the year pass judgement on a dark, surreal 2016', *The Conversation*, 22 December 2016; 'Truthiness and alternative facts: Meaning is a moveable feast', *The Conversation*, 27 January 2017; 'Lies, damned lies, and executive orders: The power of words and the Trump presidency', *Diggit Magazine*, 17 February 2017; 'Is Donald Trump really giving a voice to the voiceless?' *The Huffington Post*, 17 March 2017; 'The obscure rhetorical technique that explains everything you need to know about post-truth politics', *The Huffington Post*, 30 May 2018.

Part One

Apocalyptic politics

1

Setting the scene

A hero of our time

This is the story of one man's mission to save the world from the forces of evil. To do battle against a corrupt and self-serving enemy bent on enslaving an innocent population. In order to achieve this, he has to venture deep into hostile territory, abandoning the comfortable existence he once had, and embark on a perilous, unforgiving journey. At each stage of this journey he's assailed by fierce and unscrupulous opponents. As he battles ever further into the heart of darkness, his allies, colleagues and even his friends begin to doubt his resolve. Some of them counsel him to abandon the mission. Others lose faith completely and end up siding with the enemy.

At his lowest ebb he faces a crisis which not only threatens the outcome of the quest but also puts his very existence in danger. Life itself is in the balance. But it's at this moment of utmost crisis that he's able to realize his true potential. This is when he looks deep within himself and discovers his true identity. Through self-belief, force of character and complete conviction in his cause he faces down the enemy in one final conflict. In doing so, he achieves the unachievable and wins a famous victory. In the closing scene he returns triumphant, not only in what he's accomplished personally but also in having saved the world from a cataclysmic future.

This is a classic story archetype. You could slot an almost endless array of scenarios into its structure and come up with the plots to umpteen Hollywood movies. The hero at its centre – usually male, but by no means exclusively – could be pulled unwittingly into an intergalactic conflict and have to do battle with a despotic imperial army. They could be fighting corruption at city hall, or battling a faceless, heartless insurance company. They could be called upon to protect the inhabitants of a small Western town against a marauding posse or to apply their forensic psychology skills in the hunt for a serial killer. The same structure could provide the blueprint for political drama, telling the tale of an innocent outsider sent to Washington to confront the vested interests and rampant dishonesty of an immoral ruling elite.

Swap out the ending and you have the story of a tragic anti-hero. It's Macbeth bewitched by ambition, seeking the Scottish throne through duplicity and murder, and then desperately fighting to maintain control of his destiny. It's Michael Corleone from *The Godfather*, responding to the attempted assassination of his father, then reluctantly embracing the family legacy. Or – occupying a morally more ambiguous middle ground – it's Walter White from *Breaking Bad*, naively stumbling into the world of organized crime as he tries to secure a stable economic future for his family, then having to learn to adapt in an environment which challenges his entire moral outlook on life.

But this structure doesn't only work as the foundation for innumerable fictional stories. It's also, almost precisely, the story of Donald Trump's candidacy for president. This same blueprint maps astoundingly well onto the narrative of Trump's run for office. The actual telling of the story – whether it's tragedy, heroic drama or farce – would obviously depend on the tone you chose. Which in turn would depend on your attitude to the man and the values for which he stands. But the basic shape of the plot – the motivation, the struggle, the climax – is practically identical.

What I aim to argue in this book is that this similarity is neither coincidental nor inconsequential. The way in which Trump's candidacy – and his subsequent presidency – has centred so completely around his character, and the way his character, when thrown into the world of politics, creates an archetypal Hollywood plot structure, is one of the driving forces behind his success. His whole saga has been compelling, if not essential, viewing. In an era of binge-watching and exemplary long-form drama, this story has dominated the ratings like no other. The narrative Donald Trump created for himself, and the way he went about telling this and manipulating the media into amplifying and broadcasting it for him, offers a paradigm example of what a persuasive tactic political storytelling can be. It was, arguably, the foundation on which his success as a political figure has been based. The structure of the Trump story was torn straight from the template of all great drama. It mixes together all the same ingredients: well-defined antagonists and protagonists; a challenging quest with an unlikely outcome; and page after page of memorable dialogue. As a result, it's had a huge influence on the shape of the political landscape. In fact, I'd argue, it's played a key role in reshaping the way we perceive not just politics but culture and society in general.

And Trump isn't alone in basing his persuasive power on strong storytelling. The Leave campaign in the Brexit vote is another forceful example of the effectiveness of a good narrative. This again fashioned an underdog story of a put-upon community fighting back against a seemingly invincible autocratic bureaucracy. And in doing so, it turned voting into an act of dramatic resistance.

It is not just politicians from the last few years who've exploited this approach. Almost all notable political figures and movements down through history are associated as much with a particular narrative as they are with a set of ideas, policies or actions. Or to put it another way, behind every successful politician is a simple but powerful story.

As we'll see, the adherence to this strategy of communication has become, over these last few years, evermore important for the way we shape not only our politics but also our understanding of the world more generally. It's become something of a modern mantra – a cliché even – that we're living in an era in which tapping into people's emotions has proved far more effective than rational argument. That people vote primarily on their values and feelings. The idea is offered up as an explanation for Trump, Brexit and Boris Johnson, for Jair Bolsonaro's take-over in Brazil and for the success of populists in Eastern Europe such as Hungary's Viktor Orbán. In each case, it's passion rather than rationalism which beguiles the voters. And one of the most powerful tools for playing on people's emotions is storytelling.

* * *

The purpose of this book is to illuminate this pivotal role that persuasive storytelling plays in society. Storytelling is an essential element in the way we interpret the entire social world. Our knowledge of the world may be built on facts and evidence – but facts only have meaning when they're placed within a context; and that context is more often than not built around a story. Although storytelling has played an important role in politics throughout history, today's combination of digital media, populism and partisanship is making it an evermore important part of the persuasive process – so much so that even when the current cast of characters get written out of the script, the storylines they've instigated will continue to resonate throughout the culture. And as I'll show, this persuasion isn't restricted to those running for office or already in power. It's also at the root of strategies of disinformation, of 'fake news' and propaganda.

It's for this reason that an understanding of narrative can provide us with important insights into the workings of power, and perhaps help us harness these dynamics so we can communicate our own ideas, perspectives and propositions with as much power and effectiveness as our opponents. The purpose of the book, then, is to show how the tools and tricks of narrative can be mastered to shape our understanding of the world. To explore how stories are structured, shared and contested. And to explain the rhetorical strategies that are used to enact them, and the language that's used to craft and narrate them.

As I'll argue, language is a huge part of this overall story. Language frequently gets blamed for breakdowns in public discourse and for the critical state of modern politics. For being in a state of decline, and for wilfully obscuring rather than clarifying our state of affairs. But language itself is simply an instrument for communication. It's how people *use* language, how they respond to it and how it comes to reflect the concerns of a community that together builds the background to our politics. To understand why things are the way they are, we need to look at how language is used, how it's manipulated and the force and effect this manipulation is having on the ideas that shape society.

Neither the language we use nor the stories we built from this language arise out of nowhere, of course. The tales we tell not only shape the times we live in but also reflect them. They need an environment in which to be embedded: a climate of ideas, ideals or fears to rub up against. Today's political climate can best be summed up as the collision of two trends in global culture: post-truth and populism. Both of these terms are bandied around with abandon in analyses of what we're meant to make of the modern world. And both of them are vague enough to mean a range of different things to different people. In order to better understand their significance for today's politics then, and to set the scene for this particular story, let's rewind a few years, and transport ourselves back to the eve of the end of the world.

Living through apocalyptic times

Let's start with a fairly straightforward, if slightly philosophical, question. When the apocalypse finally arrives – that is, when we reach the climactic chapter in the human story – how are we best going to deal with it? Should we see it as a chance to rebuild society from the scorched earth upwards? Reboot civilization and discover afresh what humanity is capable of? Rethink our attitude towards sustainable power and the relationship we have with technology? Finally take decisive action against climate change?

Or should we just embrace it as a marketing opportunity? Hope that our faith in the power of consumerism can banish the doomsday gloom?

Unsurprisingly perhaps, it was this last option that was chosen by various large multinational corporations when faced with the possible ruination of human civilization in late 2012. For much of that year there'd been growing disquiet about a prophecy (or at least, an internet rumour) related to the ancient Mayan calendar system, which was predicting that the end of the world was nigh. Not only was it nigh, but it would also be arriving on precisely 21 December.

Various natural disasters were mentioned as the likely catalyst for the cataclysm, including that the planet Nibiru was spiralling through space on a direct collision course with Earth. The source of this prediction was a woman who claimed she'd been receiving messages from extraterrestrials from the Zeta Reticuli star system. They'd chosen her to be their mouthpiece, she said, so she could warn humankind of its approaching annihilation.[1] Such was the concern about this that NASA felt it necessary to step in and debunk her predictions.[2] Yet even with calming strategies of this sort, as the date drew near there were reports of panic-buying across the globe, of desperate, reassuring statements from the Russian 'minister of emergency situations',[3] while on the day itself the *Guardian* live-blogged the whole nerve-racking drama as it unfolded.[4]

For advertisers, this was too good an opportunity to miss. Jell-O, the gelatine-based desserts people, produced a commercial in which a crate of pudding was offered up as a sacrifice to the Mayan gods in the hope that it would persuade them to cancel the cataclysm. Picking up the narrative a little further along the timeline, Chevrolet had an advert showing a Silverado cruising through the post-apocalyptic wilderness to the sound of Barry Manilow. When the driver finally met up with his fellow survivors, they all lamented the fact that their unfortunate companion Dave, who'd been driving a Ford (the damn fool) hadn't made it. This didn't go down too well with the people at Ford, who took umbrage at the idea that their product would be found wanting after the fall of civilization. They threatened Chevrolet with a cease-and-desist order,[5] proving that even come the apocalypse, corporate lawyers will still be in great demand. Then there was Durex, who encouraged us all to celebrate oblivion with the slogan, 'The end of the world shouldn't be the only thing coming.'

For most people of course, the Mayan apocalypse was a bit of a joke – what the political media consultant Tobe Berkovitz calls a 'water cooler catastrophe'. While it's fine to exploit this vision of human calamity as a way to sell puddings and prophylactics, you're much less likely to see 'commercials making fun of the fiscal cliff', he notes.[6] Real social and cultural upheaval, when it arrives, probably won't involve alien communiqués or planetary car-crashes. But its mundanity will make it all the more difficult to come to terms with.

We're now further into the twenty-first century than our ancestors were with the twentieth century when the First World War fundamentally changed the character of that century. Have we already experienced an event of equal magnitude that will set the agenda for the rest of our lifetimes? Given that it turned out not to be the Mayan cataclysm, what's likely to stand as our moment of fundamental change when the history of this century gets written?

The global financial crash of 2008 would be one candidate. Its ramifications are still reverberating through the fabric of society in disturbing and unexpected ways. Yet it doesn't perhaps have the symbolic resonance that other major historical turning points have had. It was undoubtedly dramatic, both as a process and in its implications. But it wasn't perhaps dramatic enough as a spectacle.

Which brings us to the events of 2016. This was, for many, a critical year of change which seemed to throw into confusion so much of what we understood of the social world we inhabit. Even as early as July, people were asking whether it was 'really one of the worst years in history'.[7] Headlines such as this obviously have a lot to do with the narcissistic hyperbole of the present moment. Yet by the end of the year the sense was that, if the apocalypse hadn't quite arrived, at the very least a deep fracture had opened up across the crust of the globe's culture. And nowhere was this more apparent than with the sense that rationality and truth seemed somehow to have lost their authority. That they no longer had the purchase they once did on civic debate. Or held sway over the way we were choosing our future.

A dumpster fire of a year

The year 2016 began in positive enough fashion. It marked the five-hundredth anniversary of Thomas More's *Utopia*, in which he outlines his vision of a perfected society. In January, there was the launch of twelve months of celebrations for this, under the slogan 'A Year of Imagination and Possibility'.[8] A special flag was designed to commemorate the occasion, showing a large smiley face emblazoned on a bright yellow background.[9] By the end of those twelve months however, that slogan and the optimistic flag waving was ringing rather hollow.

A simple primer for seeing how the world experiences the year is to look at the way the major dictionaries attempt to capture the spirit of the times with their 'Words of the Year'. The stories these tell provide an intriguing insight into how the drama and trauma of 2016 was experienced, and how, instead of a year of utopian dreams, it turned out to be one of 'paranoia' and 'post-truth', of ongoing 'refugee' crises, 'xenophobia' and a close shave with 'fascism' (plus the odd Australian obsession with sausages).

During the autumn of 2016, a campaign was launched to have the phrase 'Essex Girl' removed from the *Oxford English Dictionary*.[10] (For those unfamiliar with the civic geography of Great Britain, Essex is a county just outside London. Over the last couple of decades it has attracted a reputation in the media as having a rather gaudy, if not vulgar culture: something along the lines of a British Jersey Shore.) Those behind the campaign were upset that the definition in the dictionary – a young woman 'variously characterized as unintelligent, promiscuous, and materialistic' – was derogatory, that it reflected badly on the county of Essex, and so needed to be expunged from what describes itself as 'the definitive record of the English language'. In turning down the request, the spokesperson explained that because it's a historical dictionary nothing is ever removed. The whole purpose of the *Oxford English Dictionary* is to describe the language as people use it, and to thus stand as a catalogue of the notable fads and preoccupations of the changing times.[11]

The 'Words of the Year' tradition is a particularly high-profile way in which dictionaries bear witness to the times. Begun with the German *Wort des Jahres* in the 1970s, the tradition has spread over the decades to other languages. In the last few years, with the rise of social media and its obsession with listing, ranking and evaluating everything, it's become increasingly popular. In 2015 – the year before our tale begins – *Oxford Dictionaries* had chosen a pictograph as their 'word' for the first time in their history: the emoji for 'Face with Tears of Joy'. By 2016 however, the verbal was very much back in fashion.

In English, there are a range of competing 'Words of the Year', as all the major dictionaries make their own choice. Many of them had a distinctly dystopian feel in 2016. For example, *Cambridge Dictionary* chose 'paranoid' because users searching for this word in its database had increased fourfold. According to their managing director, this was clear evidence that people are 'less trusting than they used to be and that the world as a whole feels a lot more uncertain than it did compared with even a year ago'.[12] Dictionary.com meanwhile went for 'xenophobia': another word which saw a sudden spike in interest. This apparently reached its zenith on 24 June, the day after the Brexit referendum, with increased traffic to the Dictionary.com site of 938 per cent.[13]

Merriam-Webster tried to stem this tide of pessimism at the beginning of December when 'fascism' started to emerge as the likely winner in their online poll. They tweeted their readers imploring them to get behind something – anything – else.[14] The strategy seemed to work. In the end, 'surreal' was chosen as being most representative of a year in which, time and again, events almost defied belief.[15]

Collins, meanwhile, chose 'Brexit':[16] a term which their spokesperson suggested had become as flexible and influential in political discourse as 'Watergate'.[17] Just as the latter spawned hundreds of portmanteau words whenever a political scandal broke, so Brexit begat 'Bremain', 'Bremorse' and 'Brexistential crisis', along with an endless stream of other somewhat strained puns. The form of the word also began being used by other political rifts: in fact, a word from the Brexit family nearly won out in Australia, where 'Ausexit' (severing ties with the British monarchy or the United Nations) was on the shortlist in 2016. Instead, the Australian National Dictionary went for the slightly more idiosyncratic 'democracy sausage' – the tradition in the country of eating a barbecued sausage on election day.[18]

Around the world a similar pattern of apprehension emerged. In France, the *mot de l'année* was 'réfugiés' ('refugees').[19] Swiss German speakers went for 'Filterblase' (filter bubble)[20] – the idea that social media is causing increasingly polarized political communities. Also in Switzerland, the Deaf Association chose a Sign of the Year for the first time. Perhaps predictably their choice was 'Trump', which consists of a sign made by placing an open palm on the top of the head, thus mimicking the president's distinctive hair style.[21] Trump's hair also played a role in Japan's choice for the year. Rather than a word, Japan chooses a kanji (Chinese character), and for 2016 it was 'gold' (金).[22] This represented a number of different topical issues: Japan's haul of medals at that year's Rio Olympics, fluctuating interest rates, the gold shirt worn by YouTube sensation Piko Taro (singer of the popular 'Pen-Pineapple-Apple-Pen' micro-song), and, inevitably, the colour of Trump's hair.

Then there was Austria, whose word was fifty-one letters long – 'Bundespräsidentenstichwahlwiederholungsverschiebung' – and means 'the repeated postponement of the runoff vote for Federal President'.[23] Referring to the seven-month period of votes, legal challenges and delays over their presidential election, this again referenced an event that flirted with extreme nationalism and exposed the convoluted nature of democracy.

All of which brings us, finally, to *Oxford Dictionaries*. Having heralded a post-language era in 2015 with the choice of an emoji, they decided on 'post-truth' for 2016.[24] Other organizations followed suit – Germany, for example, chose 'postfaktisch', which has much the same meaning.[25] 'Post-truth' also won the American Dialect Society's 'Political Word of the Year', but lost out in the general category to 'dumpster fire', defined as 'an exceedingly disastrous or chaotic situation'.[26]

Just to round out the picture, it's worth also noting the winner of Germany's 'Non-word of the Year' (*Unwort des Jahres*). Not content with having begun the Words of the Year tradition, scholars in Germany also choose a representative *unwort*: a word or phrase that's considered to have the most offensive recent history.[27] Again, these almost always focus on the close relationship between language and politics, and often have direct equivalents in Anglophone countries. Recent winners have included 'Lügenpresse', a Nazi-era equivalent of 'fake news'; 'Alternative Fakten', and, in 2016, 'Volksverräter' or 'traitor of the people', another Nazi-era term which was revived by anti-immigration right-wing groups, and which was selected by the panel 'because it is a typical legacy of dictatorships'.[28]

Not that this pervasive sense of gloom was shared by everyone. For some, the moroseness and endless moaning was symptomatic of how out of touch those in the media and academia (the 'intellectual elite') were. Putting aside celebrity deaths and a crisis in opinion polling, 2016 saw significant progress in important areas such as medicine, life expectancy and scientific knowledge. For the commentator and arch-contrarian Brendan O'Neill, it was a year of 'disruption', both scientifically and politically – but that's all for the good.[29] 'If you must weep over 2016', he wrote, 'it should be with joy' – presumably much like 2015's signature emoji was doing.

So what it is? Are we really living in a post-truth era which is a threat to social democracy as we know it? Or is this talk of post-truth itself part of a partisan battle? Just a means of spinning political disappointment; an anxiety hyped in the mainstream media, as, in the words of media scholar Tim Crook, 'journalism's key institutions sense a crisis'?[30] Is it all just a matter of trying to rationalize a world which never had much of a relationship with rationality in the first place? And how does it all relate to the double feature of Trump and Brexit, two populist uprisings which gave the year its dramatic arc, and were symptomatic of broader shift in the political mood across the globe?

2

Let's begin with the facts

Fact-checkers and other bad people

If we want to answer any of the questions raised in Chapter 1, it might help if we knew exactly what we were dealing with. What precisely is this idea of 'post-truth' that everyone's so alarmed about, and why is it supposedly so significant for understanding the current state of society? Is it simply a euphemism for lying? In which case, why do we need a new term to describe this type of behaviour? And how is it any different from what humans have been doing ever since they first developed the ability to speak?

The subject I'll address in this chapter is why, following three centuries of scientific endeavour since the Enlightenment, we're still arguing with such rancour over the significance of factual- and evidence-based reasoning. And, equally importantly, what implications does this scepticism of evidence-based reasoning have for modern politics, as well as for the stories we tell ourselves about our culture and identity. Lying is, after all, a form of fictional storytelling, of replacing real events with imaginary ones. So perhaps the trend in political discourse for controlling the narrative has, inadvertently, led to this breakdown of trust in what counts as the truth? Or is it the other way round, and the drift towards post-truth in society has prompted a fad for storytelling in political rhetoric? But to answer any of these questions, we need to begin with some facts ourselves.

* * *

Given that we've begun with a discussion of dictionaries, it seems sensible to start with a dictionary definition of 'post-truth'. When announcing it as their Word of the Year, *Oxford Dictionaries* offered the following definition: post-truth refers to circumstances 'in which objective facts are less influential in shaping public opinion than appeals to emotion and personal belief'. The president of the dictionary, Casper Grathwohl, wrote that '[f]uelled by the rise of social media as a news source and a growing distrust of facts offered up by the establishment, post-truth as a concept has been finding its linguistic footing for some time'.[1] It's a concoction of the effects of modern media technologies, anti-establishment opinion and emotional conviction. As phenomenon it had been stealing up on society for a while; it just needed a suitable term to describe it.

As is the way with all words though, no sooner had the term been coined than people began debating its 'real' meaning, and arguing about where and how it should properly be used. Soon, it was being applied to almost any phenomenon associated with the circulation of false information, or any situation where there was an explicit intention to mislead. But the whole point of adding a new word to the lexicon is that it acts as a way of marking out something new or different in the culture. Of identifying something which we haven't experienced in quite the same way before. So 'post-truth' isn't simply about a blurring of the boundaries between facts and falsehood. Or about why humans find it so difficult to locate this boundary. It's as much to do with the rhetoric around truth as it is with truth itself, with how people can be persuaded of ideas through appeals to subjective rather than objective reality (assuming that such a thing exists) and how these tactics of persuasion have come to play such a major role in the way that the politics of today are conducted.

'Words of the Year' act as a miniature version of the keywords concept – the way that certain terms (either single words or noun phrases) come to define the concerns of a culture. The use of keywords as an entry point for an analysis of the issues dominating society at any one time was pioneered by the cultural critic Raymond Williams back in the 1970s.[2] In his book of the same name, Williams traced the historical development and current usage of a hundred or so terms that defined the intellectual concerns of the period, and in doing so, he pieced together the story that society was telling about itself. The keywords concept is a very useful technique for getting to grips with the mindset of a community, not least because it reveals just how freighted with specific meanings particular words can become, and how these then act as the building blocks with which we write contemporary history.

The best way to get a feel for the meaning of any term is to look at some of the canonical incidents that have come to define it. These are examples which have been plucked from the endless outpouring of opinion and argument that constitutes political discourse, and are then held up by the media and other commentators as indicative of trends in contemporary thought.

One of the most symbolic examples of post-truth thinking is British politician Michael Gove's comment, when declining to offer up the names of any economists who were publicly backing Britain's exit from the European Union, that 'people in this country have had enough of experts'.[3] In the wake of the 2008 financial crash, which had mysteriously taken nearly all economic experts by surprise, the authority of the intellectual elite was badly compromised. And anyway, people were never likely to get that excited by detailed, evidence-based analysis of phenomena. Then there was Aaron Banks, co-founder of the Leave.EU campaign, explaining that the 'remain campaign [in the Brexit vote] featured fact, fact, fact, fact, fact. It just doesn't work. You have got to connect with people emotionally.'[4] This same point – using almost exactly the same language – was also tellingly made by an executive of the infamous Cambridge Analytica in Channel 4's undercover documentary about them. 'It's no good fighting an election campaign on the facts', Mark Turnbull said, 'because actually it's all about emotion.'[5]

There was also former Speaker of the House of Representatives Newt Gingrich arguing with a reporter in 2016 about crime rates in the United States. Despite definitive evidence from the FBI that violent crime across the country was down, Gingrich continued to argue that this wasn't the experience of the bulk of the population. People were *feeling* more threatened now than ever before. This was another, equally valid 'truth', he insisted. And if the facts didn't support it, well, he stated, 'as a political candidate I'll go with how people feel and let you go with the theoreticians.'[6] As the political economist William Davies notes, 'Telling people that they are secure is of limited value if they *feel* that they are in situations of danger.'[7] Expertise is of relative importance if it contradicts the experiences people have in their own, everyday lives.

As a sidebar to this, it's worth noting that voter behaviour has an ambiguous relationship with the notion of expertise at the best of time. As we'll see later, a key element of any narrative in electoral politics is change. And one way in which change is symbolically enacted in election cycles is by voting in a relative newcomer who promises to reshape or re-energize the nation's fortunes. In this respect, expertise which derives from prior political experience only has limited value for a position such as the president of the United States. In an article in the *Atlantic* back in November 2015 – that is, precisely a year before the US presidential election – journalist Jonathan Rauch explained what he called the '14 year rule' in presidential politics.[8] The pattern had first been identified by the speech-writer John McConnell, who'd noticed that throughout the history of the US presidency, no one had been elected who'd taken more than fourteen years from their first gubernatorial or Senate victory to the top job. The two likely candidates for the job at the time that Rauch was writing were Hillary Clinton and Jeb Bush. And both had already exceeded their fourteen years. As Rauch noted, the electorate tend to prefer people who have a certain level of experience, but who can also exude a freshness of approach. His prediction at the time was that this rule was less likely to be broken by the election of a seasoned politician as by 'someone with no political experience at all'. As we now know, this turned out to be very prescient, not only for the United States but also for countries around the globe.

But back to the main thread of our tale. It's not simply facts themselves that have fallen out of favour in recent years. So too, it seems, are those who check them. In a bizarre aside at a New York fundraiser in 2018, Donald Trump gestured towards the reporters at the back of the room and sighed, 'They'll go and check it … Ah, they are bad people'.[9] Nor is this sort of sentiment an isolated Trumpism. For instance, when Facebook's fact-checking service debuted in Brazil in the spring of 2018, it sparked accusations of censorship and left-wing bias in certain sectors, and led to trolling and abuse of some of the fact-checkers on social media.[10] Facts and their fans are thus both viewed with a hostile suspicion in some quarters. Or, as national security expert Tom Nichols puts it, we've 'reached a point where ignorance, especially of anything related to public policy, is an actual virtue' for many in society.[11]

But setting the issue up as one of facts (and fact-checkers) versus emotion isn't quite the whole story. Post-truth doesn't merely suggest that hard facts are less valued in political debate than they once were. There's also the sense that they aren't quite what they purport to be. What, after all, is a fact anyway? Isn't my perspective on the world just as valid as yours? A post-truth world doesn't simply downgrade the value we place in truth. It questions its very nature. It produces what the philosopher Lee McIntyre refers to as a general indifference to reality.[12] Facts become 'subordinated' to political values, with politicians pushing their version of events irrespective of what the evidence illustrates. And such is the trend for this that, for some commentators, we're now witnessing the very 'death of truth'.[13]

The language of alternative facts

The paradigm example of how debates around this were played out in public was the controversy over the intriguing idea of 'alternative facts', which ushered in the Trump presidency. Back in early 2017 this was the infamous phrase used by White House spokesperson Kellyanne Conway when defending her colleague Sean Spicer's claim that Donald Trump had attracted the largest crowd for a presidential inauguration ever. Interviewed on *Meet the Press* two days after the inauguration, Conway was asked why Spicer had been sent out by the president to 'utter a provable falsehood' about the size of this crowd. Photos comparing the event with Barack Obama's inauguration eight years earlier clearly showed that 2017 had attracted a far sparser collection of people. So why was poor old Sean Spicer, who was White House press secretary at the time, trying to put across such an obvious lie to the American people?

Conway's spirited rebuttal was that this wasn't a falsehood at all. Rather, Spicer was merely offering 'alternative facts' to the press's biased assertion about the size of the crowd.[14] When the interviewer, Chuck Todd, then challenged her that 'alternative facts are not facts. They're falsehoods', she simply doubled down on the claim, thus provoking the epistemological frenzy that followed.

What was, in effect, a throwaway phrase, has turned into an emblematic concept for critics of post-truth politics. It's become another keyword for our times, and, almost inevitably, showed up in Word of the Year lists. (It won the Plain English Foundation's Worst Word of 2017.)[15] As such it has transcended this original context, and come to signify anything that smacks of excessive political spin. But the context in which it was first uttered is worth dwelling on for a moment. There are interesting parallels here with Michael Gove's celebrated comment earlier. Just as Gove was using the tarnished reputation of post-2008 economic experts as a basis for his anti-expert outburst, so Conway was able to point to the way that nearly all the major media outlets had miscalled the result of the election two months earlier. All the 'scientific' evidence that the newspapers and television broadcasters had accrued via opinion polls ended up being as good as worthless. 'Maybe this is me as a pollster', she said, justifying her position, but 'I don't think you can prove those numbers one way or the other.'

And of course, there's a kernel of truth in this. It's not quite as provocatively contrarian as it might at first sound. Facts don't exist in a vacuum. They're selected. Their importance is evaluated. Their implications are argued over. And ultimately, their meaning derives from the context in which they're presented.

The comedian Stuart Lee had a joke in his 2005 stand-up routine mocking the excuse that 'you can prove anything with facts'.[16] But in a way, this is precisely what you *can* do. As far as meaning goes, facts are only ever one part of the equation. Equally important is the choice of which facts get presented and the interpretation you put on them for the argument you're making. An advert which claims eight out of ten dentists recommend a certain product, and then, in the small print, notes that the company only actually surveyed a grand total of ten dentists, is using facts to prove whatever it wants. The same goes for politicians cherry-picking the most persuasive statistics as evidence for the truthfulness of their claims. These facts are simply plot-points in a broader narrative.

This strategy isn't limited to advertising and politics. Scientific studies also struggle with the extent to which their conclusions are justified by the sample they've investigated or the types of question they've asked. This is why science is never static. There are always better, more accurate methods on the horizon for refining the knowledge we have of the world, for updating the facts. As the linguistic anthropologist Nick Enfield puts it, we only derive meaning from facts when we interpret them; the act of interpretation is basically a form of storytelling: 'Only with a story can the facts be communicated, and only then can they become part of the received knowledge that drives the very possibility of scientific progress.'[17]

Then there's the way that scientific knowledge is the result of the everyday work practices of real people, complete with all the everyday stresses, limitations and institutional politics that constitute these practices. The implications of this were first discussed by the sociologists Bruno Latour and Steve Woolgar back in 1979 in their book *Laboratory Life: The Construction of Scientific Facts*, and have been much argued about ever since.[18] Scientists don't simply 'discover' facts, Latour and Woolgar contended. They also interpret and present them. They're in the business of persuading colleagues, funding bodies and the public at large that the facts they've discovered are scientifically sound and significant. Rhetoric, in other words, plays a part even in the practices of the hard sciences.

Not that any of this is to say that we should give up on the idea of stable facts altogether, of course. Far from it. But it explains, perhaps, why a strict either/or approach to truth is so vulnerable to counter narratives.

Being trolled by the dictionary

For most people, however, the concept of an 'alternative fact' was a straight-out oxymoron. It managed to upend the very idea of what a fact surely was. One organization that certainly thought this was the dictionary *Merriam-Webster*. In response to Conway's comment, and to help clarify matters, they tweeted their own definition of the word: 'A fact is a piece of information presented as having objective reality.'[19] They also observed, with ironic understatement, that '[i]n contemporary use, *fact* is generally understood to refer to something with actual existence.'[20] If you start applying it to phenomena which never actually happened, you're wilfully misusing it.

Merriam-Webster has made something of a habit of trolling the Trump administration over their slipshod attitude to language. For instance, when Trump himself took multiple attempts to correctly spell the word 'pore', the dictionary was quick to offer him assistance. In a textbook example of Murphy's Law – the idea that 'if you write anything criticising editing or proofreading, there will be a fault of some kind in what you have written'[21] – Trump's original tweet read as follows: 'After having written many bestselling books, and somewhat priding myself on my ability to write, it should be noted that the Fake News constantly likes to pour [*sic*] over my tweets looking for a mistake.'[22] In response to which *Merriam-Webster* posted a simple tutorial for differentiating between homonyms. 'Pore over' means 'to read or study very carefully', they tweeted, whereas 'pour over' means 'to make expensive coffee'. For good measure they added: and 'comb over' means 'to comb hair from the side of the head to cover the bald spot'.[23]

The trouble is, just as the meaning of a fact is not quite as straightforward as one might at first suppose neither are the meanings of many other words. Language is continually open to being twisted and manipulated. We may mock how blatantly Conway was manipulating things in this particular case, but disputing the meanings of words is, and always has been, a central part of politics.

As *Merriam-Webster*'s intervention highlights, a usual first move when there are disagreements over linguistic meaning is to consult the dictionary. We all tend to 'take what the dictionary says as authoritative', the lexicography scholar Howard Jackson writes: 'If the dictionary says so, then it is so.'[24] The problem with this belief is that it rests on a rather flawed conception of what dictionaries actually do. Despite the fact that the dictionary, much like the Bible, gets talked about as if there were only a single canonical version (*the* dictionary), this clearly isn't the case. The *Oxford English Dictionary* may brand itself as 'the definitive record of the English language' (thus upsetting the women of Essex), but other dictionaries are also available. Lots of them, in fact. Each of which includes a slightly different set of words, all defined in slightly different ways.

The way dictionaries work is to record, as best they can, conventional usage as it exists at any one time, and in the case of a dictionary based on historical principles such as the *Oxford English Dictionary*, to document the way that language has changed over the decades and centuries. A key point here is that language is *constantly* changing. The meanings of words shift, based on the way people use them. Sometimes this shift can result in a complete volte face. For example, in Middle English (c. 1300) the word 'nice' meant 'foolish', 'silly' or 'ignorant', being originally derived from the Latin *nescius*, 'ignorant' or 'not knowing'. It gradually changed in the late Middle Ages, firstly to refer to actions which were 'fastidious' or 'fussy' (c. 1400) and then, in the Early Modern period, to become a synonym for 'refined or cultured' (c. 1580). By the mid-eighteenth century, it had begun to acquire its modern meaning of something 'agreeable' or 'pleasant', thus completing a journey which witnessed a complete U-turn in its beliefs, from 'ignorant' to 'agreeable'.

It's not only processes of historical change which can significantly alter the meaning of words. The way they're interpreted by different factions in society can become the battleground for opposing value systems. As Raymond Williams puts it, we may on the surface all be speaking the same language, but our uses of individual words can often be significantly different, 'especially when strong feelings or important ideas are in question'.[25] Take the word 'theory' when used in the context of science, for example.[26] For some this means a generalized description of phenomena in the world. A theory is an abstract explanation of how the world actually is. It's a fact of nature. For others, it's a mere guess at how the world might work. It's an acknowledgement that we don't actually know the truth about things, so we're forced to invent fanciful hypotheses about them: 'It's only a theory.' Here again, the word can mean two almost contradictory things, although in this case, both in the same period of time.

The internet, with its pluralism and user-based authorship, has brought this subjectivity around meaning clearly into focus. There's an active online community dedicated to documenting and discussing vocabulary. One of the most prominent examples of this is Urban Dictionary. This acts as a forum for diverse communities of people to add their own definitions of an ever-evolving vocabulary, thus archiving a huge variety of different types of English, most of which wouldn't normally find their way into more conventional dictionaries. As its founder Aaron Peckham notes, while '[m]ost dictionaries are objective ... Urban Dictionary is completely subjective. It's not presented as fact, [but] as opinions.'[27] And the opinion-led nature of the definitions means that the dictionary can be used as an explicit arena for political debate. Here, for example, are two entries for the headword 'Obamacare' (both written during the Obama presidency).[28]

> A term invented by impoverished, dumb-ass neocons to apply negative connotation to the bi-partisan, congressional health care plan.

> also known as socialism. giving all Americans cheap bull shit health care. a plan to destroy the quality of health care.

Two 'definitions', both of which represent widely held beliefs about the Affordable Care Act (as it's officially named), and which reflect the way the term is commonly used in society. But which are also antagonistically different from each other.

Contradictory truths

So what does this all have to do with alternative facts? A few months after her appearance on *Meet the Press*, Kellyanne Conway gave an interview to the political journalist Olivia Nuzzi, in which she attempted to explain what she'd meant by the phrase. It refers to things such as 'Two plus two is four. Three plus one is four. Partly cloudy, partly sunny. Glass half full, glass half empty.' It's the idea that for any given event you can always supply 'additional facts and alternative information.'[29] In other words, it's the idea that there are always two sides to every story. That facts – or at least the way they're interpreted – are always subject to the overarching story in which they're presented.

An acknowledgement of this – and particularly the part that language plays in it all – was something that led the website AllSides. com to create a glossary focusing specifically on terms that often provoke controversy because of the way they end up meaning starkly different things to different people. Their aim was to offer perspectives on various issues from contrasting sides of the political spectrum, working from the proposition that 'until we understand what a term means to others, we don't know the issue and can't effectively communicate'.[30] It's the idea that we speak metaphorically different languages if we don't share the same values or belief systems. (Po-tar-to/po-tai-to, but for ideological connotations.) Of the word 'fact', for example, AllSides write that while for many it's a common sense means of referring to the actual reality of things, for others it's come to be used 'as an attempt by one person or community to establish its position as unquestioned and irrefutable'.[31] In other words, there are always alternative collections of facts which opposing sides in any argument will cite, and thus facts in and of themselves do little to help the discourse along. Or to put it yet another way, you can indeed prove anything with facts.

Acknowledging this type of subjectivity and pluralism isn't to imply that linguistic meaning is a free-for-all; that like Humpty Dumpty in *Alice in Wonderland* we can use a word to mean whatever we choose it to mean. Or at least, we can't normally do this. If one has enough clout and authority, it's apparently possible to recast the meaning of even the most commonplace of words. For instance, when Facebook claimed that its video-on-demand service 'Watch' was attracting 75 million daily visitors, it arrived at this figure by purposefully stretching the meaning of what counts as a 'minute'. As the news website Axios explained, Facebook's statistics were based on a chain of decidedly idiosyncratic definitions.[32] A 'daily visitor' referred to anyone who spends at least one minute on the site per day. This is the same criterion TV networks use, so there's nothing that controversial there. But where Facebook diverged from the standard TV network measurement – and where, in the process, they redefined one of the fundamental units of time – was that for their purposes, the sixty seconds that constitute a minute don't need to be consecutive.

Tricksy legalistic exceptions such as these aside, for the most part language has the ability to be surprisingly stable, despite its constant evolution and endless variety. But what this perspective does point to is the way that meaning also resides in dialogue and negotiation with other people. In making sure you're both talking to the same purpose. That it's dependent on the context in which the words are used – a context which is often shaped by some overarching narrative to which people are committed.

There's one final point worth making about the 'alternative facts' controversy. One of the things that Kellyanne Conway succeeded in doing with her performance in that interview was to shift the focus of the discussion away from the size of the crowd at Trump's inauguration and on to how the media had gone about reporting it. By refusing to accept the fundamental premises upon which the broadcaster's questions were based, and provoking the controversy about truth and relativity, she altered the subject of the debate to one about the trustworthiness of journalism. In other words, she changed the focus of the narrative. She was able to foreground the way that everything we understand about the world, outside of our own narrow frame of immediate experience, is mediated. It's mediated by newspapers and television; it's mediated by the language used to describe it; it's mediated by the narratives we use to interpret it. And in such a mediated landscape, it surely makes sense to foster a healthy scepticism about what we do and don't believe. Or as Russian state-funded broadcaster RT (formerly Russia Today) puts it in their corporate motto, 'Question everything'.

Many of the quotes discussed here have become greatest hits in the account of the rise of the post-truth society. Whatever other vexations it might have produced, the first few years of the Trumpozoic era have proved to be exceptionally good for maxims. This select handful of phrases has become the most quoted lines of dialogue from the whole drama. Alongside Gove's 'people have had enough of experts', and Conway's 'alternative facts', honourable mention needs also to go to Rudi Giuliani's 'truth isn't truth'.[33] And then there's what is, perhaps, the most direct statement of the post-truth mentality of the lot. This came from American political commentator Scottie Nell Hughes, when she was trying to explain away the controversy over Trump's false assertion that millions of people had voted illegally in the 2016 election. What was interesting, she said, was 'that people that say facts are facts – they're not really facts ... Everybody has a way of interpreting them to be the truth, or not truth. There's no such thing, unfortunately, anymore as facts.'[34] An assertion like this calls to mind Nietzsche's aphorism that there are no facts, 'there are only interpretations'.[35] But whereas Nietzsche was making the point that what we take to be 'truth' is always as much to do with the power of those promulgating it as it is with scientific evidence, someone like Scottie Nell Hughes is using the idea to undermine the legitimacy of anyone she disagrees with.

All these examples reveal, and have come to symbolize, a blatant disdain for the hegemony of fact-based reasoning. But is it really the case that they're representative of a major shift in the tide of contemporary culture? Or are they themselves merely cherry-picked examples which have been wrenched out of context and then endlessly repeated as a means of attacking the other side in the debate? Or to put it another way, is citing this handful of quotes a way of manipulating the facts of the matter itself?

A slave to the passion

It's certainly the case that much of what gets referred to as post-truth politics isn't necessarily new. The ways in which the stability of certain words comes under sustained attacked by the process of politics, and the importance that emotional provocation can have on people's decision-making, are both issues with a long track record in the history of ideas. As far back as the fifth century BC, the historian Thucydides wrote of the way the relationship between language and reality becomes one of the first casualties in any military conflict. In his *History of the Peloponnesian War,* he illustrates how the liberties that those in power took with language brought about a culture which ultimately led to the collapse of the democratic order.[36] Those in command, he writes, 'reversed the usual evaluative force of words to suit their own assessment of actions'. As people began manipulating the language they were using to describe current events, it led to a general breakdown of meaning, which in turn licensed the aggression and violence which ushered in a state of tyranny.

Many of the remarks Thucydides makes could apply perfectly well to politics today. When he writes that the 'dominant men on each side … employed fine-sounding terms, claiming espousal either of democratic rights for all or of a conservative aristocracy', this could be referring to the populism of Brexit or Trump denouncing the political establishment. When he says that 'division into opposing ideological camps created widespread distrust', it could apply to practically any form of social media-based politics. And the assertion that those 'who could put a euphemistic gloss on a distasteful action had their reputations advanced' fits almost too perfectly with the actions of Conway, Spicer and many others.

Alongside the assault on language there's also the important, but seemingly all too often overlooked, role that emotion plays in decision-making. When Aaron Banks says that you've got to 'connect with people emotionally' if you want to win them over, he's basically quoting Aristotle (although he may not, of course, realize this). A hundred or so years after Thucydides had tackled the subject of linguistic spin, Aristotle, in his *Art of Rhetoric*, wrote of the way that an orator needed to play on the audience's emotions.[37] Effective persuasion, according to his formula, consists of three fundamental elements. First, there's 'logos', or pure argument, which involves creating a rationally convincing case – of marshalling your facts. Second is 'ethos', the character and status of the speaker. An audience is more likely to be persuaded by someone they trust, like and feel, who has authority over the subject matter. Finally, there's 'pathos' – the mood created between speaker and audience. '[T]hings do not seem the same to those who love and those who hate, nor to those who are angry and those who are calm', Aristotle says. The aim of rhetoric is to guide the audience towards making a particular judgement about the matter at hand. It's therefore important to create the conditions that are most likely to lead them to this judgement. And emotions such as anger, pity and fear 'are those things by the alteration of which men differ with regard to those judgements'. Or to put it another way, provoke a sense of anger, fear and resentment, and you engineer a mood which is more amenable to your battle cry of taking back control.

A further few centuries down the line, the Scottish philosopher David Hume made a very similar case. He was addressing the nature of decision-making rather than persuasion, but here again, he argued, emotion always lies behind our practical reasoning.[38] Then there's the role these ideas played in the fascist movements of the mid-twentieth century. In the late 1950s, the author Aldous Huxley reflected back on the themes he'd dealt with in his most famous novel *Brave New World*.[39] He'd written the book in the early 1930s, and now, a quarter of a century later, he asked himself to what extent the world had come to resemble the vision he'd outlined back then. In the 1930s, he fully believed that the scenario he was imagining had every possibility of coming to pass. He could already see signs of the rise of totalitarianism and of a future dominated by dictators. His conclusion twenty-five years later was that the world was moving towards such a future at a much faster pace than he'd originally supposed. And the clearest example of why and how this was happening was the rise of regimes such as the Nazis, and particularly the way they'd been so successful in manipulating people's emotions. Describing Hitler's approach to propaganda, Huxley writes that the behaviour of the masses 'is determined, not by knowledge and reason, but by feelings and unconscious drives ... To be successful a propagandist must learn how to manipulate these instincts and emotions.' He goes on to quote a passage from *Mein Kampf* where Hitler explicitly states that power over the masses is never achieved through scientific teaching, but by inspiring devotion: 'Whoever wishes to win over the masses must know the key that will open the door of their hearts.'

These assertions have been borne out in dozens of recent studies in psychology. In the 1970s, the prevailing idea in the social sciences was still that people were generally rational when it comes to making decisions, and that any misjudgements they might make were the product of thought processes being corrupted by emotions. Influential research by psychologists Daniel Kahneman and Amos Tversky on systematic errors in everyday decision-making processes played a key part in altering these assumptions, and led to the current state of scientific thought where 'emotion now looms much larger in our understanding of intuitive judgements and choices than it did in the past.'[40]

We may still cling to what we think of as the Enlightenment idea that we're rational animals; that our decisions about important issues are the product of sober deliberation; that we weigh the facts, probe their consequences, and then come to a balanced and reasoned decision on which we can then act. But this simply isn't the case most of the time. Instead, we make decisions based on the way we feel about an issue – and in political contexts, how that issue relates to wider notions such as identity and political affiliation. Rationality is more often than not simply used to justify the decision. It's a rhetorical strategy that helps bolster the decision we've already made.[41]

If the core ingredients that make up post-truth were clearly articulated centuries, if not millennia ago, then, why is there such renewed concern about them now? If it's always been the case that in times of social unrest those in power exploit the flexibility of language, and tap in to people's emotional responses to sway public opinion, is there anything much more to say about the state of modern politics than that it was ever thus? The answer, of course, is that the distinctive nature of the current situation lies in its details. It's not just that spin and emotion have always played an intrinsic part in politics. It's how precisely this manifests itself. And how it combines with other trends and developments in modern culture to create the state in which we now find ourselves.

3

Popular fiction

Populist uprisings

The events of 2016 weren't characterized by post-truth politics alone, of course. The two major election shocks in the United Kingdom and United States were also seen as the result of an upswing in populist politics. They were explained as the revenge of 'ordinary' voters on an out-of-touch elite. These two cases both happened to be right-wing populist victories, but with the resurgence at the same time of Jeremy Corbyn's Labour Party in the United Kingdom, and with Bernie Sanders giving Hillary Clinton a close run for her money in the democratic primaries in the United States, there was a broader trend for the ideas and rhetoric of populism across the political spectrum – a trend which has continued in the years since. In telling the story of contemporary politics then, populism is another fundamental part of the background context. Increasingly, its values and beliefs are something that politicians either orient towards or react against. In fact, we could go a step further and say that populism is one of the major narratives of modern politics – and one which is built around a surprisingly simple plot line.

* * *

In late 2018, the *Guardian* published research that indicated quite how popular populist parties have become in recent years. The report showed that one in four Europeans were voting for populist politicians at the end of the 2010s, up from a mere 7 per cent two decades earlier.[1] In the late 1990s there were only two European countries with populist politicians in government: Slovakia and Switzerland. Twenty years later that had risen to eleven. And this pattern is not limited to Europe. At the time of the *Guardian* report, populists also held power in the United States, Brazil, Mexico and the Philippines. As the political scientist Cas Mudde notes, the word was rarely used throughout the twentieth century, whereas it's shaping up to be one of the defining features of the twenty-first century.[2]

All this prompts the question of whether there's an intrinsic relationship between post-truth and populist politics. Do they share certain characteristics; and if we have one will the other always follow? Or was their emergence in the cases discussed earlier mere coincidence – two unrelated phenomena which both happened to flourish at the same time, coalescing (in the United Kingdom and the United States at least) around the same candidates and causes?

To answer these questions let's start by taking an example of a political narrative which draws on populist ideas to fire up the sympathies of its followers. In the summer of 2017 the National Rifle Association (NRA) in the United States broadcast a series of promotional videos outlining its aims and values.[3] The message at the heart of these was that the NRA had no intention of surrendering quietly to the 'elites' who, it alleged, now 'threaten our very survival'. Against background footage of a world in distress – rioters raging against the police, hooligans smashing shop windows, delinquents setting fire to the American flag – the NRA spokesperson Dana Loesch warned that '[t]he times are burning and the media elites have been caught holding the match'. Taking aim at the *New York Times* in particular (so often seen as the poster child for the liberal media elite), she declared that 'we-the-people have had it ... with your narratives, your propaganda, your fake news. We've had it with your ... refusal to acknowledge any truth that upsets the fragile construct that you believe is real life. And we've had it with your tone-deaf assertion that you are in any way truth or fact-based journalism.'

In one angry outburst this ties together all the main buzzwords we've discussed so far, while mixing in a few more for good measure. It name-checks 'truth', 'facts' and 'narrative', along with an intense scepticism of the social 'elite' and a righteous appropriation of the concept of 'we the people'. In terms of political vocabulary, it's an almost seamless blend of populism and post-truth.

While populism and post-truth politics are clearly not synonymous, and not even necessarily trussed together in a symbiotic relationship, there is a complex set of relations between them. The overlap in the Venn diagram is centred predominantly around ideas of emotion. Simplifying things rather crudely, populism is based mostly on an emotional idea: that the establishment – and particularly the institutions of economic, political and cultural power – have ignored the needs and aspirations of ordinary, everyday citizens; that they're out of touch with normal people's concerns; out of touch with their struggles and hardships, and instead focused solely on protecting and boosting their own personal interests. The term, in other words, is closely associated with an emotional reaction to politics – and specifically with perceived feelings of anger, frustration and a sense of betrayal on the part of ordinary people.

By this formula, populism is more about attitude than it is about content. It's not an ideology in the same way that, for example, socialism, libertarianism or conservatism are ideologies. Instead, it's a basic framework for viewing the world which works alongside another set of beliefs – what's often referred to as the host ideology.[4]

You can thus have both right-wing and left-wing populist movements, with very different agendas but using an almost identical rhetoric. On the far-right, for example, there are parties such as Fidesz in Hungary, the Sweden Democrats and Germany's Alternative für Deutschland. On the other hand, both the Spanish Podemos and Greek Syriza are populist parties with a left-wing host ideology, while Italy's Five Star Movement is something of a mixed ideological bag.

This ideological ambivalence can have important implications for understanding the evolving political landscape. Dominic Cummings, who was campaign director for Vote Leave during the Brexit referendum, explicitly formulated their populist campaign message so that it was neither right nor left-leaning, but based instead on a very different paradigm. His rationale for this was that the traditional right-versus-left narrative may be something that politicians in Westminster and the media obsess over, but it doesn't reflect the reality of politics as lived by the majority of people.[5] In the context of the Brexit referendum, there were as many issues that united parts of those on the left and right as there were that divided them.

The rhetoric of populism is structured around a narrative that, in the words of Roger Eatwell and Matthew Goodwin, 'prioritizes the culture and interests of the nation, and which promises to give voice to a people who feel that they have been neglected, even held in contempt, by distant and often corrupt elites'.[6] In many ways the story it tells is as simple as this. The general populace is being taken advantage of by a self-serving establishment, and the populist leader, as the only person able to represent the 'real people', will take the fight to this establishment on behalf of the common man and woman.

Given that populism is more about attitude than content, it tends to privilege emotion over fact. It doesn't necessarily call into question the very idea of facts in the way that post-truth politics does. But it plays strongly on a clamorous us-versus-them narrative, the ordinary populace pitted against the condescending elite. In fact, it goes further than this, viewing the establishment not simply as condescending but as crooked, lying, deceitful and generally morally corrupt – all of which can lead to an intensely felt scepticism towards those who see themselves as the arbiters of facts. Thus, when Michael Gove dismissed the value of economic experts, he was channelling the anger and disillusionment felt by the electorate, and using this as a means of dismissing the inconvenient views of the whole of the academic economics community. Drawing on the populist narrative, he was able to use a form of prejudice rather than evidence as his main tactic of persuasion.

There's another key connection between populism and emotion. For the writer Paul Mason, the rise of populism is in no small part a reaction against the neoliberal agenda of the last two decades.[7] One way of looking at neoliberalism, Mason says, is as a process of political decision-making which has been drained entirely of emotional considerations. In running everything from universities to health care systems according to the logic of free-market capitalism, basic human needs and desires have been squeezed out of the equation. As workers, students and patients are increasingly viewed as little more than fodder for the money-making machine, concepts such as identity, security and aspiration have dropped out of view. Populism, Mason contends, is simply a backlash against this, offering an 'emotional narrative with an inspirational core offer' where neoliberal political approaches still cling to the idea of people-as-statistics.

The nature of populism as a political phenomenon is, of course, more complicated than my brief sketch makes out. Many of the factors which have contributed to its current prominence predate the events of 2016 by several years, if not decades, so it's by no means a new trend. Equally, its high profile isn't necessarily matched by its impact on society, although there is a growing sense in some quarters that the major political battle lines in society are shifting away from the tradition of left-versus-right, and will soon come to be replaced by those representing the establishment versus anti-establishment.[8] But my focus here is less on the phenomenon as a whole, and more on populism as a style of politics. On the particular rhetoric which populist politicians use to persuade the electorate. In this respect, the formula is very straightforward. Populism is itself a simple and well-defined narrative. And it's a narrative constructed from three very simple building blocks, each represented by a keyword.

We the people

The first of these keywords is 'the people' themselves, who act as protagonist in the story – although often, in practice, with the populist leader standing in as their representative. As noted, the underlying structure of populism involves intense scepticism of the establishment along with equally impassioned reverence for the common people. But who exactly are these people? For the Argentine political theorist Ernesto Laclau, it's the very fact that the term is difficult to define – that it's so broad and unspecific – that makes populism such a powerful idea.[9] The phrase has a flexibility which allows politicians to project their own agendas onto it; while it also has a moral weight which can underpin almost any argument about the democratic process ('the people have spoken').

There are two main ways 'the people' get defined by populist movements. The first is by identifying a shared culture and set of values which unite a disparate group of individuals and transform them into a cohesive whole. The second is in contrast to the elites against which they're pitted. A good example of the first of these is the way that nationalist populism (i.e. the brand of populism practised by Trump and the majority of those in favour of Brexit) promotes the idea of a set of symbols and values which the citizens of a nation hold dear and consider to be a fundamental part of their group identity. The political scientist Benedict Anderson famously described nationalism of this sort as the product of an 'imagined community'.[10] A nation consists of millions of people, most of who will never meet in person. They aren't, in a practical sense, a community – certainly not a physically cohesive one. But while they may not personally interact with each other, they all buy into a shared idea of what they have in common: namely a set of communal myths, symbols and values which are circulated by both politicians and the media. The nation's sense of community is thus a product of the collective imagination. But just because it's 'imaginary' doesn't mean it's not extremely powerful. People can be compelled to fight and even die for their country after all, based solely on the commitment they have to this shared culture.

A notable example of how this works was the front cover of the UK's *Sun* newspaper the day before a key vote in parliament about plans for Brexit. The headline, leaving little doubt as to the paper's position on the issue, declared: 'As [Members of Parliament] vote on Brexit today, we say to them: You have a choice … Great Britain or Great Betrayal.'[11] This reflects the classic populist formula: 'we', the voice of the people (in this case represented by the newspaper), versus 'them' the political establishment. The rest of the front page was filled almost entirely with a collage of images representing an idyllic picture of Great British culture. It looked like bad Peter Blake fan art. There were sheep grazing in green fields, the Loch Ness monster craning its neck towards the horizon, the Houses of Parliament and Windsor Castle, a Mini pootling around a country lane, a fish-and-chip shop, the Shard towering over the landscape – and all of them jostling together in a composite of what it supposedly means to be British. Each of them symbolized an essential part of national identity, creating a story of what was at stake if 'we' didn't wrestle back our sovereignty from the technocrats in Brussels.

Of course, the whole thing was a carefully crafted fiction. As a chorus of critics on social media immediately pointed out, most of these symbols of British identity were either the product or property of immigrants or people from overseas. The Mini was designed by a Greek, Alec Issigonis, and the company was bought by BMW in 2000; the Houses of Parliament were currently being restored by contractors from the United States; the Shard was designed by an Italian architect, Renzo Piano, and was owned by Qatar investors; Windsor castle was built by a Norman duke who'd conquered half the nation. And the *Sun* itself, of course, was owned by an Australian-born US citizen. In other words, the factual details behind the collage were subordinate to the overarching story. The idea of Britishness for which 'we' were supposedly fighting was very much a fictional construct – as national cultures always are.

Such is the flexibility of the term 'the people' that it can often be a matter of who gets to appropriate the rhetoric first. During the Brexit campaign, for instance, those on the Leave side employed a narrative that was laden with populist tropes. They stuck to this throughout the skirmishes over the terms for the withdrawal deal itself. But as the saga dragged on, and the Remain side pushed harder and harder for a second referendum, they too picked up on populist vocabulary, campaigning now for a '*People's* Vote'.[12] Whereas, in the original campaign, the Remain argument had been framed around what experts were advising was best for the country, the idea of a 'People's Vote' returned responsibility to the population at large. The basic arguments hadn't changed – Remain were still convinced that the whole endeavour would be both economically and socially ruinous – but the language had.

The second aspect of the definition of 'the people' is what they're *not*. As with all good fairy tales, the protagonist needs an antagonist to help define them. And while the phrase 'the people' may sound inclusive, it is, in fact, quite the opposite.[13] Those who don't count as 'authentic people' are of two types. They can be either the outsiders (which, in nationalist populism, usually means immigrants) or the enemy within, the mythical 'elite'.

Pointy-headed professors

In the context of contemporary politics in the West, almost any use of the word 'elite' immediately orients the discussion towards populist sentiments. There are a cluster of words which work in this way: if they're not being used critically, terms such as the 'mainstream media' and the 'deep state' are similarly likely to signal an affinity with a particular perspective on the workings of power. As soon as someone drops the phrase 'deep state' into their conversation, for instance, you can tell they probably adhere to a very specific conspiratorial view of world politics. The phrase has become inextricably linked to a conspiratorial narrative so that simply using it indicates an alignment on the part of the speaker with the belief system encoded in that narrative.[14] And for the word 'elite', the narrative that's conjured up is a populist one.

As with so many of the words we've been looking at, the way the meaning of 'elite' is understood is far from straightforward. At times, in fact, it's downright contradictory. Here, for example, are Donald Trump's thoughts on the word, as discussed with the crowd at a rally in Minnesota. 'They always call the other side *the elites*', he mused. 'Why are they the elite? I have a much better apartment than they do. I'm smarter than they are. I'm richer than they are. I became president and they didn't.'[15]

It's a fair point, if one understands the word 'elite' to refer to a small section of society which is viewed as being superior in terms of qualities, ability or privilege when compared to the rest of the population.

Back in the mid-1970s when Raymond Williams published his seminal *Keywords*, 'elite' was one of the terms he examined. The word's origins come from the twelfth-century French 'elire', meaning to choose between different people or things, or to elect a person to an office. The elite, in other words, were those who'd been elected to a particular role. From this, it gradually developed its modern meaning of a small group of people holding or wielding a large amount of wealth, influence or power within society. As Williams notes, there's a nice irony in the fact that the forgotten roots of the word relate to elected officials, not least in the way that scepticism of career politicians once again elides elected officials with ideas of elitism.[16]

How, then, is the word actually used in political argument these days, and how can this help explain the conundrum that Trump was struggling with at his rally in Minnesota? The simple answer is that the meaning shifts depending on your perspective. For left-wing populists, the elite are those hoarding economic and political power: the bankers, the media barons, the corporate lobbyists – most of whom were born into a position of influence and privilege.[17] For right-wing populists, the elite are those in the culture or knowledge industries – actors and filmmakers, journalists and what the US politician George Wallace once called 'pointy-headed college professors who can't even park a bicycle straight'.[18] According to the conservative mindset, these groups see it as their right to shape what people are allowed to do and say in society. And in this way, they chip away at the 'traditional' values associated with a mythical stable and homogenous culture.

In both cases therefore, the word has a similar indicative meaning: people whose status give them an outsized influence on society. But the two political perspectives have different overarching stories to explain the problems of the world, and these stories influence the way that elitism gets categorized. A stereotyped version of the left-wing story is that everything's the fault of unchecked capitalism, and thus the enemy becomes those who manage or promote the capitalist machine. For those on the right it all stems from an assault on the stability of tradition, so the blame lies with those who shape the culture.

An example of these conflicting perspectives can be seen in an advert that was run in the *Times* back in October 2018, at the height of the calls for a second referendum. The advert had a red line drawn through the words 'People's Vote', and above this were scrawled the words 'Losers' Vote'. Underneath this it asserted, 'The second referendum campaign is a con promoted by elitist losers who cannot accept democracy unless it goes their way.'[19] The advert duly did the rounds on social media, being either celebrated or denounced. Among those reproving it was the campaign group 'NHS Against Brexit' who rhetorically asked: 'When did [National Health Service] nurses, dentists, paramedics, mental health workers, students, porters, administrators, healthcare assistants, midwives, pharmacists, etc. become the elite? (Clue: They aren't.)'[20]

In a sense, this question is precisely the same as that asked by Donald Trump. And the paradox is explained when one realizes that in the context of national populism, 'elite' refers to anyone with a role in an establishment institution whose job involves them, as William Davies puts it, 'claiming some disembodied, dispassionate perspective, not available to the ordinary' person.[21] In other words, elitism in this conception isn't to do with a person having wealth and influence, it's to do with them being related somehow to the authority of the system.

The problem, of course, is that we've reached a situation now where the word 'elite' can include almost anyone whose views you disagree with. It's the bogeyman of populist-inflected politics. And its use is usually a sign that the speaker is less interested in engaging in political dialogue than in simply vilifying the views of their opponent.

Giving a voice to the voiceless

The final element of the populist formula is 'the will of the people'. Given that the populist leader presents themself as the principal representative of the people, they become the channel through which this will is enacted – and for this to happen they need to hear, appreciate and understand that will. The people's *voice* and the people's *will* are thus inseparably bound together in this equation. Populism is built on the idea of giving political voice to the underrepresented in society so that the will of the people is both heard and acted upon. This, in effect, is the quest at the heart of the populist plot.

It's no surprise then that this becomes a central theme in the election campaigns of populists such as Marine Le Pen and Donald Trump. In the 2017 French presidential election, Le Pen tried to rally the youth vote by promising she would 'be the voice of the voiceless'.[22] For Trump it was the laid-off factory workers he'd met on his travels, the communities who'd been affected by 'horrible and unfair' trade deals – 'People who work hard but no longer have a voice.' For them, he vowed, 'I am your voice!'[23] He continued with his use of this language in his first presidential address to Congress. When announcing the formation of a new agency for dealing with what he called 'immigrant crime', he declared that this would be a way of 'providing a voice to those who have been ignored by our media, and silenced by special interests'.[24] He even named the initiative 'Victims of Immigration Crime Engagement'. Or VOICE for short.

In Trump's case, not only is his use of the term a textbook example of populist rhetoric but it's also a telling example of the contested nature of these key terms. In choosing this acronym for his anti-immigration initiative, he was both translating his anti-immigration pledges from the election campaign into policy in a very literal way and also strategically co-opting the language of the opposition. Giving a 'voice' to the experiences of those marginalized by history and politics is a key aim not only of populist movements but also for development and postcolonial studies.[25] It's a way of challenging the inequalities that are embedded in society, and critiquing the way these are reproduced in institutions such as the law. This use of the word is reflected in advocate organizations such as America's Voice, whose stated mission is to 'harness the power of American voices and American values to enact policy change that guarantees full labor, civil and political rights for immigrants and their families'.[26]

Trump's 'VOICE' initiative ('Victims of Immigration Crime Engagement'), on the other hand, has the effect of further stigmatizing migrant communities; of directly associating the immigrant experience with a trend for criminality. It does this despite the fact that several studies show that immigrants are less likely to commit a crime than people born in the United States.[27] But according to the zero-tolerance logic of the Trump administration, statistics such as these are simply irrelevant. As Trump's former deputy assistant Sebastian Gorka said when justifying the programme, it's targeting those who have 'already broken the law by being here'. Gorka further pressed the argument by framing the issue as one about the essentials of American identity: 'If you object to [the principles behind the policy]', he said, 'you are in favor of pain, in favor of tragedy, and in favor of chaos, and that is un-American.'[28]

This use of the word 'voice' in this context then is not in any sense inclusive, as it is in development studies. Instead, it's purposefully erecting barriers around what it means to be a legitimate citizen in Trump's America by defining 'the people' along nativist lines.

So while Trump's point would likely be that he's also providing a voice for the disenfranchised, that he himself is speaking out for the powerless and standing with them against a political tradition which has marginalized them in recent years, he's doing so by pitting different disenfranchised groups against each other. He's assigning roles to these different groups – protagonist to the one, antagonist to the other – and in doing so, shaping the everyday reality of their lives according to the narrative upon which he's basing his politics.

By conflating the will of the people with the actions of their leader, the populist politician creates a straightforward rhetorical strategy which not only deflects but actually thrives, on criticism. Whenever an opponent attempts to criticize them they can re-frame it as being actually meant as criticism of their supporters. Likewise, any criticism that's made of their policies can be re-framed as a betrayal of the will of the people. And these two simple steps can generate an ongoing 'betrayal narrative', which further fires up the electorate against the political establishment.

* * *

The argument of these first few chapters has been that our knowledge of the world may be built on a combination of facts and evidence, but facts only have meaning when they're placed within a context – and this context is invariably structured around a story. The words we use to describe the world absorb their meaning from these stories, and often become sites of political struggle between alternative stories. It's the stories that prove to be most convincing that then come to shape the culture in which we live. In the last few years, populism has emerged as one such story. A story in which the people are pitted against an elitist establishment for control over the mechanisms of power. And the emergence of this story has led to a profound scepticism that has shaken the stability of our democratic institutions.

Does this mean then that an understanding of the art of storytelling can help explain popular or effective political movements? Can it translate into a blueprint for political success? To answer these questions we need to look in more depth at why precisely storytelling is so fundamental to politics. We need to look at what counts as an effective story in this context. And at what's involved in the way that political stories are narrated and spread.

Part Two

Shaping the story

4

Explanatory stories

The political-entertainment complex

Before we get to the structure and composition of political stories – to the ways in which they're narrated, and the effects they're put to in political discourse – it's worth first looking at the broader relationship between storytelling and politics. As the journalist Christopher Ingraham recently wrote, for 'many Americans, politics has become simply another form of entertainment'.[1] As a phenomenon, this isn't by any means restricted to the United States. Politics has become an increasingly popular spectator sport in countries around the world in the last few years. Not that this should come as much of a surprise; the ever-closer convergence of politics and entertainment has been happening for a while now. But the various ways in which the two complement each other, and in which the one draws upon other, can explain a great deal about the importance of narrative for the political state we're in.

* * *

Ingraham was referring to the influence that a changing media environment has had on the way people consume political news. If the term hadn't already been co-opted for something else, we could call this the '*Network* effect', after the 1970 Sidney Lumet film. It's the result of the way that cable TV's rolling news coverage brought about a shift from reporting to commentary and how this in turn pulled the focus from policies to personalities. The premise of Lumet's film is that when news shows start vying with entertainment shows in the schedules, the content of the two begin to mix. Any broadcast environment that's chasing ratings will seek out conflict and sensationalism; it will look to coerce or manufacture drama. This has a fundamental effect on the way we view the very idea of politics. When you then add to this the more recent culture of ceaseless ticker-tape updates that fuels the business of social media, you get the political-entertainment complex we now live with.

Ingraham was writing about politics in 2017. But in many ways it's been ever thus. The symbiotic relationship between politics and entertainment – and between politicians and entertainers – is by no means a recent development. It was as far back as 1966 after all that Ronald Reagan famously observed that 'politics is just like show business'[2] (or as the Hollywood studio executive Robert Evans put it, 'nothing more than second-rate show business'[3]). It shouldn't be too much of a surprise then that the history of twentieth- and twenty-first-century politics is littered with leaders who've nursed literary or acting ambitions, and who've channelled their frustrated creative aspirations into political careers. For some reason this tendency has been particularly strong among totalitarian leaders. The author and journalist Daniel Kalder has written a whole book analysing the literature written by twentieth-century dictators[4] – a genre that Will Self gleefully baptized 'dic lit'.[5]

Highlights of the genre include Mussolini's bodice-ripper *The Cardinal's Mistress*, written when he was twenty-six and working as assistant editor for the socialist newspaper *Il Popolo*. Then there's Franco's fictional reworking of events from the Spanish Civil War,

Raza (Race), which was duly turned into a propagandist film in 1942.[6] Saddam Hussein, meanwhile, was the author of four novels. These included his final work, *Begone, Demons*, supposedly completed only a day before the American troops invaded Iraq.[7] And the trend continues in the current crop of authoritarian leaders, with Turkish president Recep Tayyip Erdoğan having written, directed and starred in a play called *Maskomya* back in the 1970s.[8]

While all of these may, on the surface, be works of fiction, they also double as rather unsubtle political allegories. Erdoğan's *Maskomya*, for instance, has a plot detailing the malign influence of the Masons, communists and Jews on global society, while Saddam's *Begone, Demons* involves a Zionist-Christian conspiracy that only runs aground when heroic Arab troops are able to invade enemy territory and destroy two large towers. As I say, the symbolism isn't that subtle.

Literary ambitions of this sort aren't restricted to despots, of course. Two of the last three Democratic presidents have tried their hand at fiction following their retirement from the White House. First up was Jimmy Carter back in 2003 with *The Hornet's Nest*, a novel set during the American Revolutionary War. A decade and a half later Bill Clinton jumped onto the presidential novel-writing bandwagon by co-authoring a thriller called *The President Is Missing* with bestselling writer James Patterson. This is a story of devious cyber-criminals threatening modern civilization, and the heroic acts of a fictional president who has to coordinate various ingenious countermeasures to thwart these threats.

In both these cases, as with the dic-lit, fiction doubles as fairly unsubtle political treatise. The consensus among critics of *The Hornet's Nest* was that, although well-intentioned, the book was more leisurely exploration of the political history of America than gripping narrative drama.[9] In Clinton's case, much was made of the almost mythical portrait the novel produced of the office of president, and how this contrasted with the artless and erratic behaviour of the current occupant.

Compared with their American counterparts, recent UK prime ministers have been rather less prolific when it comes to literature of the imagination. Prior to 2019, you had to go right back to Winston Churchill to find a fiction-writing prime minister. Churchill wrote one novel, *Savrola*, at the turn of the twentieth century, before then devoting the writing-side of his career to history books. A few decades earlier, Benjamin Disraeli had also been a prolific author, writing over a dozen novels, along with an epic poem and a dramatic tragedy in blank verse. Disraeli's early novels were examples of the 'silver fork' genre, focusing on the social mores of the upper classes. As his literary career progressed, so his work became more expressly political, grappling with topics such as the conditions of the working class and the social disparity between privileged and marginalized in society.

The 120 odd years since Churchil"s one and only novel were rather a dry spell for prime-ministerial fiction. The drought was only finally broken by the premiership of Boris Johnson who, in 2004, wrote the comedy-thriller *Seventy-Two Virgins* about a terrorist plot which is narrowly averted by the smart thinking of a bicycle-loving Tory MP. In managing to squeeze literary endeavours in between his various other commitments, Johnson was following in the footsteps of his father, Stanley, who has been both politician (he was a Member of the European Parliament in the early 1980s) and prolific novelist. Johnson senior has never, of course, been talked of as a future prime minister. But one of his novels is worth mentioning here because it deals with a subject which had, up until recently, inspired relatively little interest among English-language creative writers. The subject in question being the state of European politics. On the few occasions in the pre-Brexit era that the EU was featured in fiction it was usually presented as a corrupt and monolithic super state.[10] Johnson's 1987 novel *The Commissioner* is very much in this vein, telling the story of a plucky British politician who has to confront a pernicious web of corruption radiating out across European Union institutions. As we'll see, this is a plot template that has since become very familiar in political discourse all around the continent.

Alongside the fiction writers there have been a good number of actor-slash-politicians. The most prominent of these is Ronald Reagan, of course. But there was also the ex-president of the Philippines Joseph 'Erap' Estrada, who was star of over a hundred films. Then there's the *éminence grise* of Polish politics, Lech Kaczyński, who was a child star with his twin brother (and former Polish president) Jarosław back in the 1960s (as lovable urchins the two of them set out to steal the moon). And of course there's Volodymyr Zelensky, the actor who played a teacher-turned-president in the Ukrainian television comedy *Servant of the People*. Zelensky somehow managed to move directly from playing an unconventional president speaking out against corruption on Ukrainian television to actually becoming the president of Ukraine by speaking out against corruption.

The most high-profile entertainer-turned-politician of recent years is, of course, Donald Trump. Since launching his political career Trump's relationship with the entertainment industry has soured somewhat. But although Hollywood and he may now be pitted against each other in the culture wars, like all good antagonists, they have a lot more in common than they're willing to admit. Not only is Trump frequently referred to as the first Reality TV president,[11] but he's also appeared in, among other things, one of the *Home Alone* films, scores of television series (from the *Fresh Prince of Bel-Air* and *Spin City* to *Sex and the City* and *Top Gear USA*), and won a Golden Raspberry Award (or Razzie) for his part in a 1989 romcom about a ghost trying to penetrate the astral plane so he can once again have sex with his wife.[12] He also has the dubious honour of being the only president to date to have had a cameo in a soft porn film.[13]

Trump isn't the only member of his administration who can boast of a quirky filmography. His first White House Chief Strategist and the architect of his election campaign, Steve Bannon, has an equally idiosyncratic background in the entertainment industry. Before getting into politics Bannon had a spell in Hollywood, working for an investment company which arranged financing for film projects.[14] During this time he tried to get a number of bizarre projects off the ground, including an erotic, futuristic adaptation of Shakespeare's *Titus Andronicus* which featured intergalactic travel and an episode of 'ectoplasmic sex',[15] as well as a rap version of *Coriolanus* which was to be set in South Central during the 1992 L.A. riots.[16] Neither of these came to fruition unfortunately, and so, after the millennium, Bannon switched from fictional projects to documentary film-making. When asked by the *Wall Street Journal* back in 2011 about his cinematic influences, he listed an eclectic mix of directors, including Sergei Eisenstein, Michael Moore and Leni Riefenstahl, propagandist for the Nazis.[17]

Which somehow brings us back full circle to the dic-lit genre. Writing of this, Daniel Kalder notes that in the formative years of many of the twentieth century's most infamous autocrats, writing acted as an imaginary dry-run for their ideas: a place where they could rehearse 'their ideological fantasies on paper in anticipation of the day when they would have entire populations at their mercy'.[18] Looking at things from this perspective, the relationship between politics and entertainment is not simply coincidental. Politics can be seen as a form of storytelling that uses a broader and more extensive set of resources than your average novel or film. And of course, one that is ultimately capable of a more profound and direct effect on the state of the world.

Strategic narratives

The development of storytelling abilities was one of the key factors behind humankind's incredible evolutionary success.[19] Speech and language were also part of the equation, of course. But without storytelling – without the ability to conjure up and communicate illusory worlds – there would be no gods or nations, no legal system, no money. It's the power we have to imagine complex sets of ideas into being, and to then share these among the community, which creates both the societies we live in and the cultures that provide the meanings for our lives. Remove stories from the human equation and civilization itself fades from the picture.[20]

Stories fulfil a host of different functions in our lives. First and foremost they provide entertainment. According to the global accountancy firm PwC, revenues from the entertainment and media industry will hit $2.2 trillion in 2021.[21] In other words, there's a lot of money being made from storytelling (although not necessarily by those who write the stories). But stories do much more besides. As the sociologist Francesca Polletta notes, these days storytelling is sold as a strategy for everything from the attainment of spiritual enlightenment and the resolving of interpersonal conflict to effective weight-loss.[22] Such is the vogue for narrative that Microsoft now have a 'Chief Storyteller' in charge of their 'Image and Culture team' (i.e. their public relations), while the US Army use narrative-based video games, co-created by Hollywood screenwriters and military strategists, as training exercises for their troops.[23]

In more general terms, stories offer us a way to help make sense of our experiences; to show us how actions have consequences and thus meaning. They're a way of processing and passing on information. For instance, Daniel Kahneman, in his book *Thinking, Fast and Slow*, frames his theoretical explanation of the psychology of decision-making as a story. Chapter One of the book is called 'Introducing the Characters', and opens with the statement that 'a brief synopsis of the plot is in order'.[24] The reason for doing this, he explains, is that the mind 'appears to have a special aptitude for the construction and interpretation of stories about active agents, who have personalities, habits, and abilities'. The teaching of anything, even abstract precepts about human cognition, is more easily achieved through narrative.

Stories also allow us to create the ties that form communities. All the identities we have as groups are based on shared narratives, woven together to form culture. We use stories to communicate with each other, to reflect on our own sense of self. And, of course, stories operate as a very effective tool for persuasion.

It should be no surprise then that storytelling is central to the business of politics. The author and Pulitzer Prize winner Viet Thanh Nguyen puts it well when he writes that 'those who seek to lead our country must persuade the people through their ability to tell a story about who we are, where we have been, and where we are going. The struggle over the direction of our country is also a fight over whose words will win and whose images will ignite the collective imagination'.[25] Barack Obama, on the eve of his second term as president, made almost precisely the same point: 'The nature of this office is also to tell a story to the American people that gives them a sense of unity and purpose and optimism, especially during tough times'.[26] This was something he felt he hadn't appreciated early enough, and thus saw as a priority for his second term. And this presidential storytelling continues even after a politician has left office, as they strive to make sure that it's their version of the narrative that gets accepted by history.[27]

The political strategist Mark McKinnon sees storytelling as central to the work of a campaign's communications team. McKinnon worked on George W. Bush's 2000 and 2004 presidential campaigns. For the 2000 campaign the basic narrative he and his team pushed was Bush as a moral and authentic antidote to the Clinton years (summed up in Bush's one-liner that under Clinton they'd 'moved that sign, "The Buck Stops Here" from the Oval Office desk to the Lincoln Bedroom'[28]). For the 2004 election it was Bush as a steadfast leader in times of war post 9/11.[29] 'Voters are attracted to candidates who lay out a storyline', McKinnon notes. Losing campaigns are a muddle of unconnected ideas and disparate information. Whereas winning campaigns 'create a narrative architecture that ties it all together into something meaningful and coherent'.[30]

This maxim isn't restricted to politics in the West. Chinese president Xi Jinping has also spoken of the way that 'telling stories is the best form of international dissemination' for boosting China's profile around the world. According to the publisher of the *People's Daily* newspaper, the art of '[t]elling stories well has been a common characteristic of celebrated statesmen and thinkers in China and beyond since ancient times – and it is a clear characteristic of General Secretary Xi Jinping's leadership style'.[31] Such is his apparent dedication to the art and power of narrative that in 2017 he published a collection of writings simply called *Xi Jinping Tells a Story*.

Historically in the West, there's been a tendency for those on the right to be better at using effective storytelling to sell their ideas than those on the left. After John Kerry lost the presidential election to Bush in 2004, James Carville, former lead strategist for Bill Clinton, bemoaned the way that Republicans were able to produce a narrative while 'we produce a litany ... They say, "I'm going to protect you from the terrorists in Tehran and the homos in Hollywood". We say, "We're for clean air, better schools, more health care"'.[32]

A decade down the line and this was still something the Democrats were struggling with. So much so that after their poor showing in the 2014 midterm elections, the Democratic National Committee planned to set up a 'national narrative project' which would help them create a cohesive story about their aims and ambitions rather than simply give a bullet-point list of policy ideas. 'The goal is to lift up the foundational ideas that unify Democrats' in order to create 'a more powerful, consistent message and engage the American people in meaningful ways'.[33] Unfortunately for them, they never fully acted on these intentions, thus ceding the advantage in the 2016 election to Trump and his years of experience as self-promoting fabulist.

Another non-traditional politician who recognized the great importance of narrative in politics is French president Emmanuel Macron. Although in Macron's case it wasn't the product of decades-long training in Reality TV, but rather a firm grounding in poststructuralist philosophy (thus playing up a little too perfectly to Gallic stereotypes). For a short time at the beginning of his career Macron worked with one of the great theorists of narrative, the philosopher Paul Ricoeur. As a 22-year-old student he was Ricoeur's assistant, helping out with clerical tasks such as referencing and note-checking, before going on to edit the manuscript of *Memory, History, Forgetting*.

There's been a great deal written in the French press on the influence that Ricoeur's philosophy has had on Macron's politics, particularly on his centrist ideology and his attempts to synthesize ideas from both left and right.[34] Equally important though are Ricoeur's ideas about narrative. For instance, one of Ricoeur's key precepts is that people's sense of self should always be seen in terms of their 'narrative identity', which is constituted by the stories they tell about both themselves and each other.[35] For Macron, this can apply to the nation as well as the individual. During the 2017 presidential election he spent a great deal of time talking of his broad vision for the state of France and of the need to reinvent the entire structure of French politics to reflect the story of the modern nation.[36] For his critics, this was viewed as a way of skirting concrete policy plans and instead indulging in the bland rhetoric of advertising. But as Olivier Duhamel, a professor at the Paris Institute of Political Studies, notes, it's also entirely in line with Ricoeur's emphasis on 'the necessity and the strength of narratives ... in that events of all kinds become visible and intelligible only as told through stories'.

It's not just political parties who recognize the importance of narrative as a political tool. As part of its Strategic Communications department (StratCom), NATO has a section on the Military Concept for Strategic Communications which is dedicated to developing 'narratives, themes and master messages for different audiences'.[37] The idea is that 'Strategic Communications' should be incorporated at the very centre of military operations and activities, from early planning through to execution.[38] The premise behind this commitment is that military strategy and strategic narrative follow precisely the same structure; the only difference being that narrative involves emotion while strategy doesn't. As Mark Laity, current Chief of Strategic Communications, explains, a narrative contains an explanation of how events relate to one's system of belief, which in turn indicates the direction of future actions. 'Narratives make sense of the world, put things in their place according to our experience, and then tell us what to do.'[39] They're an organizing framework for our thoughts.

For the television producer and author of the highly engaging *Into the Woods: A Five-Act Journey into Story*, John Yorke, this relationship between narrative and our understanding of the world is the essential explanation of why we're so attracted to stories. The way we perceive the world, Yorke argues, always involves an attempt on our part to impose some sort of order on it. And the form this ordering takes is the very same form that narrative takes. Narrative isn't simply something that helps us make sense of things; it's the actual mechanism that structures understanding. Or, as Yorke puts it, storytelling is the codification of the very method by which we learn.

And one way in which we can witness the power that stories have in this respect is by looking at how people instinctively reach out to existing narratives whenever they're struggling to understand the seemingly random and unpredictable events that are unfurling in the world.

The crystal ball of fiction

In the autumn of 1917 the writer Aldous Huxley took a teaching job at Eton. The previous year he'd volunteered for the army but was rejected on health grounds due to his bad eyesight. Both his parents had been educators however, so taking work in a school presumably felt like a natural enough step for him. Among the pupils he had in his short stint in the classroom was a fourteen-year-old called Eric Blair.[40]

Thirty-two years later Huxley was to write to Blair, who by this time had adopted the penname George Orwell, congratulating him on the publication of his novel *Nineteen Eighty-Four*.[41] After offering a fair amount of praise for the book, Huxley goes on to voice slight reservations. Despite the obvious power of *Nineteen Eighty-Four*, Huxley felt that his own novel, *Brave New World*, actually gave a better picture of how society was evolving. Both novels offer prophetic visions of a future dystopia and a populace under the yoke of totalitarianism. But for Orwell state control was administered through fear and brute force, while for Huxley it was distraction and vapid entertainment.

The philosopher Raymond Williams recalled how, back in the 1950s, 'along almost every road that you moved, the figure of Orwell seemed to be waiting ... if you engaged in any kind of socialist argument, there was the enormously inflated statue of Orwell warning you to go back.[42] That same sort of fascination, and the determination to use him as a touchstone for any sort of political critique, seems to be repeating itself in the early part of the twenty-first century. Although both Orwell's and Huxley's novels have been popular ever since publication, there's been an increased spike in interest in both of them over the last few years.[43] According to Google Trends, internet searches for 'George Orwell' remained pretty much constant throughout the 2010s – except, that is, for the week of 22 to 28 January 2017 when they saw a sudden surge. It's not difficult to pinpoint the reason for this – 20 January was the date on which Donald Trump was inaugurated as president, and 22 January was when Kellyanne Conway introduced the world to 'alternative facts'. Writing in the *Washington Post* following Conway's comments, the columnist Margaret Sullivan argued that the incident was evidence that society has now 'gone full Orwell'.[44]

For many people, the phrase 'alternative facts' was startlingly reminiscent of Orwell's idea of Newspeak, the engineered language used by the novel's totalitarian government to control how the population thinks. It's Newspeak which creates the slogans 'War Is Peace', 'Freedom Is Slavery' and 'Ignorance Is Strength', building on an idea that Orwell had previously given to Squealer, the pig-community's propagandist in *Animal Farm*, who was able to 'turn black into white'.

While Newspeak is fiction, there's at least an element of truth to the way it illustrates how language is never a register of completely stable meaning and is always open to manipulation. But an equally interesting aspect of the comparison between Orwell's imaginary linguistics and today's political rhetoric is the fact that people instinctively seem to turn to literature for ways of making sense of what was going on in the world. This is another key element in the relationship between narrative and politics. Stories from literature, along with other forms of narrative culture, are regularly used as a way of talking about current affairs – and some of these then become conceptual reference points around which people structure their debates about the politics of the day. In the last few years, for instance, along with Huxley and Orwell, Sinclair Lewis's *It Can't Happen Here* has once again become a bestseller thanks to its eerie parallels with the rise of Trump, while the imagery of Margaret Atwood's *The Handmaid's Tale* has become a mainstay in political resistance movements.

So why is this? In his exploration of *Future Politics*, Jamie Susskind queries why, 'if we want to understand the world as it will be in 2050, should we ... rely on a work of fiction from 1949?' (or, he could have added, from 1932, 1935 or 1985).[45] What it is it about fiction that helps illuminate the practical political realities that confront us in our lives, both today and in the immediate future?

There are a number of possible reasons. A general answer is perhaps the fact that, in the words of the philosopher Hannah Arendt, 'storytelling reveals meaning without committing the error of defining it, that it brings about consent and reconciliation with things as they really are'.[46] Or, as the Elizabethan poet Sir Philip Sidney put it in his *Apology for Poetry* back in the sixteenth century, poets and storytellers 'yieldeth to the powers of the mind an image of that whereof the philosopher bestoweth but a wordish description, which doth neither strike, pierce, nor possess the sight of the soul so much as that other doth'.[47] Stories are a way of turning abstract theories about the changes in the world into concrete scenarios, of translating philosophical reflection into vivid experiences. They help us better understand not only the dynamics of what we're witnessing but also the consequences and emotional fallout. Shared stories link the private realm of our individual consciousness to the public realm of politics; they offer us a way of stepping temporarily outside of the stream of actual events so that, paradoxically, we're able to better contemplate and comprehend them.

But there's something more specific in these particular examples. It's notable that the majority of these novels – *Nineteen Eighty-Four*, *Brave New World*, *It Can't Happen Here* and *The Handmaid's Tale* – are set in the future. They're speculative predictions about what life might be like if politics were to take a wrong turn somewhere up ahead; predictions that are, for the most part, based on worrying evidence that the politics of the day was very likely to do exactly that. In other words, they're thought experiments on the part of their authors for just how frightening society might become if we choose (or inadvertently allow for) one type of future to unfold at the expense of another.

One element of their appeal then is reading them as metaphoric prophecy. In Orwell's case he was imagining a specific year, not that distant from the time he was writing. There's a sense that his novel is partly a prediction of life a couple of generations down the line. As it turned out, the 1980s weren't quite as bleak as he imagined. But perhaps he just got his maths wrong. Perhaps he should have doubled up on his forecast, and rather than setting his totalitarian future in 1984, set it instead in 2019. Either way, there's a certain fascination for the reader in being able to contrast the way things have turned out with the way the story-world of the novel predicted they might.

The same is very much the case with *The Handmaid's Tale*. As the journalist Jane Mulkerrins says, its huge success – both as a book and a TV series – has been helped by its sense of 'prescience'.[48] Set in the bleak aftermath of a Second American Civil War, where groups of women are sexually subjugated by the state and forced to bear children for the elite of society, its themes are seen by many as frighteningly relevant to political developments in parts of the world in the late 2010s.

But it's not just the way these novels seem to have predicted elements of modern-day society that fuels their popularity. As Huxley suggested in his letter to Orwell, they're also viewed as manuals that can help us understand the nature and implications of the events we're living through. They reveal the strategies and techniques of despotic regimes, and the circumstances that create the environments which allow these types of events to take place. If Orwell or Atwood in some sense predicted elements of the reality we're now living through, perhaps they can offer further clues about the way our current situation is going to play out. In a world which seems so unpredictable, the well-crafted logic of the stories they're telling offers us a sense of what our future may hold. Atwood, in fact, has referred to her novel as an 'antiprediction'. It wasn't intended as a prediction of the future, when she wrote it, because the future simply can't be predicted in any meaningful way. Instead, she says, her approach was that 'if this future can be described in detail, maybe it won't happen'.[49] By creating these nightmare visions, their authors hoped that humankind would have the good sense to ensure they never actually came to pass.

Hollywood diplomacy

In the autumn of 2018 a company called Yandy, who style themselves as a 'Lingerie Store and Adult Halloween Costumers', ran into a storm of bad publicity when they advertised a sexy *Handmaid's Tale* costume as part of their new holiday line. There was outrage on social media, causing them to promptly withdraw the item and issue a statement explaining that while the outfit had been meant as 'an expression of women's empowerment', they now saw that it could just as easily be mistaken for 'a symbol of women's oppression'.[50] However misguided this was as a business adventure – not to say naïve in its understanding of empowerment – it illustrates just how deeply embedded in the culture the iconography of *The Handmaid's Tale* has become. Since the TV adaptation was first broadcast in 2017, the image of the long blood-red cloak and starched white bonnet has become an enduring part of the vocabulary of contemporary politics. It's a regular symbol of resistance at political demonstrations and a staple in memes addressing women's rights.[51] And it works in this way because the simple but eye-catching image represents a whole set of interrelated themes that are woven into the narrative of the novel.

Drawing on the shared knowledge of pre-existing stories is an integral part of the way we communicate with each other. In some instances these allusions become part of the everyday vocabulary of a language. When the *Washington Post*, for instance, creates a 'Pinocchio Ranking' of politicians, we know exactly what this is going to be about because we know that the eponymous character from Carlo Collodi's children's novel is a conventional metaphor for compulsive lying. Pinocchio has become one of the modern myths of Western society, and allusions to these myths work as linguistic shorthand for more complex concepts.

Allusions to literature and films don't need to be quite as established as this however. There are various other ways in which we draw on shared knowledge of pre-existing stories to help us argue a political point. There are one-off analogies, where cultural reference is used to help explain a particular situation or event. A recent example from the world of international relations centred around the film *50 First Dates*, an American romcom staring Drew Barrymore and Adam Sandler. The film has a very high-concept premise: Sandler's character meets the beautiful young Barrymore and falls in love, only to find that she has short-term memory loss causing her to forget all about him the following day. As such he's forced to woo her over and over again, leading to some broad comedic misunderstandings. It's not traditionally thought to be a classic in the genre. But for the Iranian foreign minister, in an interview with the *New Yorker*, it offered the perfect comparison for diplomacy with the Trump administration.[52]

The use of cultural references like this is an easy way to make a straightforward point, and there's no need for the reference itself to have much political meaning. In this instance, the analogy is simply between the recurring amnesia at the root of the movie's plot and the lack of any consistent logic in dealings with the Trump team. It's also probable that the rather unsophisticated nature of the film is part of the comparison. Trump and his team don't warrant a more highbrow analogy.

It's unlikely that Adam Sandler or Drew Barrymore will become regular features of today's political vocabulary. But a second use of pre-existing stories is where characters, iconography or phrases from a work of fiction become repeatedly used for expressing a particular position in political discourse. This is precisely what's happened with *The Handmaid's Tale*, which now offers people a simple and arresting way to make a range of points about women's rights.

Another notable example of this phenomenon is the way that the actress Carrie Fisher's death in late 2016 led to the use of the Princess Leia character from *Star Wars* as a similar symbol of resistance. Fisher died a few months after Donald Trump had been elected president and a few weeks before he was inaugurated. The day after his inauguration, hundreds of thousands of people took part in the Women's March in cities across the country, protesting against the values and policies he stood for. Images of Fisher were one of the most visible symbols used by demonstrators on these marches. As the designer Hayley Gilmore commented in an interview for *Wired*, 'Carrie Fisher's portrayal as Leia in the Star Wars film franchise resonates with many women because she is a fierce, intelligent, charming, and powerful woman ... It makes sense [marchers] would gravitate towards Leia, especially after Carrie's death.'[53]

Gilmore herself created a poster for the event, based around the Princess Leia character, which was adopted by scores of people taking part in the demonstrations. Using an image of Leia holding up her blaster above the slogan 'A Woman's Place Is In The Resistance', the poster brought together various different cultural elements to make a political statement. First, there's the refashioning of the proverb 'a woman's place is in the home', here given a decidedly less patriarchal spin. The use of the word 'resistance' then brings to mind historical events where grass-roots groups have been pitted against authoritarian regimes – the French Resistance during the Second World War, the independence and civil rights movements led by Mahatma Gandhi and Martin Luther King respectively.[54] But 'the Resistance' also happens to be the name of the group of rebels founded by Princess Leia in the third trilogy of *Star Wars* films. The real-life political movement is thus able to tap into the emotional attachment that people have to the fictional world of *Star Wars* and its narrative of a small group of resistance fighters led by a powerful woman winning out against a despotic evil empire.

In cases such as this, allusions to fiction achieve a number of things. Not only do they make the issues instantly recognizable and relatable to a large audience, but they also co-opt the emotional attachment that people have to the original story. By aligning themselves with a character such as Leia, the demonstrators align themselves with the moral values of the story she's a part of, as well as the heroic optimism this story represents for them.

An important aspect of this process, however, is that a shared cultural vocabulary can be appropriated by all sides of the political spectrum. It's not reserved for those whose values most obviously match the content of the original narrative. For instance, these days you're just as likely to see people from the right invoking Orwell, especially when complaining about what they see as overt political correctness and the supposed policing of people's speech.[55] When, in August 2018, the then foreign secretary Boris Johnson provoked a calculated storm of outrage by comparing women who wore burkas to pillar boxes, the *Daily Mail* described the criticism he received as a witch hunt which was '[d]isturbingly Orwellian'.[56] The allusion here isn't to the complexities of the world of *Nineteen Eighty-Four* itself, of course. It's to a hollowed-out version of the idea of Newspeak, a version pulled roughly from the context of the novel's value system. Yet despite this, it's still working as a particular – and particularly effective – type of political shorthand.

Likewise, just as those on the left can appropriate ideas from *Star Wars*, so also can the right. Ronald Reagan famously described the behaviour of the Soviet Union as the 'aggressive impulses of an evil empire' (a reference to the Galactic Empire from the *Star Wars* saga) in 1983, and when, a few weeks later, he then made the case for a space-based missile defence system the media almost immediately started calling it the Star Wars programme. The name took hold to such an extent that Reagan felt the need to clarify the purpose behind the programme, arguing that 'isn't about war, it's about peace … It isn't about fear, it's about hope, and in that struggle, if you will pardon my stealing a film line, the force is with us.'[57]

There's even political mileage in embracing this sort of iconography when it's being used specifically as an insult. For instance, when asked if he objected to being likened to the chief villain in the *Star Wars* saga, Vice-President Dick Cheney replied that the answer was a simple *no*. 'After all, Darth Vader is one of the nicer things I've been called recently', he said.[58] Not only did he not object, but he also played up on the idea: he occasionally used the Darth Vader theme, the Imperial March, as his entry music at political appearances, and reportedly dressed his black Labrador up in a Darth Vader costume for Halloween one year.[59]

So why would someone willingly associate themselves with the villain of a story? How can there be any political capital in that? There are a couple of possible explanations. The first is that the villain of the piece invariably possesses great power. They may use it for malign and misguided purposes, but there's no denying the effectiveness of their ability to impose their will on the world. And as a politician, it's far better to be associated with effective rule than with incompetence. As Steve Bannon has said, 'Darkness is good … Dick Cheney. Darth Vader. Satan. That's power.'[60] Then there's the fact that in classic dramatic structure – especially that used in Hollywood – the villain is often as compelling a character as the hero. In the words of George Lucas, 'Obviously everyone likes the villain better than they like the heroes, that's sort of a tradition.'[61] As we'll see in the next chapter, protagonists and antagonists share virtually precisely the same dramatic DNA. Thus, comparing someone to a classic Hollywood bad guy isn't quite the searing critical insult one might assume.

The final use of allusions to pre-existing stories in politics is slightly different from the others. It involves the retrospective reference to literature as a way of justifying or explaining an event or behaviour. An interesting, if slightly confusing, example of this comes from Paul Dacre, the former editor of the British newspaper the *Daily Mail*, a few months after he'd retired. At the height of the never-ending arguments over the Brexit process, the High Court in England ruled that Parliament should be given a vote over whatever deal was finally decided by the government. The *Daily Mail*, as a staunchly pro-Brexit paper, took up an editorial position which was strongly opposed to this. They felt that the judiciary was interfering in issues which the government alone should rule on. So Dacre reported the story with a front-page headline describing the three judges who'd made the ruling as 'enemies of the people'.

The term 'enemies of the people' has a long provenance, having been used by everyone from Robespierre during the French Revolution, through Lenin in the Russian Revolution, to Joseph Goebbels during the Third Reich.[62] It's also a classic trope in populist rhetoric. But according to Dacre, the headline in his paper was actually meant as an allusion to the Henrik Ibsen play of the same name.[63]

The reference here is a strange one. Ibsen's 1882 play tells the story of a man who exposes the truth about troubling events in society and is then punished for doing so. The argument that underpins the play is that the truth must be given a voice however unpopular this may prove to be, and that those exposing the truth will very likely be branded 'enemies of the people'. The play is more about the dangers of groupthink than about the populist struggle. In the 1950s, at the height of the McCarthy era, there was a notable English-language adaptation written by Arthur Miller, which addressed the way that a climate of paranoia can wreak havoc on society.

Quite how all this accords with Dacre's allusion in the context of a judicial ruling about the rights of parliament to vote on one of the most consequential events in a generation, it's difficult to say. What the allusion does perhaps do is attempt to elevate the intellectual standing of the headline. In other words, it's the opposite of the *50 First Dates* example. Where the Iranian foreign minister was indirectly likening the Trump administration to a crass Adam Sandler vehicle, Dacre is recasting the political struggle between the people and the establishment as classic drama – and specifically aligning himself and his paper as cultural commentators in the same way that writers such as Ibsen are.

Storytelling thus has a relationship to politics in a variety of different ways. References to pre-existing stories provide a shared vocabulary for people to discuss or argue about their politics. In certain cases stories can act as explanatory toolkits to help us make sense of the times we're living through. Down through the years there's been a continued attraction between politicians and the storytelling arts, and many politicians have explicitly stressed the need for storytelling abilities in politics. But for all these close ties, none of what we've discussed so far explains precisely how storytelling works in political contexts. To understand this, we first need to take a closer look at what makes an effective story.

5

What makes a good story?

An abundance of story

Raymond Williams's *Keywords* project was updated in the 2010s by a new generation of scholars for a new century. One of the words they added for the revised version was 'narrative'. Over the last twenty years, they write, this 'has seen a sharp rise in frequency ... especially in such phrases as "change the narrative" and "take control of the narrative," which have become unavoidable in political commentary'.[1] In this respect it's not only a keyword but also a buzzword, co-opted by countless individuals and institutions as a way of aligning their actions with the linguistic zeitgeist. What rarely gets examined, however, is what constitutes a narrative in these contexts. What does a political narrative look like when used on the campaign trail or as part of the persuasion tactics behind a policy or ideology? And why is it that narrative has become such an integral part of the political toolkit?

* * *

The importance that storytelling has for human civilization, rivalling language in the way it shapes everything from cognition to culture, means that the relationship it has with politics extends much further than just a fad for voguish terminology. Stories are used in a myriad of ways, for a host of different purposes, and can take various different forms. On the most general level, narratives can shape the way we understand our experiences, and how we see the world. They help us view certain value systems as normal or natural, thus contributing to the ideologies embedded in society and culture. The overarching idea of patriarchy, for example, is encoded in the simple story of Adam and Eve (God created man in his own image, with woman as his helpmate), and thus underpins the whole of Judeo-Christian culture.

In the late twentieth century, the enduring influence of cultural narratives like this came under sustained attack with the rise of postmodern theory. The French philosopher Jean-François Lyotard argued that the postmodern age was characterized by intense scepticism of the traditional 'master narratives' and the ideological shadow they cast over the culture. Instead, he said, we were witnessing an era of competing narratives, each championed by different communities with different cultural experiences of the world.[2] The history of the world could no longer be seen as a single, linear chronology; it was fragmented, made of multiple perspectives and characterized by contestation and struggle as people from all parts of society tried to get their side of the story heard. That's not to say that the master narratives had lost all influence. They're still retold and reinforced in much of mainstream culture, particularly in the media, and they still act as the taken-for-granted context against which other stories about people's individual actions and aspirations are presented.

In the day-to-day business of politics, people tell anecdotes about personal experience, relate political issues to their life stories and provide testimonials about the consequences of events. Each of these produces a slightly different form of story, and each can be used for a range of different purposes.[3] For instance, the political scientists

Judi Atkins and Alan Finlayson have looked at the way that political leaders use personal anecdotes, and particularly those about their encounters with 'ordinary' people, as evidence of the success of their policies.[4] They'll talk of meeting an average mum-of-three, or a struggling pensioner, in a market town in the north–east, or on a housing estate in the midlands, who'd personally told them of their recent troubles and how these had been alleviated by the common-sense policies advocated by the politician. In cases such as these, the testimony of everyday citizens is used as proof of a more general point the politician is trying to make. And, as Atkins and Finlayson put it, with populism on the rise, these sorts of 'real life' anecdotes have 'a special authority to validate and legitimate claims about the world and what is to be done about it'. A few home truths from Brenda from Basingstoke or Malik from Manchester can often be far more persuasive as evidence than highlights from the executive summary from a report by the Office for National Statistics.

Research by psychologists Melanie Green and Timothy Brock gives an insight into why this type of persuasive strategy might be so prevalent nowadays.[5] They found that when people use narratives rather than argument as a means of persuasion, the audience is less concerned about the credibility or perception of the speaker. When a speaker uses rational argument, people are more likely to believe them if they find them trustworthy or authoritative. When people are told a story, on the other hand, they're more likely to be swayed by its content than by their feelings towards the person doing the telling. Which leads Green and Brock to suggest that storytelling can be used to advantage by 'low-credible sources or by speakers who lack cogent arguments' – a finding that seems to be borne almost too neatly by the current crop of world leaders.

The idea of narrative as a form of rhetoric is in no sense new, of course. It goes back at least as far as Aristotle, who talks of dramatic art as having a cathartic effect on the audience, and purifying or purging strong emotions in the listener. As Green and Brock again point out, the long history of censorship for types of storytelling such as novels and films points to just how effective they can be in influencing people's view on the world. You wouldn't go about banning books, after all, if you didn't think they had a very powerful effect on people's behaviour.

Today, the prevailing idea seems to be that stories have a more immediate impact on an audience than arguments do. Again, this is borne out by research. Neuroscientists from Princeton and New York University have shown that brain activity that takes place when people are listening to a story isn't limited solely to those regions associated with language. It also involves regions related to emotional, sensory and motor systems, suggesting that listeners don't merely comprehend the content of a story, but they actually experience it.[6] You get psychologically caught up in a story in a way you simply don't with a series of well-balanced claims, counterclaims and corollaries. So stories offer a more intuitive way of conveying a political message, grounded as they are in the dramatization of everyday experiences coupled with collective cultural aspirations. And one of the ways in which they do this is by tapping into cultural archetypes.

The Cinderella Man

James Braddock was a boxer in the 1930s. Early in his career he suffered problems with his hands, which led him lose a string of fights. At the same time as he was struggling with this, the Great Depression was sweeping through America. Braddock was forced to take work on the docks to make ends meet, and when this didn't provide enough to support his family, he had to sign up for financial aid from the government. In the mid-1930s he began his comeback. This reached a climax in 1935 when he was matched against reigning champion Max Baer for the world heavyweight title. Baer's people had picked Braddock because they assumed he'd be a pushover given his patchy history in the ring. The bookies had him as an 8-to-1 underdog.

For the writer Damon Runyon, the fight produced the greatest pugilistic upset in modern history. It was the perfect example of a 'fistic fairy tale', Runyon wrote, as Braddock, the one-time down-and-out, was '[b]rought back from Hasbeenville by the magic wave of the wand of sheer chance' to beat the reigning champion.[7] Labouring the metaphor a little, Runyon described how the contest culminated 'with the poor abused hero finding his pumpkins of failure turned into prancing white steeds of glittering success and his feet incased in the glass slippers of happiness'.

It was Runyon who gave Braddock the nickname the 'Cinderella Man'. His story embodies the classic fairy tale arc of struggling local fighter transformed into global champion. It's a feel-good narrative about perseverance set against the backdrop of the Great Depression, as the child of Irish immigrants overcomes physical and financial hardships to pull off one of the great sporting upsets.

According to the folklorist James Deutsch, the Cinderella story has a particularly strong resonance for the United States.[8] This is because the story's basic plot is exactly the same as that of the American Dream. With perseverance, self-belief and hard work anyone can achieve greatness. When a statue of Braddock was unveiled in his hometown in 2018, the owner of the local boxing gym said, 'His story is representative of the Irish immigrants back then, but it also applies to immigrants now … [H]is story of struggle to attain the American Dream is universal.'[9]

The point I want to illustrate here is a simple one. All stories have a structure to them, and these basic structures resurface over and over again. James Braddock's story has exactly the same basic structure as Cinderella's story – so much so that this became his nickname. And the reason the story resonated so much both then and now is that this, in turn, has precisely the same structure as the ideals that constitute the American Dream. The parallels between fairy tale and national psyche are partly centred around the rags-to-riches trope. But the Cinderella story also enacts the rewards of virtue and the punishing of evil. The little gal/guy wins, not through chicanery and cheating, but by sticking to their principles. As Deutsch puts it, 'You rightly deserve your prince (or princess), just as the United States deserves its pre-eminence, or so most Americans believe.'

There are two upshots of all this. The first is that Cinderella can be seen as a political story. We can see how this plays out in, for instance, the allure of the underdog in political contests. In a 2009 research study, the social psychologists Nadav Goldschmied and Joseph Vandello looked at the way that candidates vie with each other to position themselves as underdog so as to downplay their chances, while simultaneously suggesting the other side has been gifted an unfair advantage.[10] In the primaries for the 2008 presidential election, for example, nearly every candidate tried to co-opt this role for themselves. Barack Obama insisted he was the underdog. So did Hillary Clinton. So did Rudi Giuliani. So did John McCain. Stories of little-fancied outsiders going on to beat the odds are a staple in history (the American Revolution, for instance), in fairy tales (Cinderella, of course), in religion (David and Goliath), in sports (James Braddock) and in politics itself: Truman's 1948 presidential win against Thomas Dewey, symbolized by the way the pro-Republican *Chicago Daily Tribune* printed the next day's headline before the polls had even closed, confidently announcing that 'Dewey Defeats Truman'. Casting oneself in this role in the drama engages the sympathy of the audience, and has them rooting for your victory.

So that's the first implication. The second is that one of the key ways for understanding how stories work is to understand how they're structured.

Man in a hole

There have been repeated attempts to come up with a formula that can explain the basic structure of all narratives. Work in this area was pioneered by the Russian folklorist Vladimir Propp, who examined scores of folk tales looking for common themes and structures. His aim was to find out whether all folk tales shared a similar set of fundamental elements, and how these then worked together. He ended up with a list of what he called 'narratemes' – narrative units – which were combined in various different ways to create the structure of a story.[11]

Although Propp's work focused only on Russian folk tales, it's applicable on a basic level to stories from pretty much anywhere. One of his main arguments was that stories are character-driven: their plots emerge from the decisions the characters make and the actions they pursue. There are a small number of archetypal characters, and stories are then built around the roles these characters play. For instance, every dramatic story has a central character or hero with whom the reader identifies, and who embarks on a challenge or journey of some sort. In addition, there are very often characters such as the 'donor' – an ally who provides the hero with something which proves crucial for the success of the journey or quest: the Fairy Godmother gives Cinderella the glass slippers and transforms the pumpkin into a golden carriage, for instance.

Propp's approach was to identify archetypal characters, along with the different situations they were involved in, and from this create a list of building blocks from which folk tales were constructed. His idea was particularly influential in suggesting that all fictional works have a shared basic structure, and that narratives can be created by weaving together elements of plot into a sequence.

Other ways of trying to track down the key to the structure of all human stories have focused more directly on the shape of the plot. This approach is based on the idea that, as the literary theorist Patrick Colm Hogan puts it, the structure of a story derives from one of a small number of universal prototypes.[12] When an author decides on a topic, this will automatically suggest a prototypical structure with which to work – a love story, a heroic quest and so on – which then gives the rough shape that the story will take, along with the key elements involved.

One of the most entertaining versions of this approach comes from the novelist Kurt Vonnegut.[13] For his master's thesis in anthropology, Vonnegut set out to show that all stories have a basic shape to them that can be sketched out on a piece of graph paper. The idea is more than just a cute recognition of the fact that we use the same verb for both *plotting* a novel and *plotting* the distribution of data on a graph. The intention was to apply scientific principles (albeit rather basic ones) to literary studies, and thus, hopefully, illuminate some of the underpinning fundamentals of narrative structure which are shared by communities all around the world.

Vonnegut's story-structure graph consists of a vertical 'G-I' axis representing the relative *good* or *ill* fortune that the hero experiences, juxtaposed with a horizontal 'B-E' axis which provides the timeline for the story from *beginning* to *end*. For instance, one of the most often-told stories is what Vonnegut called 'man in a hole'. (Although, as he qualified, it needn't be about a literal man or a literal hole; rather, it's someone gets into trouble, and then gets out of it again.) The graph starts with the hero experiencing slightly above-average fortune.

Calamity then strikes, and this fortune takes a notable dip. But the protagonist then works their way out of the predicament until, at the conclusion of the tale, they're slightly better-off than they were at the beginning. The graph is thus just a large, faintly lopsided U-shape mapping out the downslide in fortune and the subsequent recovery.

As simple as this conception of narrative shape sounds, it does in fact underpin many of the most popular stories in our culture. The 'scientific' element of Vonnegut's analysis has been borne out by a recent research study from Cornell University.[14] Using a data-scientific approach to analyse trends in the reception of Hollywood movies, the study showed that the emotional arc that was most successful at the box office was the aforementioned 'man in a hole', which, they note, 'results in financially successful movies irrespective of genre and production budget'.

Vonnegut identified eight archetypal shapes in all. Along with 'man in a hole' there are the following:

- *Boy meets girl*, in which the hero finds something he or she desires, loses it, but then manages to find it again (and this time, to keep it). This is the structure of pretty much any romcom you wish to name.

- *Cinderella*. Something starts out badly but then gets better. This is drawn on the graph as a diagonal line sloping upwards but with a wobble in the middle as events experience a relapse in fortune halfway through the story, before going on to end with a distinct up-tilt – the classic 'happily ever after' ending.

- *From bad to worse*. In this pattern things start off a little below par and steadily get worse. Vonnegut gives the example of Kafka's *Metamorphosis*, in which the story starts out with the hero living a tedious existence, only for things to take a turn for the worse when he wakes up one morning to find himself transformed into a cockroach.

- *Which way is up?* In this scenario various different things happen, but it's difficult to discern whether they're either good or bad. Plotted on the graph, it's basically a straight horizontal line across the middle of the page. According to Vonnegut, this is much how life itself is experienced, so this pattern accounts for most realist narratives, as well as existential dramas such as *Hamlet.*

- *Creation story.* Humankind is given a series of increasingly positive gifts from God.

- *Old Testament.* The same as the Creation story, but with humankind experiencing a sudden and brutal fall from God's good graces at the end of it all. An example in novel form is Dickens's *Great Expectations.*

- *New Testament.* Precisely the same graph as the Old Testament story, but with yet another extra episode at the end in which the fall from grace is reversed, and eternal salvation is ensured.

One of the interesting things that Vonnegut noticed – and which encouraged him to think that the approach was more than simply an amusing pastime – was that the 'New Testament' graph resembles the 'Cinderella' one almost precisely. The emotional arc starts with a sharp incline in fortune, before dipping treacherously in the middle, but then righting itself and eventually leading to eternal bliss/ marriage-to-the-prince. From a structural point of view then, there are intriguing links between the founding myth for Christianity, a canonical fairy tale and the ideals that comprise the American Dream.

There have been a number of other attempts to create taxonomies that account for all the various types of story structure. In the late

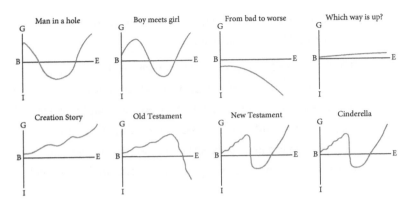

Figure 1 *Kurt Vonnegut's eight archetypal plots.*

nineteenth century, the French writer Georges Polti could only whittle his archetypes down to thirty-six situations. The writer and academic Ronald B. Tobias, meanwhile, put the number at twenty master plots.[15] The screenwriter Blake Snyder slimmed things down to ten basic plots.[16] More recently, researchers at the University of Vermont analysed over a thousand works of fiction from Project Gutenberg to see how the language of the stories reflected different emotional arcs.[17] Along with 'man in a hole' and 'Cinderella', they also identified patterns which they describe as *Rags to riches* (a progressive rise in fortune/positive emotions); *Tragedy* or *Riches to rags* (a progressive fall in fortune/positive emotions); *Icarus* (a rise followed by a fall); and *Oedipus* (a fall followed by a rise followed by a fall). If we were to translate these into Vonnegut-style graphs, we'd end up with a full range of diagonal lines pointing both down and up, U-shapes and inverted U-shapes and truncated sine waves.

Reduced to essentials like this, the whole exercise is in danger of looking a little simplistic, of course. But as Vonnegut's observation about the parallels between 'Cinderella' and the 'New Testament' illustrate, it's not the shapes themselves that are interesting, but the way they can help us see structural similarities and connections which in turn reveal further implications about the nature of narrative.

With that in mind, one of the most influential recent classification systems is Christopher Booker's 'seven basic plots'.[18] In his 700-page analysis of the way fundamental patterns are recycled and reworked across all the narrative arts (from novels and plays, to opera and film), he identifies the following archetypes: There's the *Quest*, most notably exemplified by Homer's *Odyssey* and Virgil's *Aeneid*, but also found in stories such as *Lord of the Rings* and *Raiders of the Lost Ark*. There's the story of *Voyage and Return*, as in *Alice in Wonderland* or the *Wizard of Oz*. There are stories of *Rebirth*, of which a good example is Scrooge's emotional trajectory in *A Christmas Carol* or the fairy tale of the frog prince. There's *Comedy*, ending in marriage or its emotional equivalent, and *Tragedy*, ending in death or similar disaster.

As far as political narratives go, however, it's the final two archetypes in his list which are the most relevant. These are *Rags to riches* and *Overcoming the monster*. The first of these is basically Vonnegut's conception of 'Cinderella', and tells the story of a young child who starts out trapped in an oppressive environment but, through a mixture of pluck and good fortune, fights her way out until finally she claims her happy ending – and in doing so, grows into a mature adult.

The second – *Overcoming the monster* – opens on a community being threatened by some evil force or monstrous beast. In response to this a hero (usually reluctant and unprepared at the beginning of proceedings) sets out to do battle with this monster. They engage it in combat, overcome various related challenges, until finally they're able to vanquish it. In doing so they restore peace to the community, while also, thanks to the experience, learning valuable moral and spiritual lessons about themselves. As the literary theorist Patrick Colm Hogan notes, this type of story tends to be used as a means of defining community identity – and especially national identity – and is thus particularly relevant for politics.[19]

As we can see, there's a slight difference of focus between Vonnegut's exercise and Booker's. Vonnegut's story structures concentrate almost exclusively on the emotional arc of the protagonist. The squiggles on the graph paper are meant to track the undulating feelings the hero experiences as events push them from one plight to next. As the sentiment analysis from the University of Vermont study shows, the payoff for all the different patterns is the emotional engagement produced in the reader or audience as they vicariously accompany the protagonist on their emotional expedition.

Booker's classifications, on the other hand, are structured more around the actions the protagonists pursue. The archetypes differentiate between the various scenarios the hero finds themself in, be it a journey, a quest or a battle. Although the focus is on the trajectory taken by the protagonist at the centre of the story, the structures also point towards the dynamics that produce this emotional journey: the interplay between friend and foe, between pursuer and pursued, between ambition and actuality. As we'll see in the remainder of this chapter, it's here that their political relevance lies.

Emotional engagement does, of course, play an important role for Booker's story structures as well. As Patrick Colm Hogan has shown in his work on narrative universals, the different characteristics of the various genres can all be explained by 'reference to differentiating features of specific emotion systems'.[20] For instance, a romantic comedy is about the individual happiness of a couple, so it has a personal goal, whereas an *Overcoming the monster* story is about restoring happiness to the community, so it has a more social goal.

The question of *why* so many narratives should be based on a small set of archetypes has various hypotheses, ranging from the evolutionary to the psychoanalytic. Booker's scheme, for instance, synthesizes work from the likes of Freud, Bettelheim and particularly Jung and his theory of psychological archetypes – the universal patterns and myths embedded in the collective unconscious of people the world over. For our purposes, however, the question of why is of limited relevance. The important point is that studies which have surveyed hundreds and thousands of stories point inductively to broadly recurring patterns such as these. And that whatever the underlying reasons, these patterns (or some rough equivalent of them) seem to be embedded deeply in the human psyche. This sort of approach can therefore help explain why some stories resonate more than others with an audience, and why and how they're used for the purposes of political persuasion.

Mob rule

To show how these archetypes translate into actual stories, and how they can help identify the parallels between ideas that are prevalent in both politics and culture, let's look at two more examples. Alongside the American Dream narrative, with its structural roots in the 'Cinderella' story, there are another two defining myths which play a central role in the formation of the American national psyche – and which, for this reason, are a mainstay in American political discourse. These are the fear of oppressive regimes (including one's own government) and the fear of mob rule.

So commonplace are these ideas in the culture that they figure as the principal themes in hundreds of novels and films. For the purposes of this chapter, let's take two classic movies as illustrations: *Star Wars* and Fred Zinnemann's 1952 Western *High Noon*. Summarizing the plots of these is probably superfluous, but here goes anyway. *Star*

Wars tells the story of a young farmer named Luke Skywalker who, when his aunt and uncle are slaughtered by Imperial Stormtroopers, sets out with an unlikely group of associates on a quest to thwart the tyrannical ambitions of the Galactic Empire. At its core, this is the story of the fight against a dictatorial regime – the 'evil empire' – and the heroism of a small band of rebels whose righteous belief in their own cause helps them overcome a series of seemingly impossible challenges in order to restore moral order to the universe.

High Noon is the story of town marshal Will Kane (played by Gary Cooper) who, at the outset of the film, is just about to retire and head off for a new life with his young bride, Grace Kelly. On his final day as marshal he gets word that a notorious outlaw is heading back to town with his gang, hell bent on revenge. Kane tries to enlist help from the rest of the townsfolk to confront the threat, but everyone is too scared to offer any support. As the clock ticks down to the hour of confrontation, his wife urges him to flee. But Kane refuses, and in the tense and dramatic conclusion, faces down the enemy alone on the dusty main street.

The central theme of *High Noon* is the fear and chaos posed by lawlessness, and how the decaying of moral values can threaten the well-being of a community. In certain respects it's very different from *Star Wars*, particularly in the way the two films portray the governing authority. In *High Noon* the danger comes from those who've placed themselves beyond the law, and it's down to the representative of the state to restore order. In *Star Wars*, on the other hand, those rebelling against the governing power are the heroes of the piece. On a moral level, of course, the members of the Rebel Alliance and Gary Cooper's sheriff are on very much the same side: the governing authority in *Star Wars* is positioned as wholly illegitimate, while the marshal in *High Noon* is the personification of appropriate institutional power.

This similarity is further borne out in the way that, from a structural point of view, they're basically telling the same story. In Booker's terminology, they're both instances of the *Overcoming the monster* plot. We can see how they fit with this archetype by simply slotting the different characters and events into the skeletal structure of the archetype:

Archetype	A community	is threatened	by a monster
Star Wars	The galaxy	The building of the Death Star	Darth Vader and the Galactic Empire
High Noon	The town of Hadleyville	Arrival of the gang seeking revenge	Frank Miller's gang

Archetype	A hero	engages the monster in battle	and vanquishes it
Star Wars	Luke Skywalker	The raid on the Death Star	Destroys the Death Star
High Noon	Marshal Will Kane	Shoot-out at high noon	Kills Miller

(As a side note, *Star Wars* also has elements of the 'Cinderella' story to it, in that it tells of an orphaned child whose personal endeavour enables him to transcend his modest beginnings and achieve greatness.)

Archetypal plots such as *Overcoming the monster* thus act as the linear grammatical structure for stories, which can then be populated with different characters, events and actions to turn them into specific narratives. Or to put it another way, the way archetypal stories work is that they combine a number of set elements (protagonist, antagonist and so forth) in a particular pattern, providing a blueprint for an untold number of stories.

As I suggested earlier, we can see exactly these same two stories at work in contemporary politics. For instance, the NRA video which warned that the government was coming for people's guns employs the same basic structure as *Star Wars*, setting up a conflict between an evil state that is abusing its power and stamping down on God-given freedoms and the normal citizens courageously resisting such attempts at oppression. This basic plot is baked into the story of America: in the mythology of the upstart nation breaking free from the shackles of a corrupt, imperialist Britain; of the pioneering frontiersmen, forever threatened by the elites back on the East Coast; and of the individualistic heroes in all walks of life, constantly being held back by the interfering state with its constraining, collective mindset.

But while rebellion is celebrated in one use of this story structure, it's feared in another. During the 2018 midterm elections in the United States, Republicans pushed the slogan of 'Jobs Not Mobs' as a way of demonizing everyone from Antifa (anti-fascist) protesters to migrants from Central America hoping to enter the country.[21] All these different groups were branded as lawless, and a threat to traditional American values and the stability of American society. In this version of the story those in power could thus frame themselves as marshals holding out against invasion, rather than as an authoritarian regime threatening the basic liberties of marginalized communities. Again, this basic plot is a core part of American folklore. The political commentator Robert Reich calls it the story of the 'Mob at the Gates', which is found in folk tales about the frontiersman Daniel Boone and his battles with indigenous American Indian tribes, in stories about Davy Crockett clashing with the Mexican army, and in the communist scare of the 1950s.[22]

What's also important to note is that these two myths can both be invoked at the same time by the same political group. In the case of the earlier examples , the fear-mongering about the abuse of government powers and about the threat from 'illegals' comes from those on the right in American politics. Although they may, on the surface, look like different, even conflicting, stories – as the narrative archetype approach reveals, at their heart they're founded on precisely the same structure.

Subtext and allegory

As it happens, both the films I've used as examples here have very specific political subtexts woven into fabric of their stories by their authors. The screenplay for *High Noon* was written by Carl Foreman, who was, at the time he was working on the film, under investigation by Joseph McCarthy's House Un-American Activities Committee, and was subsequently blacklisted for his supposed communist sympathies. In the book *High Noon: The Hollywood Blacklist and the Making of an American Classic*, Glenn Frankel explains how Foreman came to see the film as an overt allegory about the Hollywood blacklist, and particularly about the complicity of the film-making community and the way it failed to take a collective stand against McCarthyism. Foreman was subpoenaed by the committee just as he was finishing the screenplay. As he's quoted as saying by Frankel, all of a sudden 'life was mirroring art and art was mirroring life'.[23] His career was threatened by this malign force, but when he turned to his colleagues for help, they were all too frightened for their own professional well-being to support him. 'I became that guy', he said. 'I became the Gary Cooper character.' And the screenplay thus became a tale of the individual hero taking a principled stand in the face of a corrupt and vengeful power sweeping through society.

Although the central premise of the film is, then, very much an American story – one of individual bravery defeating the forces of chaos and disorder – it's possible to read its political message in very different ways. The interpretation of the whole depends on your interpretation of what counts as mob rule. So while presidents such as Dwight Eisenhower and Bill Clinton have loved it, an arch-conservative such as John Wayne could still consider it to be 'the most un-American thing I've seen in my whole life'.

Star Wars also has an element of political fable to it. Its creator George Lucas has spoken on various occasions of the way that the Nixon administration and the Vietnam War had an important influence on how he shaped the plot of the early films in the saga.[24] The impact that these two events had on America in the 1970s started him thinking about the ways in which democracies can fail, and how they deteriorate into dictatorships when corruption goes unchecked. He's quoted as saying that Nixon – who he viewed as having subverted the Senate and as acting in an increasingly imperialistic way – was the direct inspiration for the Emperor Palpatine, the supreme leader of the 'evil empire' in the first *Star Wars* trilogy.[25]

Twenty years later, when the prequel trilogy was released, the political dramatis personae had changed, but the general fears and warnings about the state of democracy remained. Lucas explained to Maureen Dowd of the *New York Times* in 2009 that he now envisaged George W. Bush as Darth Vader and Dick Cheney as the emperor.[26] He even lifted elements of dialogue directly from contemporary political discourse to use in the films, having Anakin Skywalker (who later transforms into Darth Vader) tell his mentor Obi Wan Kenobi that 'if you're not with me then you're my enemy' – a manipulative assertion that Bush had made to the international community in the build-up to the Iraq War.[27]

For those interested in pursuing this rather niche topic further, the website Conservapedia, which aims to counter the supposed liberal bias in its more famous cousin Wikipedia, lists a host of other ways in which Lucas encoded his 'liberal' message into the films. These include supposedly creating negative depictions of the military and of capitalism (there's a lot of ruckus around trade federations in Episodes I and II), along with abstruse allusions in the naming of some of the peripheral characters (the first name of the evil Nute Gunray, for instance, is a homophone for then-Speaker of the House of Representatives Newt Gingrich).

What's of note here is that this subtext is very different from the political stance in the examples of the fear of oppressive regimes and the fear of mob rule that I cited in the previous section. *High Noon* and *Star Wars* were envisaged by their creators as having a liberal message, and had specific Republican politicians as the inspiration for their villains. The NRA's scaremongering about gun control, and the Republican Party's 2018 campaign for 'Jobs Not Mobs' are both firmly rooted in conservative politics, on the other hand. The narrative structure itself is entirely impartial, of course. It's the way it's populated with specific characters and specific ideas that turns it into a vehicle for the persuasion of a specific political message.

Single storyism

For the political commentator David Brooks, American politics has always indulged in what he calls 'single storyism'.[28] This is the way that politicians, especially during an election cycle, reduce complex situations into simple fables, usually by drawing on the narrative archetypes outlined earlier.

Brooks was writing about this in early 2016, in the midst of the primaries for the presidential election. He singled out Donald Trump and Bernie Sanders in particular as giants of the single-storyist phenomenon. For both of them, he said, almost all the issues they address get reduced to the same *Overcoming the monster* narrative. There's always a corrupt or tyrannical group that is the cause of the disorder in society. For one of them it's illegal immigrants; for the other it's Wall Street bankers. The single – and simple – story they then tell is that the populist leader is the only person who not only appreciates and understands the concerns of everyday citizens but also protects them from this monstrous threat to their livelihood and to the well-being of the American way of life.

This phenomenon isn't limited to American politics, of course. A great deal of politics is based on the perception of events rather than their practical details. Populism, as we've seen, is structured around a singular, straightforward narrative. As former Italian prime minister Matteo Renzi said in an interview with the *Guardian*, the 'narrative of the populist is a message that presents the future as a place of problems – about jobs we will lose and how migrants will steal the future'.[29] The narrative is based on the fear of migration rather than any actual evidence of its effects. But then, this fear makes for a much less ambiguous plot than the economic and cultural complexities that actually result from patterns of global mobility.

The same narrative outline is equally popular and prevalent in UK political discourse. Take, for instance, attitudes to Europe and the EU. The writer Fintan O'Toole suggests that there are only a select few basic narratives at play in mainstream attitudes to the British relationship with the continent.[30] One of the most enduring of these – at least for conservative or reactionary mindsets – is the idea that Britain has fallen from the status of proud owner of an empire to become an occupied colony (or, as the popular metaphor has it, a vassal state). This view of the world is founded on a simple dichotomy. One can be either master or slave, colonizer or colonized. Despite the fact that the Second World War was won by Britain and its allies, the suspicion lingers that those same battles continue, and that the European Union is just another form of German-led domination. Brexit thus becomes a confrontation between a plucky little island-nation and the imperialist ambitions of its unscrupulous continental neighbours. As O'Toole writes, this may seem like a bizarrely dystopian fantasy, 'but in the English reactionary imagination, dystopian fantasy was and is indistinguishable from reality'. Instead of nuance and complexity in the issues that govern the UK's political relationship with Europe, the rhetoric falls back on a simple story of nationalism and national enmity.

The use of overly simplistic stories not only distorts the truth but also distorts the idea of what the truth should or could be. Take, for instance, the controversy that ensued when the UK's shadow chancellor, John McDonnell, was asked to give a one-word answer to the question of whether Winston Churchill should be seen as a hero or a villain. While there may be a creative tradition of writing very condensed memoirs,[31] reducing the life story of a politician and soldier whose career spanned seventy years, and who was involved in many of the major political crises of the twentieth century, to a single word is clearly nonsensical. Nevertheless, McDonnell took the bait and gave an answer. Citing the Tonypandy strikes in South Wales, to which Churchill, as home secretary, had decided to dispatch the army, he answered 'villain'.[32] This one-word judgement on Churchill's legacy was, naturally enough, picked up by various news outlets which sensationally reported that 'McDonnell calls Churchill a villain', and that the remarks 'could stir a lot of trouble'.[33] The narrative being performed here is, of course, as much about McDonnell's identity (as a left-leaning politician with a long history in protest politics) as it is about Churchill's. But the ingredients – an absurdly unnuanced summary of a complex political life; the way an evaluation of this life was reduced to a simple good-versus-bad narrative; and a political controversy generated and relayed by media coverage – are emblematic of how the simplistic story can gatecrash the news agenda and sideline the serious business of reasoned political debate.

Brooks adapted his idea of the 'single story' from a lecture given by the author Chimamanda Ngozi Adichie.[34] Her talk was a warning about the way that complex human situations can be reduced to stereotypes because of the simplistic stories that get circulated in society about them. The dominant story about Africa, she argued, was of the inhabitants of the continent as desperately poor and in need of pity and aid. This is almost the only mainstream narrative about the millions of citizens of the fifty plus countries of the continent, and it frames the perspective of those with no first-hand experience of interactions with the diverse cultures and demographics of Africa. Single stories such as these are used by those in power to shape the way we understand the world.

David Brooks uses the 'single story' idea as plea for more nuance in public discourse. Every policy, he argues, has its positive and negative effects, and is likely to alleviate some aspects of a situation while compounding others. In other words, no policy will act as a panacea for the complexities of social life – and recognizing this is fundamental for having properly productive conversations about how we can best address the challenges in society. For this reason, says Brooks, the 'only way forward is to elect people who are capable of holding opposing stories in their heads at the same time, and to reject those who can't'.

Brooks's suggestion of the need for nuance in our politicians is doubtless sensible advice. But politics always has two broad sides to it. It's half persuasion, half policy. When campaigning – which was what Sanders and Trump were engaged in at the time of Brooks's article – the focus is on persuasion. In this context, a simple story is a very powerful tool. As we've seen, archetypal stories provide ready-made structures for thought. By inserting different elements into the structure, you automatically create a narrative perspective on those elements. The easiest way to demonize the European Union as an institution is to cast it in the monster role in the *Overcoming the monster* plot. Whatever facts you then throw at the argument will be repelled by the logic of the narrative.

Archetypal plots frame people, events and ideas in particular ways. They allow you to slot these events into a ready-made value system, and one which, importantly, has a dynamic quality to it. You're not simply branding the government or the European Union or illegal immigrants as evil. You're highlighting the fact that they're engaged in evil *actions*; that they're actively behaving in ways which threaten the well-being of you and those you care for in society, and that this action needs to be stopped.

6

Dramatic structure

The monomyth

You can distil the structure of a story down in various way. You can examine how its components coalesce around different dynamics and themes – men in holes, overcoming monsters and so forth – as we saw in the previous chapter. Or you can look at the combination of details which provide for the mechanics by which the story works. This chapter focuses on this latter approach, and does so with specific reference to the structure of drama. There are two reasons for choosing dramatic narratives as the basis for the discussion. The first is that the starting point for the book as a whole is that stories are a powerful way of emotionally engaging the electorate, so drama is ideally suited to this purpose. The second is that much of political storytelling involves enacting a narrative; it involves the politician playing a leading role in the story they're telling, and turning issues and debates into dramatic spectacle. It's not called 'political theatre' for nothing, after all.

* * *

In October 2018, Donald Trump held a press conference in the Oval Office with one of his most vocal supporters, the rapper Kanye West.

Their conversation ranged far and wide. Most of it was dominated by a monologue from Kanye, in which he speculated that if he ever decided to run for president himself it wouldn't be until 2024, as he wouldn't want to unsettle Trump's second term ambitions. Although, as he then added, 'time is a myth' so best not hold him too literally to this promise. He also had a few thoughts about the multiverse, and why he was campaigning for the release from prison of the Chicago gang-leader Larry Hoover. As he noted, there are theories floating around that there are an infinite number of alternative universes across the time-space continuum. For this reason, he said, 'it's very important for me to get Hoover out, because in an alternate universe, I am him'.

Among his philosophical musings one assertion he made, that came across as perhaps a little more lucid than some of the others, was the justification of his support for the president. As he astutely remarked, 'Trump is on his hero's journey right now.'[1] The reference here is to an idea put forward by the mythologist Joseph Campbell. The 'hero's journey' is an archetypal story pattern which can be traced from ancient myths to modern dramas. And for the study of story structure, it's a seminal idea.

A story, at its most basic, is something that can be told in which something happens. It's a recounting of the actions taken by a person (or other anthropomorphized character) as they try to achieve a goal of some sort. The drama is their struggle to attain this goal and the changes that take place as part of this struggle. Or to put it in slightly more technical terms, a narrative is a sequence of chronologically ordered events (often the product of human agency) that are causally linked, which include some sort of complication and which move towards a particular goal.

A basic dramatic narrative has three steps to it (often conceptualized as three acts), which are succinctly summarized by John Yorke in the sequence: 'I exist; I experience the world; I change.'[2] Or, as the literary critic Tzvetan Todorov explained it, there's a move from a sense of equilibrium at the beginning of the story, through a period of disruption, and then back again to a renewed sense of equilibrium by the conclusion.[3]

Along with this process of change, there's also a chain of causes and effects. Events don't simply happen one after the other. One thing happens *because* of another. It's the pattern created by these causal links which constitutes the plot. As we saw in the previous chapter, there appears to be a cultural stock of basic plots: a set number of archetypal structures which provide the foundations for all stories. The importance of this, as the sociologist Francesca Polletta says, is that 'we believe a story because it is familiar … we find a story coherent because it resonates with stories we have heard before'. And this, in turn, sets up a certain inevitability about the plot.[4]

Crucially, a good story will also have some sort of meaning. It's not just about what happened, but about how we *feel* about what happened. It's this aspect of stories which makes them such an important form of emotional engagement. In fact, we could say that we primarily understand a story in emotional terms, empathizing with the hero, detesting the villain, getting caught up in the jeopardy of the narrow escapes and sudden reversals in the plot.

One of the most influential expositions of how these various elements combine together into dramatic structure is Joseph Campbell's 'hero's journey'. Campbell, whose professional life was spent studying comparative religion and folklore, devised what he called the monomyth – a template for a huge category of stories in which a hero embarks on an adventure, suffers various trials, before finally emerging victorious and returning home spiritually enriched. Campbell's own summary of the structure reads as follows: 'A hero ventures forth from the world of common day into a region of supernatural wonder: fabulous forces are there encountered and a decisive victory is won: the hero comes back from this mysterious adventure with the power to bestow boons on his fellow man.'[5] As we can see, this has precisely the same three steps identified by Yorke: (1) a person embarks upon (2) a journey into difficult environment which (3) leads, ultimately, to self-knowledge.[6] Equilibrium ⟶ disruption ⟶ equilibrium.

Critics of Campbell have complained of the way the idea has come to be seen as a somewhat brittle formula for the creation of engaging plots, and has thus ended up stifling originality. This is partly because his work has been particularly influential in Hollywood, and features at the core of nearly all screenwriting manuals. Another criticism is that it's simply too vague and general to be a useful means for analysing stories. There are doubtless elements of truth to both these points. But despite this, Campbell's ideas still offer an excellent starting point for an understanding of the structural basis of dramatic storytelling, and for the key elements involved in it.

The classic three-act structure

So what are the classic ingredients for a traditional drama? What follows is a very condensed summary of 2,500 years of distilling the basics of narrative structure in drama, from Aristotle's *Poetics* through Campbell to the proliferation of modern writing guides by authors such as Syd Field and John Yorke, as well as narratologists such as Patrick Colm Hogan. It's inevitably somewhat truncated, but it sketches out the main elements of dramatic structure, and how they relate to each other.

First, you need a protagonist. This is the hero or anti-hero of the story, the figure to whom things happen and who, in turn, makes things happen. The hero is the character with whom the audience identifies: the one who acts as the audience's avatar, a cipher for their emotional engagement and empathy.[7] We don't necessarily have to like the protagonist, we just need to care about their cause. To get caught up in the struggle they have to confront. To battle alongside them as they try to extricate themselves from the various difficulties they find themselves in. The best protagonists are distinctive and compelling characters, which often means they stand out from the crowd in some way (the maverick cop, the school misfit and so on).

Secondly there's the antagonist. This is the person or phenomenon that the protagonist must confront and attempt to vanquish. Without an antagonist there is no protagonist. It's the antagonist who creates the conflict, which is the central component of any drama. As the screenwriter Syd Field puts it, 'All drama is conflict. Without conflict, you have no action; without action, you have no character; without character, you have no story.'[8] Conflict is based on opposites. The conflict is between the life that the protagonist has now and the one they desire; between wish and wish-fulfilment. The antagonist then stands in the way of the protagonist attaining the desired object, and the plot is the means by which they overcome this obstruction and attain their goal (assuming the story has a happy ending). Or, to return to Yorke's three-part sequence, a story occurs when someone is confronted by their opposite, learns how to successfully overcome this, and thus changes.

In compelling dramas, protagonist and antagonist are two sides of the same coin, with the antagonist the dark mirror image of the protagonist. The antagonist often embodies qualities that are absent in the protagonist, and which they need to embrace in order to successfully attain their goal. But the antagonist also creates a sense of moral outrage in the audience. They may be a worthy adversary, but at the same time their moral code is in direct contradiction to all the hero believes in. The relationship with antagonist thus provides the moral structure for the film. One of the reasons that *Overcoming the monster* stories are so pervasive is that they enact a basic moral outlook on life that's embedded within human consciousness – the idea of defeating evil and seeing righteousness prevail.

Linked to the antagonist is the inciting incident. This upends the protagonist's otherwise settled existence and propels them into an unfamiliar environment – an environment which is usually both hostile and embodies the opposite of all their cultural values. The inciting incident is the event which instigates the journey or challenge which they need to pursue. Or to put the whole thing into aphoristic terms: a problem appears which requires the hero to seek out a solution.

The goal that is sought – the solution to the hero's dramatic need – represents some sort of primal human desire. As Blake Snyder puts it in his screenwriting manual, 'Make the hero want something real and simple: survival, hunger, sex, protection of loved ones, fear of death.'[9] These basic desires and instincts provide the motivation for the action. The antagonist threatens them; the protagonist needs to find a way to attain them. This is the basic formula for all drama.

Along with the initial inciting incident which kicks off the action, there are typically two more decisive moments that underpin the structure of the classic three-act plot. The first of these is what John Yorke calls the midpoint, when the challenge faced by the protagonist suddenly escalates. By this stage the hero has come too far to be able to abandon the quest and turn back, yet at the same time they suffer a setback which threatens to jeopardize all they've achieved so far. If a man has fallen into a hole, this is when he's at the very bottom of that hole. But the midpoint is also the point at which the protagonist embraces the quality they need to master the challenges they're facing. They discover some inner-truth about themselves, which, in a classic formulation, is the opposite of what they started out as. The second half of the plot then sees them struggling to embrace this truth, and in doing so, adapting themselves for the challenges to come.

Along with the midpoint there's also always a crisis: the point at which the final dilemma is crystallized, and the protagonist has to decide who they really are. They face a choice between denying change and therefore returning to their former self, or confronting their innermost fears and ultimately being rewarded. Inciting incidents and crisis points are both invitations to venture into an unknown world. They're both choices the protagonist needs to make: people don't take the call immediately – they struggle with the decision; they don't accept change immediately – they struggle to accept it. Once the crisis has been confronted, however, the hero can move swiftly on to the climax – the final showdown with the antagonist – and the resolution which follows.

All this translates into the classic three-act structure of drama as follows: Act 1 sees the establishing of the protagonist and their current situation. In Act 2 they're confronted with their opposite in the shape of the antagonist. In Act 3 the two are synthesized – their dispute is resolved – thereby achieving a sense of balance. By the end of the drama the hero has thus found the answer to how to control the disruptive events that were unsettling their world. Or to put it another way, they've taken back control of their destiny.

The play's the thing

So how does this work in practice? Before applying it directly to the world of politics, let's have a look at how it plays out in literary drama, and in a play that, while in one respect works as political drama, is also a lot more besides. In Kurt Vonnegut's schematic, the shape of

Hamlet was a straight horizontal line. It began about halfway down the G-I (Good-Evil) axis, and meandered along without ever moving either up or down. It's not that nothing happens in the play, but simply that, for Vonnegut, it's difficult to tell whether what happens is good or bad.

Hamlet is informed by his father's ghost that he was murdered by his uncle, but he doesn't know whether to trust the ghost – or indeed whether it really is the spirit of his father at all, or instead some malignant demon trying to lead him astray. He stages a play so as to provoke his uncle into reacting in a way which will provide tangible evidence about what actually happened – but the plan doesn't work out quite as he'd hoped, and leaves him still racked with uncertainty about what he should do. The drama ends with Hamlet being killed in a duel, but given his ambivalent attitude to matters of faith and spirituality, there's no telling whether he's destined for heaven, hell or none of the above. On one level then, *Hamlet* is a very poor dramatic story. But as Vonnegut adds, there's a compelling reason for why it's considered one of the masterworks of world literature, and this is because it dramatizes a fundamental truth about existence: that 'we know so little about life, we don't really know what the good news is and what the bad news is'.[10]

While *Hamlet* may flatline in Vonnegut's schema, it fits neatly into the structural outline I've sketched out in this chapter. As protagonist we have Hamlet, prince of Denmark, who's centre stage for most of the play. He's variously flawed, and thus compelling – but by the end of the story, he's overcome the character traits that were hampering him from achieving his goal at the beginning (namely chronic introspection and existential angst), and his actions have resulted in order being restored to the state. (Throughout the play, the political themes, centring on the struggle for a just and healthy monarchy, are intertwined with the personal drama of Hamlet's inner struggle.)

As principle antagonist we have Hamlet's uncle Claudius – a 'remorseless, treacherous, lecherous, kindless villain'[11] – who's accused of murdering Hamlet Senior in order to steal the throne. There are an assortment of lesser antagonists as well, ranging from the spying duo of Rosencrantz and Guildenstern to Hamlet's seemingly morally duplicitous mother, to his adversary in the final duel, Laertes. And, of course, there's Hamlet's own conscience and character, against which he wages continual battle.

As an aside, *Hamlet* illustrates the well-crafted plot structure extremely well; all the key components are there, all working in harmony to effortlessly power the narrative. The slight problem for an exercise such as this is that it uses the structure a little too well. Each component is multi-layered; ambiguity coexists with dramatic purpose; and the whole structure plays on the way that drama is constructed. As a result, its subtle use of these conventions means that it not only works as a supremely powerful piece of theatre but also acts as a commentary on the nature of drama.

Take Laertes for example, who ends as the surrogate antagonist for Hamlet in the final conflict. By the last act of the play Laertes has become a mirror image of Hamlet: another son pushed to revenge his father, with family honour and righteousness on his side. Laertes becomes the embodiment of the symbolic idea that the conflict that Hamlet himself is fighting is an inner conflict; a struggle with his own sense of self. And to avenge his father he needs, in effect, to transcend and kill his own character.

The incident that incites the drama, and sets Hamlet on his journey of both inner and outer conflict, is the appearance of his father's ghost, ordering him to avenge his murder. This acts as the manifestation of a sense of disquiet Hamlet has felt ever since his father died and his uncle married his mother. The goal he's aiming to achieve, superficially at least, is to find out whether the ghost's revelation was truthful, and if so, to follow its command and avenge his father and bring justice to the state of Denmark. The primal desire motivating the quest is family honour and the moral imperative to punish wrongdoing.

The midpoint of the drama comes with the Mousetrap scene – the play within the play – where Hamlet employs a troop of actors to stage a scenario which parallels the way in which Claudius is alleged to have murdered the former king. This is set up as a means of resolving the doubts about the veracity of the ghost's revelation. But of course, it fails to satisfy Hamlet's ethical concerns, and instead leads to a series of accidents which end with him killing the innocent Polonius, thus being transformed into precisely that which he was trying to avenge. This is his point of no return. He is now fully committed to the undertaking.

The whole drama comes to a climax in the swordfight between Hamlet and Laertes, which somehow manages to tie up nearly all the loose ends, mostly by finding ingenious ways in which the main characters end up killing each other. Structurally the play delivers on everything that's led up to this point, while doing so in a final flamboyant action scene which, as the Russian director Grigori Kozintsev remarked, was probably one of the reasons why *Hamlet* was such an audience favourite.[12] This isn't quite the end of proceedings however: the drama is provided with its resolution by Fortinbras (another son of another recently slain father) arriving to give his verdict on the whole sorry tragedy, and offer a brief eulogy on Hamlet's life and his potential as the leader of state.

And there we have it. An extremely condensed synopsis of one of the most enduring and complex dramas of world literature. But by concentrating almost exclusively on the skeleton of the plot, and the way its component parts cohere, the aim has been to illuminate the archetypal structure of so much drama and to show how this simple pattern underpins nearly all dramatic storytelling.

Trump: The movie

We've drifted away somewhat from the world of politics. But the point of outlining the structure above is to provide a model for how narrative works not only in drama and fiction but for political persuasion as well. Hamlet may be set within a charged political environment, and have a political subtext, but it is not an overt work of political persuasion. The test, then, is to see whether this structure maps on to the way that ideas and issues are communicated in the context of political discourse. As I began the book with a précis of Trump's story, let's see whether this still conforms to the archetype now that we've expanded it with more detail. Do these elements of plot structure find easy and obvious parallels in the Trump-narrative that's become such an everyday part of our culture over the last few years? And if so, how do they help create emotional engagement around issues for the electorate?

If you wanted to illustrate Trump's self-styled story in two sentences you could do worse than the assertion he made to an audience at the NRA conference in May 2018. 'Your Second Amendment rights are under siege', he warned. 'But they will never, ever be under siege as long as I am your president.'[13] Both grammatically and logically this is nonsensical. After all, he was already in office at the time – he'd been president for nearly a year and a half. The two assertions thus seemingly contradict each other. *Second Amendment rights are currently under siege / they're not under siege while I'm president (which I am at the moment).* Yet they also illustrate the simple, single story that's at the core of Trump's appeal to a particular section of the electorate. This story is structured very clearly around the *Overcoming the monster* archetype. And seen within the context of his narrative of political outsider doing battle against an elitist political class, the two sentences somehow manage a perverse coherence.

But there's a little more texture to his narrative than just this. The story I'll use as an example is the one enacted in his 2016 election campaign. There are obviously countless ways of approaching the story of Trump's political career, and the telling you choose will be determined by your attitude to his politics and their influence, by the purpose you have in narrating this, and by the format in which you're doing so. For the purposes of this chapter however, the aim is to look at how his campaign was pinned around a particular story, and how this was 'narrated' through his pronouncements, actions and engagement with the press. Importantly, it's the story he fashioned for himself, not one that others tried to tell about him – although the way it was told relied in great part on his interactions with the media and how they reported on this interaction. This particular version of his story begins with him deciding to run for office and ends with the result of the election itself.

The protagonist in Trump's story is, of course, Trump himself. He pulled from the shelf a very standard archetype (a caricature, even) for his political character: that of outsider to the political establishment. This then allowed him to present himself as a notable exception in the initial crowded field of contenders. As the writer Mark Pack notes, choosing the character of 'pseudo-outsider' also offers some practical advantages for campaigning. It's much easier 'to sound principled and consistent if you've not actually done anything' and have no real track record in politics, whereas it's 'quite hard to be principled and consistent [with all the] countervailing pressures that are on you when it comes to making decisions' when you're in office.[14]

In setting himself up like this, Trump's character was also able to exemplify the theme of the narrative itself. The same dynamic is at work for most populist leaders: they frame themselves as being the antithesis of career politicians, and in this way can position themselves as the individualistic hero, not beholden to anyone else, and thus free to represent the will of the people. In Trump's case, all the actions he took – his blunt and combative style of speaking; his lack of concern over the traditional etiquette expected of elected officials – all spoke to his character, which in turn represented his narrative. He also had help in promoting this narrative from a rich array of sources. For example, a report from US intelligence services noted how Russian state media was consistently putting out stories which portrayed Trump as 'an outsider victimized by a corrupt political establishment and faulty democratic election process that aimed to prevent his election because of his desire to work with Moscow'.[15]

In the UK, Boris Johnson has adopted precisely the same basic script (although perhaps without the ambivalence over ties to Russia), arguing that the electorate are fed up with the cagey, equivocal way politicians usually speak, and prefer instead someone who says what's on their mind, even if this occasionally offends certain people. As he noted himself in his biography of Winston Churchill, 'Character is destiny, said the Greeks, and I agree.'[16] And as much as any politician, he's built his political career around this axiom.

Another excellent example of politician as dramatic protagonist is Ronald Reagan. Walter Fisher, who introduced what's known as the narrative paradigm to communication theory, posed an interesting question about common perceptions of Reagan's political image.[17] How was it that Reagan was almost universally thought of as the 'Great Communicator' when he regularly diverged from the facts, was inconsistent in what he said, and often skirted around rational argument? There seems to be a stark paradox here.

According to Fisher, there are three factors which explain the enigma. First, there was the use that Reagan made of the classic American Dream myth. Then there was the character he was able to construct for himself which paralleled this narrative. As Fisher says, the perception of character is vitally important in selling the narrative.

If you view someone as essentially trustworthy or on your side, you can overlook several scattered lapses of fact or misjudgement. And finally, Reagan brought his audience into the narrative themselves, positioning them as heroes in the American story he was enacting. As Fisher puts it, 'Reagan's notion that America and its people are essentially heroic' and that by being true to this idea of the American people the nation can embrace its destiny, created 'an audience of poetic auditors rather than argumentative judges'. By seeing an endorsement of their own values and concerns in the character of the politician, the electorate views that person almost as an extension of their own selves, as the public representative of their individual views and beliefs.

In a political story then, the protagonist is always working on behalf of a community that's under threat and in need of a champion. The threatened community in Trump's story are a mixture of blue-collar workers whose standard of living has deteriorated or who've lost their jobs, along with those who feel that their cultural and moral values are being threatened by changes in society. In Boris Johnson's pitch to take over as prime minister from Theresa May, the community were those who felt they'd been betrayed by May's government over the implementation of Brexit. In the imagery of the archetype, these are the villagers who need a hero to step forward to protect them from the monster who's threatening the homestead.

Which brings us to the antagonists. Having identified a threat to the home community, the next step is to personify that threat in terms of specific people or groups, and in this way to create a concrete target against which to fight. It's here, of course, that Trump excels most as a storyteller. As we've seen, a protagonist is nothing without an antagonist against which to define themselves. And Trump's tactic of picking fights wherever he can, and never apologizing for the litany of *ad hominem* attacks he makes, gives him an endless list of opponents. Ultimately, however, it's not specific individuals he's in conflict with. The personalities are interchangeable. Jeb Bush and Hillary Clinton, for example, represented exactly the same values in the structure of narrative he was telling, despite being on different sides of the political divide. Once he was done with the primaries he could move seamlessly onto the head-to-head with the Democratic challenger without changing strategy.

For Trump it wasn't just political opponents. The antagonist in his story are foreign or outside interests threatening American prosperity, along with those who support or defend these outside interests. This includes everything from Mexican immigrants to Chinese business to the liberals and career politicians who facilitate all of the above – not to mention the media which is constantly misrepresenting him and thus aiding the enemy's cause. In each case these antagonists represent a set of values and a particular moral stance which is antithetical to everything Trump himself purportedly stands for. He may make endless *ad hominem* attacks on adversaries, but he always identifies a moral trait he disagrees with when formulating these attacks. And the solution for dealing with these problems and people? Build a wall, shred the punitive trade deals, drain the Washington swamp and take the fight straight back to the press.

The inciting incident for Trump's drama was his decision to stand for president in the first place. This is the call to action, the transition from Act 1 to Act 2 in the script. It was motivated by national pride and a sense of duty. And as such, he didn't simply decide to run, but felt compelled to do so. As he narrated it himself in a tweet when justifying some of his business deals, 'I am a very good [property] developer, happily living my life, when I see our Country going in the wrong direction (to put it mildly). Against all odds, I decide to run for President.'[18] This is the narrative in microcosm; the logline for the story. A comfortable existence sacrificed to the sense of duty he felt towards his country, and to the simple goal of making American great again. It adheres to the structure to the point of cliché.

Again, this is typical of a certain populist ideal of the approach to politics. For instance, almost exactly the same pattern can be found in the campaign video that Alexandria Ocasio-Cortez used when running for Congress in 2018.[19] 'Going into politics wasn't part of the plan', she says in her voiceover to the video. But seeing and experiencing the struggles of people in her community compelled her to take this path. Again, this creates a narrative of the outsider being the one who, simply by dint of who and what she is (from a humble background, part of a new generation, unfettered by the staid conventions of the established political classes), will bring change to the culture in Washington.

The compelled-by-national-pride narrative is very clearly one constructed for the purposes of campaigning, however. Trump's former lawyer Michael Cohen, who ended up in jail for the part he played in 'touting the Trump narrative for over a decade', offers a very different version of the call to action: 'Donald Trump is a man who ran for office to make his brand great, not to make our country great. He had no desire or intention to lead this nation – only to market himself and to build his wealth and power.'[20] Unsurprisingly, this isn't the narrative frame that Trump himself decided to tell.

As we've seen, the quest itself is never straightforward in compelling drama. The hero has to undergo a series of challenges, all of which help to reveal more about their character. Each conflict Trump generated, each controversy he provoked, each obstacle he ploughed past was a way of further delineating the persona he was promoting of himself. In this respect, generating conflict was an important element of the narrative strategy. After all, a passive protagonist, simply experiencing and reacting to the world, doesn't make for engaging drama. And Trump has been anything but a passive protagonist.[21]

One of the most interesting ways in which this happened was with what could count as the midpoint of the drama. Two days before the second of the scheduled presidential debates, the *Washington Post* unearthed video footage of Trump from back in 2005 talking in crude and sexist detail about his seduction habits. The view in the media at this time was that his campaign was already faring badly – the first presidential debate had been seen as a clear win for Hillary Clinton – and with these sudden revelations from the Access Hollywood tape it looked as if his candidacy was now damaged beyond repair. The nature of his comments would have had most people fired from their jobs immediately; surely the same standards should apply for someone running for the highest office in the land?

In drama the midpoint is the moment of truth. All crisis points demand a decision from the protagonist. What are they going to do? How are they going to adapt to the needs of the moment? And what will this reveal about their character? Throughout the campaign, the press were continually speculating about the so-called pivot. As the linguistic anthropologists Michael Lempert and Michael Silverstein note, the media often cover a candidate's campaign as if it were a story of personal development and growth, with the incidents that occur during the course of the campaign presented as challenges that test the candidate, and that provide an opportunity for them to reveal their true character.[22] For Trump's campaign, this often translated into media speculation about this mythic 'pivot': the moment at which Trump himself would fully appreciate the weight of responsibility that comes with the presidency, and how he would be changed by the nature of the office for which he was running.[23] The Access Hollywood revelations then provided the perfect opportunity for this to happen. The midpoint of the story would see an emotional and existential pivot, and set the scene for a tale of redemption and self-knowledge. This, at least, was the story arc that the majority of the press seemed to be subconsciously imposing on events.

After intense criticism, Trump did make a vague apology. But then, almost immediately, went back on the offensive. He obstinately refused to drop out of the race. Refused to acknowledge there was anything fundamentally wrong with the behaviour on display in the video. And instead, turned the attack around and began targeting Bill Clinton's history of infidelity. In other words, he remained consistent to the character he'd established for himself, and used this incident as a way to further bolster his credentials as brash nonconformist. He refused the chance to undergo any form of change himself, insisting instead that the expectations of the office of president should change.

As Lempert and Silverstein write, these sort of "'defining moments" are, of course, in the eye of the beholder'.[24] They're *created* as much as narrated by the media pundits covering the election, and often only in retrospect does their significance for the developing plotline become apparent. But this incident, at least in the way in which it was reported, further bolstered a storyline of nonconformist outsider versus the legacy politics of the Clinton brand.

The climax of Trump's story is the election result itself. The format of a presidential election is a straightforward clash between two opposing forces and thus a ready-made culmination point for a narrative. We know that this event will provide the drama of the climax from the very beginning of the story, so all the events and actions that take place along the way are focused in this one direction. But again it's only in retrospect, with Trump's win, that these events gain their real meaning. If he hadn't won, the interpretations of his actions would need to be given a very different spin, and would result in a different type of story. As it is, the outcome sets up a resolution that sees this as one of the great upsets of political history, an episode of historical significance which produced a seismic shift in the established political order.

Of course, Trump's story, at least this version of it, is not *Hamlet*. It's more akin to the structural approach of an action movie than something with any real depth or complexity. In good drama, the protagonist goes on a journey of self-discovery in order to find out who they really are. As we've seen, there's little sign of an internal journey in this telling of the story. But then emotional engagement for political purposes is different from theatrical drama. Or at least, it works to a greatly simplified template.

Where does it all end?

One of the stranger examples of the way that George Orwell's work has been co-opted for political purposes was its use by the American government as anti-communist propaganda. Both *Animal Farm* and *Nineteen Eighty-Four* were adapted into movies financed by US intelligence agencies in the 1950s. And to optimize their effectiveness as anti-Soviet allegories, in both cases the endings of the stories were changed.[25]

In Orwell's original, *Animal Farm* ends with the farmyard animals looking back and forth from the pigs, who've taken over the role of tyrannical leaders, to the humans, and finding it impossible to tell the difference between the two. The only thing the revolution has succeeded in doing is replacing the autocratic rule of one group with another. In the 1954 animated film, however, the humans were removed from the story completely. The film was secretly financed and distributed by the CIA, after Howard Hunt, who was later to feature as a key actor in the Watergate scandal, had bought the rights from Sonia Orwell.[26] By cutting the humans from the story, Hunt and his colleagues turned it into a simple parable about the evils of communism (the pig-regime), without the equally damning critique of the capitalist system represented by the humans.

A very similar change was made to the 1956 film of *Nineteen Eighty-Four*, directed by Michael Anderson. In this case, funding came from the US Information Agency. At the end of Orwell's original, the protagonist, Winston Smith, has had all his revolutionary ideals thwarted. The novel concludes with him reconciled entirely to the state ideology, summed up in the damning last line: 'He loved Big Brother.' For the film version that was shown to audiences in the UK this was apparently too bleak. It represented too great a surrender to the tyranny of communism. So instead, Winston and his lover Julia are transformed into revolutionary martyrs, and the pessimism of the ending is replaced by defiance.[27] They're gunned down in the final scene, but only after Winston has let out a strangled cry of 'Down with Big Brother!'

In his memoir on Hollywood, the screenwriter William Goldman uses the simile of an endless piece of string to describe the events of life.[28] What the writer does in turning this life into a story – and deciding which story to tell – is to choose the two places in which to cut the string. The choice of beginning, and particularly of ending, will determine almost everything about the type of story you tell. Christopher Booker makes a similar point in his introduction to his *Seven Basic Plots*. Despite how obvious it may seem, the fact that stories have either a happy or unhappy ending is 'the most important single thing to be observed' about them.[29] Stories result in a sense either of satisfaction and fulfilment or of frustration and discontent. In defining what a dramatic narrative is, a vitally important component is the simple fact that they always have an ending.

So why is this important? It's because the ending influences both the way stories are structured, and the way the audience interprets them. In terms of the telling of the story, knowing what ending you're moving towards determines the way the rest of the elements of the plot fit together. The literary theorist Peter Brooks argues that as readers of a story, we assume that what's to come later will help us make sense of what we've read up until that point.[30] We keep reading in order to access a full understanding of the meaning of the story, knowing that we can only do this successfully in retrospect, once we're in possession of all the available information. The ending acts as a frame for all the events that proceed it.

The end of a story often appears to have an inevitability to it, especially in retrospect. This is partly because stories are so often based on archetypal structures. There's a good argument, for instance, that with the 2016 presidential election, the media set the scenario up in such a way that the only really satisfying resolution would be a win for Trump. From the point of view of dramatic structure, his victory offered the perfect conclusion (the dramatic twist in the plot) to the events that proceeded it. By constantly focusing on the incongruous nature of his candidacy, on the insurmountable troubles he faced, on the endless setbacks, the press inadvertently structured the contest as an underdog story. And their obsession with his candidacy, reflected in the way he dominated news coverage, positioned him very much as the main character in the drama. Perversely, the media created the expectation of – and thus circumstances for – an upset.

Another important aspect of the ending is that they provide a meaning for the story as a whole. The sociolinguist William Labov noticed from his research on the everyday stories that people tell that they nearly always include an evaluative component, something that indicates why they're worth telling.[31] It's as if the narrator is anticipating a 'So what?' response to their tale, and they get in first with the justification. In a broad sense this is true of nearly all stories. There's always a purpose to them in the way that they illuminate or comment upon something about the world. If I tell a story about a colleague at work, about something they did or said, it's likely not just meant as an amusing anecdote, but also to be an indirect comment on their character (they're not to be trusted; they're particularly good at their job; I'm secretly enamoured of them; or whatever it may be). And it's often the conclusion of events which provides this evaluation. The ending resolves the troubles with which the story begins, and in this way, allows the narrative to act as an explanation of some aspect of the world.

A good way to illustrate this is with the ongoing saga of Brexit. In an article in the summer of 2018, Matt Kelly, editor of the *New European* newspaper, offered a brief analysis of the narrative arc of Brexit as it was playing out at the time.[32] Underpinning what might have appeared as an unruly mix of confusion and chaos was, he suggested, a classic three-act structure of the sort used in all good drama. Each act was bookended by a sudden reversal in fortune – dramatized, in this case, by three unexpected election results – which shifted the story forward in new and bewildering directions.

Act One: in 2015 the prime minister at the time, David Cameron, accidentally wins a general election he assumed was going to result in a hung parliament. He's obliged to see through his manifesto pledge to hold a referendum on Britain's membership of the EU; a commitment that was only ever included in said manifesto as a desperate attempt to stop the nationalist UKIP party from eating into the Conservative vote. Act Two: the Leave camp unexpectedly wins the referendum, much to the surprise of many of its main proponents, who'd simply been using the campaign as a way of furthering their own careers. Act Three: faced with the daunting task of carrying out a policy that lacks shape and detail, the new prime minister, Theresa May, calls a snap general election in the hopes of boosting her bargaining power. All doesn't quite go to plan however. She ends up with a reduced majority, thus making the task of extricating the government, and the country, from its self-inflicted miseries even more difficult than it had been before.

As Kelly writes, one the many side-effects of all this has been the spectacle of the Conservative Party collapsing in upon itself – a state of affairs that, with perfect dramatic irony, is 'the very thing the entire episode was designed to prevent'. Telling the story in this form would undoubtedly make for a good drama, with the perennially relevant idea of political folly as its motivating theme.

But the story of Brexit as narrated here is, of course, missing one key component. It lacks an ending. As suggested above, a powerful plot sets up a particular ending, and then projects a series of actions all of which appear to lead inextricably towards that ending. If you buy into the idea that Brexit is the story of the British people emancipating themselves from the yoke of European Union tyranny, for example, then a happy ending requires the country to symbolically break free from this abusive relationship. If, on the other hand, you see the Brexit story as one in which a handful of self-serving politicians misled the public with covert backing from a malign foreign power, then the happy ending will include the restoration of moral probity and good sense, and the country being rescued from economic disaster in the nick of time. Depending on which of these you choose, the story becomes a very different beast.

Kelly wrote this article as part of his push for a second referendum on Brexit. By narrating the story up until that point as a tale of three elections (the 2015 general election, the 2016 referendum and the 2017 general election), he was suggesting that a second referendum would produce a nice dramatic symmetry. In other words, the story he was choosing to tell about this period in the UK's political history was the classic 'man in a hole' archetype, with the UK, led by various Conservative politicians, as the 'man', Brexit as the 'hole', and with a proposed second referendum as the means by which the country then hauled itself out of the hole. (In actual fact, the fourth election in the cycle turned out to be the 2019 European Parliament elections, which unleashed the Brexit Party on the world.)

Another good example of the influence of endings can be seen in the television film, *Brexit: The Uncivil War*. This was screened in early 2019 (i.e. while negotiations about how exactly the UK might leave the European Union were still under way), and told the story of the referendum campaign itself, with a central focus on the role played by Dominic Cummings, Campaign Director of Vote Leave. The climax of the film is the referendum result and the Leave campaign's victory. But this is followed by a brief coda which shows Cummings giving evidence to a parliamentary committee four years later. In real life, Cummings persistently refused to appear before Parliament to answer questions about his activities, and this scene is thus entirely invented (albeit with the content based on comments he'd made on his blog and elsewhere). It's what the writer James Graham called an 'imagined future' for the story. In an interview with the journalist Carole Cadwalladr, Graham explained why he'd used this ending, despite the fact that it wasn't a true reflection of events.[33] In this final, fictionalized scene, Cummings admits to misgivings about the impact the referendum has had on British society, and there's the sense that he's unsure – repentant even – about the chaos he's helped unleash on the country. Although the dramatic arc of the story itself is the election campaign (the motivations behind it, the strategies used and the personalities involved), the ending aims to broaden the meaning of the piece to make it a commentary on the troubled nature of British political and cultural identity more generally, despite the fact that, at the time it was written, there was still no sense of how the whole thing would turn out.

Six months later, there was another twist in the plot in real life, as Cummings was hired as a senior adviser to the new prime minister. In

March 2019 (i.e. a few weeks after the screening of *Brexit: The Uncivil War*), he was held in contempt by Parliament for refusing to appear before the select committee.[34] But when Boris Johnson replaced Theresa May as prime minister in July of that same year, he appointed Cummings as his de facto deputy chief of staff, thus offering a very different ending to the story.

In the context of politics, there's one further important point to make about the role played by endings. This is the fact that an ending in narrative drama is also always the beginning of another story. To briefly return to *Hamlet*, the plot of the plays ends not with all the characters having killed themselves, but with Norwegian crown prince Fortinbras arriving and, in the absence of any surviving members of the Danish royal household, laying claim to the throne. The end of the reign of the Hamlet family dynasty in Denmark thus marks the beginning of Fortinbras's reign. The king is dead; long live the king.

This same dynamic is true in the way that political events become structured as stories. From Tony Blair announcing that 'a new dawn has broken' as the sun rose on the morning after his landslide victory in the 1997 general election, to the Leave campaign anointing 23 June – the day of the Brexit referendum – as the UK's 'Independence Day', the end of one episode always acts as the beginning of another. The way you frame the ending of your story determines the type of future you can look forward to.

Part Three

Language and rhetoric

7

Hope and fear

A new hope

The political strategist Mark McKinnon argues that all good political campaigns have a simple emotional appeal at their heart. The formula for creating a political narrative, he says, is straightforward. You pin your story around one of two emotions: hope or fear.[1] This is what drives the desire for change; it's this which leads to the conflicts which give shape to the plot. The narrative structure we looked at in the previous chapter produces the struggles that the protagonist undergoes on their journey towards their goal, but the motivation that fuels their quest comes from these basic emotions.

As simplistic as this may sound, it has a proven success rate. For instance, if we look at the strategies used by the last two Democrat presidents, we can see that they both adhere to McKinnon's formula in the most literal of ways. And they do so by telling biographical stories which exemplify the set of values that are symbolized by their chosen emotion.

* * *

There have been major Hollywood films about the last two pre-Trump presidents. Both films were made after their subjects had left office, and the narratives are framed by our knowledge of their political legacies. In Oliver Stone's *W*, on the life and presidency of George W. Bush, this legacy is the highly ambiguous status of the Iraq War and its aftermath. For Vikram Gandhi's *Barry*, it's Barack Obama's status as the first non-white president. The stories told by both these films are actually mostly about troubled relationships between fathers and sons rather than politics.[2] Stone has turned Bush's life story into a personal drama of a man's struggle to live up to the expectations of his father, with geopolitical concerns being simply the means by which he tries to resolve this inner struggle. *Barry*, which narrates Obama's early adulthood before he entered politics, is a story about growing up with an absent father, and the experience of being mixed-race in a society still very much working through its racial identity issues. In both cases, the emotional core at the centre of the plot is the main character's desire to be accepted and loved.

Long before either film was made, both politicians had carefully reworked their own biographies as part of the construction of their political personas. In Obama's case, this involved presenting the outline of his life story as an exemplar of emotional foundation that supports the American Dream.

Obama's breakthrough political moment came with his keynote address to the 2004 Democratic National Convention. The title given to this speech was the 'Audacity of Hope'. Two years later this would also become the title of his second book. The phrase was taken from a sermon given by his former pastor, Jeremiah Wright, which in turn was based on a painting by G. F. Watts, simply called 'Hope'.

Obama's book was published with the subtitle *Thoughts on Reclaiming the American Dream*, and the narrative structure of his pitch to the American people – both in speech and in book – was based very much around the Cinderella archetype. With belief, persistence and hard work, anyone in America can achieve both acceptance and success. He rounds off the 2004 speech with a litany of examples of groups who've held onto hope in times of trouble: slaves singing songs of freedom, immigrants setting their sights on a better life in the United States, navy personnel on active service abroad and, finally, the self-referential 'skinny kid with a funny name who believes that America has a place for him, too'.[3] The idea of hope is used as a mantra throughout the speech, drawing together themes of opportunity and aspiration – and Obama, standing there addressing the conference, is able to put himself forward as a paradigm example of this. Later, of course, this one word became inseparably linked to his image through its use on the iconic poster, with its red, blue and white portrait of the president, designed by Shepard Fairey.

Twelve years earlier, Bill Clinton had used almost precisely the same straightforward message for his election campaign. He too had positioned himself as the personification of what was possible for Americans and for America. Again, there was no great subtlety to the way he expressed this – helped in his case by the fact that the town he'd been brought up in was actually called Hope.

For the 1992 Democratic National Convention at which Clinton accepted his party's nomination, his team produced a short film to introduce him to both the delegates in the hall and the country more broadly. The media critic and historian Joanne Morreale has identified three different subgenres of campaign films in American politics.[4] First, there are biographical films, which paint a picture of a candidate's identity. Secondly, there are résumé films, which outline the candidate's accomplishments. And finally, there are visionary films, in which the candidate outlines their aspirational outlook for the future for the nation. Challengers in an election tend to emphasize biography, given that they don't yet have accomplishments to boast about. Incumbents, on the other hand, are more likely to focus on achievements, on the assumption that the electorate already know all about their background. Clinton's film, which was simply called 'The Man from Hope', was a mixture of the first and the third of these categories. It was a short biographical portrait of Clinton as he looked back over his childhood and the transition to adulthood, of how he felt called to a political career, and of what the idea of America meant to him.

The storyline of the film is straightforward. It begins with the nostalgia of small-town America, of picket fences and a community where no one locks their doors at night. His was a happy childhood, the narration says, but not without its hardship. His father died while he was still young, so he had to take on the responsibilities of man of the house. Some years later, when his mother remarried, these responsibilities included confronting his drunken and abusive stepfather. At the same time, his family provided him with a strong moral grounding, and a belief in the importance of education and a love of one's country. These are the private virtues that will guide his public demeanour. The hopes and convictions that small-town America instilled in him, and which he will embody as president. The film closes with a speech in which he presents himself as a unifier, still believing in the promise of America, still believing in a place called Hope.

There is nothing about policy either in the Clinton campaign film or in Obama's convention speech. Instead they're entirely about identity and values – of the candidates as individuals, of their party and of the American people. And although both of these pitches are about as far from Trump's narrative as you can imagine, they share with it a simple, classic structure, which aims to engage the audience on a primarily emotional level.

Likes and clicks (with Ikes and Dicks)

Along with hope, the other major emotion that powers political narratives is fear. Back in the 1828 presidential election, when the incumbent John Quincy Adams was struggling to fight off a challenge from Andrew Jackson, his campaign staff decided that their best bet was to paint an apocalyptic vision of what would happen if Adams wasn't re-elected. They employed an early version of the Project Fear strategy – or what political scientist Daniele Albertazzi calls an act of 'dramatization', bewailing all the many tragedies that would befall the community if it were to reject the present leadership.[5] In this case, if John Quincy were to lose the election, his campaign warned, America would be overwhelmed by hatred, plague and pestilence, with Satan himself stalking the land.[6]

This message was conveyed to the electorate by means of the campaign song, 'Little Know Ye Who's Coming' ('Fire's comin', swords are comin' / Pistols, guns, and knives are comin' ... / If John Quincy not be comin'!'). These days, jingles of this sort are a sadly neglected aspect of modern-day presidential persuasion strategies. The soundtrack for a campaign today is nearly always third-party songs. Music is still an important part of live campaign events – it sets a particular mood and helps build emotional engagement with the audience – but it doesn't have the same storytelling function that bespoke jingles did in the past.

Campaign jingles were still popular up until the 1960s, with the face-off between John F. Kennedy and Richard Nixon producing an intriguing pop-cultural battle. Today, the Kennedy/Nixon election is best remembered for the impact that television had on public perception of the candidates – the relaxed and photogenic JFK contrasted with the scowling, sweating Nixon during the TV debates. But it also produced a classic duel of the jingles. Kennedy was able to draw on his showbiz connections to get Frank Sinatra to produce a slightly reworked version of his 1959 hit 'High Hopes', tweaking the lyrics so that Jack had what the rest lack, was on the right track, and so on and so forth.[7] But Kennedy also ran the less-remembered

'Kennedy, Kennedy', which painted a lyrical picture of a man who was 'old enough to know and young enough to do'.

Neither of these was quite as catchy as Nixon's campaign song, however. Taking a leaf out of the 'I like Ike' minimalist rhyme approach, Nixon's team came up with 'Click with Dick', which encouraged voters to 'Come on and / Click with Dick / The one that none can lick'.[8]

While the days of the jingle are no more, the aphoristic nature of their lyrics lives on in campaign slogans. Slogans are often seen as a vital part of election politics. They're meant to summarize a campaign's main theme, and to do so in a memorable way. After all, there's often great power in simplicity. Or at least, that's the intention. For the most part, they're a ubiquitous but entirely forgettable element of the communication strategy. In the worst cases they can even be counterproductive, providing critics with a ready-made line of attack.

For instance, the unfortunate Malcolm Turnbull chose to run for prime minister of Australia in 2016 under the slogan 'Continuity and Change', not realizing quite how similar this was to the vapid 'Continuity with change' that was used by the fictional politician Selina Meyer in the television series *Veep*. Simon Blackwell, writer and executive producer for *Veep*, explained that the intention behind this slogan was to come up with something that said 'absolutely nothing but seem[ed] to have depth and meaning'.[9] So you pick an oxymoron consisting of two abstract buzzwords. The lesson of the story for Turnbull being that if you're going to accidentally plagiarize something, it's probably best not to rip off a phrase that was intended as satire in the first place.

A similarly strategic misjudgement was Republican candidate Barry Goldwater's 1964 slogan: 'In your heart, you know he's right.' Almost immediately this was lampooned by his critics with alternative versions such as 'In your guts, you know he's nuts' and 'In your heart, he's too far right'.

Even when they don't backfire quite as spectacularly as this, they can still be a liability to a campaign. Hillary Clinton's 2016 campaign tested eighty-five different slogans before settling on what they hoped would be a winning phrase.[10] As Figure 2 shows, these mostly contained some combination of words such as 'fairness', 'families', 'future' and of course 'America'. ('Building a fairer future today'; 'Fairness First'; 'A fair chance for families'; 'American strength from American families'; and so on.) The campaign ended up choosing the undistinguished 'Stronger together'. But the fact that they'd road-tested so many, and that the alternatives all sounded like computer-generated proposals of what a worthily progressive rallying cry *should*

Figure 2 *Word cloud of the most frequently used words in Hillary Clinton's 2016 presidential campaign slogans.*

sound like, seemed to be symptomatic of the lack of dynamism in the campaign as a whole.

Clinton isn't alone in having slogan problems. By far the vast majority of recent presidential campaign slogans haven't been particularly memorable, and probably barely registered for the voter. In 2008, John McCain ran under the slogan 'Country First'. Four years later Mitt Romney went for 'Believe in America'. While Bob Dole's 1996 slogan was 'The Better Man for a Better America'. In 1976, Gerald Ford ran with 'He's making us proud again'. Not only are these nearly all variations on a theme, but they're often also remarkably similar to those used by their predecessors on both sides of the political divide. For instance, John Kerry's 2004 slogan was 'Let America Be America Again', which seems like a badly phrased attempt at 'Make America Great Again'; while George W. Bush's slogan the same year was the Obama-esque 'Yes, America Can'. Every now and again of course you get something a little idiosyncratic, such as Herbert Hoover's 1928 'A Chicken in Every Pot and a Car in Every Garage'. But these are few and far between.

On certain occasions, however, a slogan can escape the trap of being too trite, and the best of them work as succinct little narratives for the campaign as a whole. This is precisely what happened with both Vote Leave's slogan for the Brexit referendum and Trump's 2016 campaign statement. Writing in the *Guardian*, the journalist Ash Sarkar noted '"Take back control" was able to tell a complex story in just three words – that voters had the opportunity to reverse national decline by participating in an insurgent political moment'.[11] Trump was a bit less focused, needing a full four words for his mission statement. (To be fair, the Brexit slogan began as four words as well, 'Let's take back control', but when picked up by the media the first word got mislaid somewhere along the path.)

So how do these work as stories? Simply put, they place the desire for change at their heart, and foreground the need for action to accomplish that change. Change-through-action is the fundamental ingredient of any dramatic narrative. Both slogans also use imperatives ('Take'/'Make'), urging participation from the electorate. This is vital given that part of the strategy is to pit the common people against the idea an establishment which thinks it knows best and interferes in matters in which it shouldn't. By encoding the idea of participation into the wording itself, the slogan thus becomes inclusive and encourages involvement. Contrast this with Hillary Clinton's 'Stronger Together' or the oddly similar slogan used by the Remain campaign: 'Stronger, Safer and Better Off'. Both of these are trying to sell the status quo, and to do so by listing a number of contrastive qualities that vaguely gesture to what might happen if we abandon what we now have. They neither invite action nor demand change. And as a result, they have very little dynamism or emotional pull.

The other crucial element shared by the Leave and Trump slogans is the evocation of a nostalgic golden age. Dominic Cummings, campaign director of Vote Leave, has talked of how he very explicitly framed the slogan to include this idea. In a speech he gave the year after the referendum he said, 'Note the word "back" triggering loss aversion: something had been lost, and we can regain what we've lost.'[12] The strategic reference to the past is precisely the same in 'Make America Great Again'. Not only does it suggest a loss which can be regained but it also invokes a sense of security – the past is a more secure and less frightening place than the future. It's psychologically reassuring simply because it's a known quantity. Then there's the way that the struggle to regain a lost paradise is a founding idea for Judeo-Christian society. The fall from innocence, from simpler, more wholesome times, is a defining narrative for Western culture – and both slogans draw on precisely this same narrative archetype.

A rose by any other name

The campaign slogan used by the British Labour Party in 1992 asserted, 'It's time to get Britain working again'. Labour had been out of power for thirteen years at the time and went on to lose the next general election despite most polls suggesting they'd win. What's notable about this slogan is the disastrous understanding it shows of what's known as 'framing'. In 1978, the year before Margaret Thatcher came to power, the Conservatives ran a highly effective advertising campaign under the slogan 'Labour Isn't Working'. With this phrase emblazoned above a photo of a long queue outside the unemployment office, the simple pun on the word 'work' linked the troubled policies of the Labour government with the growing number of jobless. Fourteen years later, for most of which time they'd been out of power, the Labour Party presumably thought it would be a good idea to try to counter this narrative with a snappy comeback. Thus, the declaration that it was 'time to get Britain working again'. Yet by paraphrasing the Conservatives' former slogan – by repeating the same pun on the same word – what they actually ended up doing was simply reminding voters of the original narrative, and all the associations between Labour and economic mismanagement that the earlier advert had so successfully encoded.

Framing is the idea that the way in which we perceive the world is structured by sets of associations – a frame – that provides us with a particular perspective on events. Language plays a central role in this because so much of our experience of social life is linguistically mediated. When you hear a given word, you think of the object that it's referring to, but also to a variety of other related ideas which you associate with it. If you hear the word 'rose', for example, your brain will likely also conjure up things such as 'red', 'flower', 'thorns' and maybe 'Valentine's day'.

And it's not just concepts that get conjured up, but emotions as well. If you hear a word which you associate with pleasant memories, for instance, your mood is likely to brighten slightly. This is the cognitive process which mentalists take advantage of when they use subliminal suggestions to manipulate a subject into thinking about a particular idea. They'll drop the words 'red', 'thorns' and 'Valentine's day' into a discussion about something else, and then, when a few moments later they ask the subject to pick a type of flower, they'll uncannily choose a rose. The upshot of all this is that when different concepts become conventionally associated in our politics – for instance, the Labour Party being associated with unemployment following the Conservative's 1978–79 advertising campaign – we begin to take an evaluative stance towards those concepts. We begin to think of the concept as inextricably linked to the values with which it's become associated, even when there's no actual connection in reality.

Take, for instance, the two phrases 'illegal aliens' and 'undocumented immigrants'. These are both ways to talk about people residing in a country without permission. They're both in common usage, especially in the United States. In many ways they're entirely synonymous. But the linguistic framing of the two is very different. It's the glass-half-empty/glass-half-full distinction. The word 'alien' doesn't simply mean 'foreign'; it also has connotations with 'non-human'. The adjective 'illegal' references the fact that someone's current status within the country isn't officially sanctioned. But it's also associated with crime, punishment and jail – it implies that the person him or herself is a criminal. This is why, in 2013, the Associated Press decided to avoid using the word 'illegal' to describe migrants, arguing that it was dehumanizing, and to replace it with 'undocumented' instead.[13] The intention was to use a less prejudicial form of linguistic framing.

In the summer of 2018, however, the United States Justice Department, which, under the Trump administration, takes a very hard line on immigration, decided to do the precisely opposite. They sent out an edict saying that attorneys' offices should always use 'illegal alien' in their documentation.[14] This was a part of an ongoing communications strategy by the administration to shift the way they talked about immigration. Earlier that same year, Citizenship and Immigration Services had cut the words 'a nation of immigrants' from its website, and had changed the name of their Citizenship and Integration Grant Program, which provides funding for English-language lessons, to the Citizenship and Assimilation Grant Program.[15] The intention was clearly to build up the associations between immigration and law-breaking, rather than ascribe to the alternative long-standing narrative of the melting pot.

Linguistic framing of this sort is central to political life – so much so that advocacy groups now counsel their supporters about the importance of using phrases which subtly support the ideology they're trying to promote. For instance, the TaxPayers' Alliance, a conservative pressure group in the UK who advocate for a low-tax society, recently put out an infographic titled 'Stop using anti-taxpayer language' which, they wrote, would teach politicians 'how to remove socialism from your daily conversations'.[16] To do this they advise that one should always use the phrase 'taxpayers' money' instead of 'government money'; should talk of 'the NHS' rather than 'our NHS'. And, slightly less subtly, instead of 'we're asking people to pay a bit more tax', say 'we will use the threat of imprisonment to force people to pay more tax'. Change the framing and you change the perspective on an issue.

If the media then adopt this terminology, they inadvertently end up endorsing this ideological viewpoint. They end up taking sides on an issue even if they don't realize it, simply by employing the framing language of one group rather than that of another. For instance, when, in 2015, George Osborne, as Chancellor of the Exchequer, branded the new minimum wage in the UK as a 'National Living Wage', and when the press then uncritically began using this terminology, they were helping to spin the idea that £7.20 an hour is something you can actually live on, that it's adequate for basic subsistence in terms of food, clothing and accommodation. In fact, as independent calculations show, such an amount is little better than a poverty wage: the campaign organization the Living Wage Foundation calculated that for someone living in London in 2016, what they call a 'real living wage' would have been £9.75, that is, about 25 per cent more than government policy ensured.[17] But this reality is obscured every time Osborne's linguistic framing is repeated. In cases such as this, as the psychologist Dale Westen puts it, 'If you let the opposition control the terms of discourse, you let them control the broadcast networks. And if you let them control the broadcast networks, they will control voters' associative networks.'[18] In other words, through careful management of language, those in power can influence the way our brains interpret important political issues, and thus influence the way we perceive reality.

There's another important aspect of the way the brain works which has an influence on the way political discourse shapes the way we see things. This is the fact that the act of repeating your opponent's well-chosen language, even to criticize the concepts it refers to, will help normalize their ideas as part of the everyday vocabulary of politics. By negating a frame, you are, in fact, simply strengthening it. The more I tell you that the UK sends the EU £350 million a week, the more you're lively to believe it. And if someone else then tells you that it's not true that the UK sends the EU £350 million a week, well, the figure of £350 million a week will just be imprinted in your mind that little bit more. This is related to what's known as the 'illusory truth effect', the way the mind tends to see repetition as equalling truth. It's a type of cognitive bias whereby repeated exposure to certain information will breed the assumption that that information is correct.[19] As the cognitive linguist George Lakoff puts it, 'Any unscrupulous, effective salesman knows how to use your brain against you, to get you to buy what he is selling.'[20] Politics today would appear to be teaming with a surfeit of such unscrupulous but effective salesmen.

The most famous example of the way negating a frame simply helps reinforce it is Richard Nixon's assertion 'I'm not a crook' during the Watergate scandal. By using the word 'crook' in this context, Nixon ensured that this was the first idea that sprung to mind for his audience.[21] He himself triggered the concept of nefarious behaviour by explicitly voicing the idea, thus achieving precisely the opposite of what he was intending to.

There's arguably a similar process going on with the word 'Brexit' which, significant, contains the idea of an 'exit' in its very structure. And, conversely, doesn't include anything to do with remaining or with Europe. In other words, every time the term is used, the idea of exiting is triggered.

The Brexit debate is rife with examples of subtle tactical framing. The coining of the word 'Brexiteer', for instance, was seen as an important strategic step for the Leave campaign. In early media reporting, 'Brexiter' and 'Brexiteer' were both used with equal frequency. But, as Michael Gove explained in an interview in the *Spectator*, 'Brexiteer brings to mind buccaneer, pioneer, musketeer ... It lends a sense of panache and romance to the argument.'[22] Adopting this as the default term for the Leave movement added a swashbuckling edge to its identity. 'Brexiteer' stands in stark contrast to the term that had previously been used to describe the same position, the far more underwhelming and negative 'Eurosceptic'. Equally important for the post-referendum debate was the coining of 'Remoaner'. In this case the blend – incorporating a suitably creaky pun – not only provided a label for one side of the debate but also added a touch of insult into the mix.

In many instances, framing works alongside narrative. The associations that build up around a concept, that become the 'natural' way of thinking about that idea, are often structured by an underlying story. Take, for instance, the way people generally think about taxation. George Lakoff, whose work on framing has been hugely influential, uses the concept of tax as an illustration of the way that ideologies in society are structured around different conceptual frames.[23] Everyday attitudes to tax, he argues, are in fact part of a far broader world view about how society should be run – and indeed, about the values and morality of society in general. The broad outline of Lakoff's argument goes as follows. For those on the political right, taxation is viewed as a burden imposed on the individual by the state. It's pragmatically necessary in many circumstances, but is antithetical to the basic ideas of self-sufficiency, individual choice and liberty upon which the conservative world view is based. This is reflected in the language we use to talk about it. In aphorisms such as 'You Can't Escape Death or Taxes', the way the verb 'to tax' means 'to make heavy demands upon', and in phrases such as 'reducing the tax burden' on citizens. Taxation subsidizes the collective at the expense of the individual, and from a conservative perspective, this is antithetical to everything they stand for. This is why conservatives nearly always run on low-tax or tax-cutting platforms. And given some clever framing over the years, this perspective on taxation has become the mainstream view in society to such an extent that tax policy is often seen as natural conservative territory.

Of course, all this is based on one very specific framing the concept of tax. It ignores, for instance, the vital part that taxation plays in the smooth running of any community. The fact that humans are a social species and rely on cooperation for their functional well-being, and that taxation is the mechanism by which this collective cooperation is organized in complex, capitalist societies. It ignores the way that any individual's personal success will always be the result of public investment.

Not only is the conservative perspective on tax a product of ideological framing – of the associations between taxation and government interference – but it's also based on the same narrative structure that underpins the American Dream. The framing that views taxation as a burden imposed on the private citizen by the state maps neatly onto the archetypal myth of the individualistic hero striving to make their own way in the world. It's the Cinderella archetype, where the community, symbolized by the family, is far from a supportive force, and the hero has to rely on their own guile and good fortune to survive. In Cinderella's case, it's not her immediate family of course, in much the same way as the members of society (whom you're supporting with your taxes) aren't your blood relatives. Instead, the wicked stepmother/government are distant authorities intent on trying to cheat her out of what's rightfully hers. The conservative position on taxation, then, closely corresponds with one of the principal narrative archetypes that underpins American political discourse. To counter this narrative, the left would need to embed their perspective in an equally engaging story. A story, perhaps, about selflessness, embodied by the doctors and nurses who care for our loved ones; about service and security, represented by fire-fighters and military personnel; about pride and investment in a shared national identity.

8

A post-truth lexicon

Wooden language

The principle behind the last few examples has been that by controlling the way society uses language you gain control over the narrative. These narratives can be condensed into short strings of words for mottos and catchphrases, and sustained and spread through the popularization of simple expressions and turns of phrase. The careful choice of vocabulary, and the strategic juxtaposition of concepts, can act on the way people's brains work – and in this way influence the way they view the world.

Language is not, by any means, the only tool we use for telling stories of course. These days especially, words work alongside images, videos, music and performance as part of the repertoire we all have at hand when communicating. A modern political party will take account of the communicative potential of the way their candidate dresses, the way they stand and carry themselves, the colours that are used in their campaign designs, as well as a host of other things, all of which contribute to the message they're trying to convey and the story they're trying to sell. Yet language remains the most flexible way we have of communicating with each other, and in this respect is still vitally important for political discourse. So much so that the ground war between the different sides in a political contest is very often fought over language as much it is over ideas and values. And as we'll see in this chapter, the tactics of this ground war can take a variety of different forms.

* * *

Many of the worst totalitarian regimes of the twentieth century were avid users of what's known as 'wooden language' – the grandiose but meaningless fragments of official text which were meant to inspire the regime's citizens with images of a glorious future, while at the same time obscuring the distressed realities of society as it actually was. Bucharest's Kitsch Museum, which documents everyday life in Romania under Ceaușescu and the communists, has a display encapsulating quite how vacuous this language could be. The display is a version of the game of exquisite corpse and involves choosing a phrase from each of the columns below, combining them together and producing a result which will be equally meaningless whichever combinations you choose.[1]

In his book *La Langue de Bois*, the historian Françoise Thom explains how wooden language delights in abstract generalizations, extravagant metaphors and a dogmatically Manichaean view of the world (socialist republic = good; degenerate capitalist state = very bad).[2] A fundamental characteristic of this language is its relationship with the workings of totalitarian power; it's the state-fashioned framing of how citizens are supposed to view their community, and their shared vision for the future of the country.

There are certain parts of the world in which the phenomenon is still active. Prior to the 2015 congress of the Workers' Party of Korea, for instance, the North Korean government released hundreds of inspirational slogans, encouraging the populace to 'turn the whole

Esteemed fellow citizens, dear voters	carrying out the tasks of transition in our country	compels us to a complete analysis	[of] existing conditions, as a result of upcoming elections.
In the same way,	the diversity of domestic evolutions and the international context	fulfils a primordial role in determining	[of] the paths we must tread in the future.
The practice accumulated in the past year	the new model adopted by the conscious political forces	necessitates the implementation	[of] the system of general participation in the consolidation of democracy.
At the same time, let us not forget that	the constant guarantee of an authentic democracy in Romania	leads to the appreciation of the importance	[of] the diverse forms of action for solving emerging problems.

Figure 3 *Examples of wooden language from the Kitsch Museum, Bucharest.*

country into a socialist fairyland by the joint operation of the army and people!' Or the even more evocative 'Let this socialist country resound with Song of Big Fish Haul and be permeated with the fragrant smell of fish and other seafoods!'[3]

This type of language isn't restricted to totalitarian regimes, of course. Anyone who's worked in a large organization will be all too familiar with it. Officialese, the language of institutions and corporations, is equally full of abstract generalizations, strained metaphors and a dogmatic commitment to overwrought, hollow platitudes. Back in 2009, the public administration committee of the House of Commons published a report aimed at curbing the use of this type of language in government bureaucracy. It cited examples such as the following, which were undermining their attempts at clear and coherent communication: 'An overarching national improvement strategy will drive up quality and performance underpinned by specific plans for strategically significant areas of activity, such as workforce and technology.'[4] The philosopher Roger Scruton has also complained that the institutional rhetoric of the EU, what he refers to as Eurospeak, has all the traits of wooden language.[5]

Despite these examples, however, it's arguable that this type of language no longer plays as significant a role in political discourse today as it once did. The purpose of wooden language, when used by autocratic regimes, is both to project an optimistic vision of the state of society and, at the same time, to mask the way things actually are. It's for this reason that writers such as Michiko Kakutani cite it as a forerunner of the post-truth tendencies spreading out across Western democracies today.[6] Yet importantly, wooden language existed (and still exists) in contexts where its status couldn't be publicly opposed. It was the dominant narrative in society because society didn't sanction alternative voices. In other words, there's a fundamental difference between the wooden language used in totalitarian regimes and the sort of officialese so beloved of the communications departments of large institutions: the former can't be critiqued or mocked in public. It is *the* public discourse. And any attempt at satirizing or subverting it is swiftly and conclusively stamped upon.

But while wooden language in its twentieth-century form may no longer exist – except of course in place such as North Korea's fisheries fairyland – this is not to say that vacuous language which obfuscates and confuses isn't still front and centre in political discourse. And is still managing to obscure reality. It's just that it works in a slightly different way these days.

Dystopian fiction

In October 2018, Jeremy Corbyn got up to speak in the House of Commons and said, 'The blindfold Brexit they're cooking up is a bridge to nowhere and a leap in the dark.'[7] It would be hard to come up with another sentence which managed to squeeze in quite as many metaphors, and to ensure they were quite as mixed, as this. Yet the phrase is strangely in keeping with the spirit of the Brexit 'debate', which has been characterized throughout by its rich use of increasingly bizarre metaphors.

Three months prior to this, Theresa May (still prime minister at the time) was sarcastically asked by one of her own MPs, Andrea Jenkyns, if she could 'inform the House at what time it was decided that Brexit means Remain?'[8] When it was coined, Theresa May's mission statement for her role as the Brexit-era prime minister, the declaration that 'Brexit means Brexit', was intended to signal her steadfast resolve as leader.[9] As the months went by, and a detailed policy definition of Brexit continued to prove elusive, one might have supposed that its rhetorical usefulness would become compromised. Yet two years later, it was still featuring as a catchphrase, albeit mostly by those on the right of her party intent on goading her. Not only was Andrea Jenkyns parodying it with her 'Brexit means Remain' jibe, but when Jacob Rees-Mogg dismissed the Chequers agreement (May's first fully formed attempt at defining what Brexit might actually mean in policy terms) by bombastically claiming it would lead to 'the greatest vassalage since King John paid homage to Phillip II at Le Goulet in 1200', he defiantly signed off with the hashtag #BrexitmeansBrexit.[10]

In grammatical terms 'Brexit means Brexit' is a tautology: it expresses a proposition which is necessarily true. And while tautologies are vacuous from a strictly semantic point of view, they can be pragmatically powerful. Rhetorically, May's catchphrase was meant as a mixture of calling a spade a spade, of saying things are what they are and that enough is enough. Or at least, it might have had that effect if there was any consensus about what Brexit actually did mean.

In the absence of a concrete definition, debate over its meaning has been mostly conducted in metaphors. A metaphor is almost the exact opposite of a tautology. Rather than explaining something in its own terms, it creates meaning by yoking together two dissimilar things. Metaphors can help us understand something we don't understand in terms of something we do. For an idea whose identity is vague or nebulous, they can fundamentally shape the way we perceive that idea. Research in cognitive linguistics has shown that metaphors are integral to the way we understand about the world. As the linguists George Lakoff and Mark Johnson explain, 'Metaphorical thought is what makes abstract scientific theorising possible ... Much of our reasoning is therefore metaphorical.'[11]

So how about the metaphors that have been used to describe Brexit? Can they help clear up the meaning of the concept? Is there a hidden pattern lurking within them that can shed light on the whole tortuous process? And what do they show about the way debate about this seismic political event has been conducted?

The most prevalent Brexit metaphors in the early days of discussion were the distinction between 'soft' and 'hard'. In very basic terms, the former implies continued membership of the single market and/or the customs union, and the latter doesn't. The trouble is that the two words aren't simply descriptive; they also assign different values to the two alternatives. They frame the decision in very different ways. As William Davies writes in the *New York Times*, 'Any Brexiteer wanting to perform machismo will reach for the "hard" option' – despite the fact that no one really has a clear idea of what this would mean in practical policy terms.[12]

Metaphoric linguistic framing has been central to the discussions over Brexit. Whereas 'hard' and 'soft' refer to two different types of outcome, another often used pair of metaphors, a 'clean-break Brexit' versus a 'cliff-edge Brexit', both refer to the same outcome: leaving the European Union without any agreed deal. Yet one metaphor casts this in entirely positive terms while the other sees it as catastrophic. Neither of them are straightforwardly descriptive; instead they're intended as calculated acts of emotional manipulation.

Of course, a great deal of politics isn't about practical detail; it's about symbolism. And the battle over Brexit has been fought from the very beginning almost entirely on symbolic grounds. This is apparent in the way that many of the Brexit metaphors draw on overarching narratives which have little to do with policy implications: narratives such as patriotism and national identity. Included in this category are Theresa May's 'red, white and blue Brexit'[13] and Boris Johnson's 'full British Brexit',[14] neither of which signify much more than that Brexit is about Britain. They are, if you will, tautologous metaphors.

The largest category of Brexit metaphors is those which simply make associations with 'things that are bad' or 'thing that are good'. These include Jacob Rees-Mogg's notion of 'a punishment Brexit' (one that keeps 'us in the European Union in all but name'),[15] or the European Research Group's 'worst-of-all-worlds black hole Brexit'.[16] There have also been train-crash Brexits,[17] and Boris Johnson's fear of a 'bog-roll Brexit', which would end up being 'soft, yielding and seemingly infinitely long'.[18] The most pessimistic vision, however, was given by David Davis when he assured the population that Brexit won't result in the country being 'plunged into a Mad Max-style world borrowed from dystopian fiction'.[19]

All the above, despite being coined by pro-Brexit politicians, create an unremittingly negative picture of the process. They're meant as a warning, of course. But as discussed in the previous chapter, the way in which one frames an idea is all important. And negating a frame actually reinforces it. By declaring that Brexit *won't* transform the country into a dystopian wasteland, the metaphor conjures up in our mind precisely that.

Even when the intention has been to liken Brexit to something positive, the metaphors have been oddly ambivalent. For instance, Jacob Rees-Mogg (him again) compared breaking from Europe with entering heaven. But to get there, he conceded, we'd need to pass through a transition period akin to purgatory, which doesn't sound that reassuring. Then there was Boris Johnson's oddly ambiguous forecast that Brexit would be a 'Titanic success'.[20]

These last two examples might in fact be better included in the category of existentially challenged metaphors. Also in this category is the journalist Philip Collins's notion of Schrödinger's Brexit,[21] and the Conservative MP Charlie Elphicke likening Labour's Brexit plans to the Hotel California where 'we check out but never leave'.[22]

All of which brings us finally to Boris Johnson's evaluation of the state of play when resigning as foreign secretary.[23] The definition that Theresa May's government was advocating at the time, he complained, was a sort of 'Brino', or 'Brexit in Name Only'.[24] In other words, after two years of negotiations, and despite endless assertions that Brexit meant Brexit, the term and its referent were still distant strangers, with no immediate prospect of being happily reconciled.

What is perhaps most noticeable about this battle of the metaphors is that it's almost entirely rhetorical – entirely a series of attempts by different factions to impose their narrative and values on the concept, with little concern for practicalities and policy. The vividness of the metaphors, and the way they often work in opposition to other drama-laden metaphors, turns the process into a clash of moral visions for the country, with no heed being paid to the complexities and nuances involved in the diplomatic and policy requirements involved. Once again the simple story – or in this case the stark metaphor – hamstrings the actual business of effective politics.

A week is a long time in politics

Such is the confusion over the whole process that it's not just the 'Brexit' part of 'Brexit means Brexit' that seems to have perplexed people. At one stage in proceedings we got to the point where the meaning of 'meaning' was also being put through the political wringer. At precisely the same time as Boris Johnson was talking about his bog-roll Brexit, the main topic of debate in the UK was whether Members of Parliament would get what was described as a 'meaningful vote' on the final Brexit bill (or Section 13 of the United Kingdom's European Union [Withdrawal] Act 2018, to give it its more prosaic name).[25] 'Meaningful', in this context, meant a vote which would allow Parliament to veto the deal if they weren't happy with it. In other words, a vote which could actually alter the outcome. As opposed, one assumes, to other types of votes which are mostly meaningless. In the end, the MP calling for the meaningful vote voted against his own amendment, thus condemning the whole convoluted process to rumble on without anyone quite knowing what it was all meant to mean. (Although at a later stage the 'meaningful vote' did again become part of the process – in fact, there ended up being a series of meaningful votes – yet right to the very end there was still squabbling about the significance these would or should have on the outcome of affairs.)

The same week that MPs were playing games with the meaning of 'meaningful' in the UK, more sinister linguistic forces were at work in the United States. In fact, that particular week, running from 18 to 24 June 2018, witnessed bizarre examples of linguistic manipulation taking place almost every day, and illustrates how politics is, at root, about persuasion and coercion and that those who practise it professionally employ whatever resources they think will best accomplish this.

In the United States, much of this centred around a scandal over the policy of the forced separation of children from parents who were seeking asylum at the southern border. One particular point of contention became how to describe the facilities in which the children, once they'd been detained and removed from the care of their parents, were being kept. For instance, Steve Doocy, host of the conservative TV programme Fox & Friends, argued that the wire-mesh structures in which the children were being confined were not, strictly speaking, cages. Instead, he said, the authorities had simply 'built walls out of chain-link fences'.[26]

Another Fox journalist, Laura Ingraham, then criticized the intense criticism that the Trump administration was receiving for the policy by suggesting that the detention centres were 'essentially summer camps' or, at a stretch, 'boarding schools'.[27] For those on the other side of the political divide the facilities resembled a very different type of 'camp'. Writing in the *San Francisco Chronicle*, the author Andrea Pitzer saw them as sitting 'cleanly within the tradition of concentration camps'.[28] Almost exactly a year later, the controversy over whether to use the phrase 'concentration camps' to describe the detention centres flared up once again, as once again the plight of detained and caged migrants again dominated the news.[29]

It wasn't just media organizations manipulating language in an attempt to influence how people viewed events. Possibly the most egregious example of this type of framing came from the US government itself, who described the detainment centres as 'tender age' shelters.[30] The use of the word 'tender' here supposedly referred to the age of the detainees, but the broader meaning seemed to imply that the shelters themselves were part of a programme of tendering for the children (the same type of juxtaposition as 'illegal' and 'alien'). As the linguist John McWhorter wrote, the 'purpose of such language is to mask the cruel detention of these bewildered children in internment compounds'.[31] It was a textbook case of doublespeak: the use of forced euphemism that's intended to conceal the real nature of what's going on.

All these instances took place before the week had even reached its midpoint. Thursday 21 June marked the summer equinox. For future historians, two news stories from this day could be taken to define a great deal about the era. And again in both cases, it wasn't the stories themselves so much as the way they were reported.

In the UK, the government finally announced its plans for the legal status post-Brexit of European nationals currently living in Britain. With the result of the Brexit vote, close to four million people who'd been living in Britain legally under the European Union's 'free movement' legislation, suddenly had their future residence status put in doubt. The plan announced by the government on 21 July basically involved those who'd been living in the country for five years or more being able to register for what was termed 'settled status' on the payment of an administrative fee. In other words, their legal right to live in the UK would be preserved, provided they satisfied some bureaucratic procedure. The front pages of the right-leaning press reported this the next morning as follows: the headline in the *Daily Mail* was '3.8 Million EU Migrants Allowed to Stay Here. That's 600,000 more than estimated – and they can bring their families';[32] the *Daily Express* wrote, 'They stay, you pay. Migrants here until 2021 … but it's £50 for you to visit EU';[33] and the *Daily Telegraph* speculated that 'four million EU nationals will get right to stay in the UK after Brexit – and violent criminals could be among them'.[34]

In all three of these headlines there is a subtle (or in some instances, not so subtle) choice of language to stoke outrage at what was a decision simply to protect the rights of people already legally residing in the country. Using verbs such as 'allow', and making unmotivated associations between British-based European citizens and 'violent criminals', a further potential influx of migrants, and visa charges for European travel once Britain has removed itself from the policy of free movement, the newspapers continued to play up a narrative of demonizing both Europe and immigration in general.

Back in America on this same day, the linguistic story that dominated the news cycle was arguably less consequential but decidedly more surreal. This was the incident of Melania Trump's coat. It occurred when the First Lady made a visit to some of the migrant children who'd been forcefully separated from their parents at the Mexico-Texas border as per her husband's policy, and who were now being confined in the aforementioned 'tender age' shelters. On her journey there and back she was photographed wearing a green jacket with the slogan 'I Really Don't Care, Do U?' emblazoned on the back. Unsurprisingly, the significance of this message provoked a great deal of speculation in the media.

A brief timeline of how the interpretation of this event unfolded goes something like this. Attempting to clarify matters following the storm on social media, the First Lady's spokesperson quickly tweeted that the message was a red herring. 'If media would spend their time & energy on her actions & efforts to help kids – rather than speculate & focus on her wardrobe – we could get so much accomplished on behalf of children. #SheCares #ItsJustAJacket.'[35]

Less than two and a half hours later, her husband was offering a different interpretation: '"I REALLY DON'T CARE, DO U?" written on the back of Melania's jacket, refers to the Fake News Media,' he tweeted. 'Melania has learned how dishonest they are, and she truly no longer cares!'[36]

By this time the coat's slogan had already been turned into a meme, with one Twitter user replacing the 'REALLY DON'T CARE' text with 'VOTE IN NOV',[37] and another one setting up a funding page *http://ireallydocare.com* where people could donate to a variety of different immigrant-support groups.[38]

By the end of the day news organizations such as the BBC were running features offering a variety of different possible interpretations, ranging from 'she really doesn't care' to 'it's just a jacket'.[39] Other outlets were posting pieces on 'What We Know about How Melania Trump Decides What to Wear', which consisted mostly of a list of designers who'd refused to dress her.[40] Meanwhile, at a Stop Separation rally at a border town in Texas, a reworking of the jacket's slogan had become the most popular protest sign.[41]

Political historians were also weighing in on the debate. For instance, Giovanni Tiso considered possible historical parallels for the 'I really don't care' phrase, linking it to the Italian slogan 'me ne frego' which was adopted by Mussolini and came to operate as 'an explicit character trait of Fascism'.[42] While Troy Patterson in the *New Yorker*, argued that the coat constituted one of 'the most significant conjunction[s] of clothing and incipient fascism' of the last century.[43]

Yet despite all this uptake and speculation, there was no consensus about its original intended meaning – or indeed, whether it actually had a meaning at all. And while this sort of indeterminacy might be something to celebrate when discussing the relationship between language and reality in abstract terms, the concrete issues here – the plight of immigrant children detained and separated from their families – are clearly highly serious. As fashion statements go then this couldn't be much more literal. Yet without the back and forth of query, explanation and clarification that plays a vital part in the determination of any expression of meaning, the phrase was simply a provocation to open interpretation. It was only several months later that Melania Trump said that it had indeed been a message for 'the left-wing media who are criticising me'.[44]

What's perhaps most noteworthy is that this same pattern of inflammatory remark followed by angry free-for-all over its interpretation has become a regular strategy in political communication. Take, for instance, Boris Johnson's comments comparing women in burkas to pillar boxes.[45] Or his metaphor likening Theresa May's Brexit proposal to a suicide vest.[46] The intention, it seems, is to exploit rather than contain the protean nature of linguistic meaning with statements like these. With the result that debate gets dragged away from discussions of the actual issues into a sideshow about interpretation. So that once again, language is being used to obfuscate rather than clarify.

Cheap heat

Provoking this sort of interpretative sideshow depends on making sure the media take the bait, of course. It just so happens that over the last few years, a specific type of journalistic method has developed which is ideally suited to this purpose.

A 'hot take' is the term used to describe a short, provocative commentary that's dashed off in reaction to a notable event. It's usually heavy on the moralizing but doesn't worry too much about facts or nuance. It's a phenomenon that's been spreading relentlessly over the past few years, driving a level of political debate which wallows in stark contrasts, promotes the emotive over detailed reasoning and jumps to snap judgements simply to attract attention.

Hot takes are part of the crowded 'marketplace of ideas'. Of the need to react quickly, attract attention and provoke a response. The classic formula for a hot take is to zero in on something about which there's a general consensus, then pronounce that 'the real scandal' is in fact a quite different thing. Here again, conflict is the key feature; the conflict in this case being generated by preaching against prevailing orthodoxy or common sense. They offer arguments that are almost too unorthodox to be believed, and that produce an archetypal reversal in the unfolding narrative structure. They're twists in the plot, but more often than not ones which are entirely gratuitous. Or to put it another way, they're the argument-based version of clickbait.

To take a random example: it was reported in the news sometime during 2017 that even though the post-Brexit economic downturn could mean people seeing family and friends lose their jobs, those who'd voted in favour of leaving were still sticking firm to their decision.[47] In response to which *Spiked* magazine declared that the fact that 'Leave voters are willing to endure economic hardship in the name of Brexit is inspiring'.[48] Unemployment and financial hardship may superficially seem to be a bad thing, but they are in fact evidence of stoic national pride.

No one writes hot takes themselves, of course. The term is only used dismissively. To impugn the writing of someone else (usually someone whose world view you disagree with) as being crass, sensationalist or simply wrong-headed. While what you yourself are writing is a thoughtful and well-balanced commentary that makes an important contribution to the national discourse.

The term originated in sports commentary in the United States. In the early 2010s it then migrated across to politics. According to the *Merriam-Webster* dictionary, the 'hot' part implies something 'of intense and immediate interest'.[49] The idea of a 'take' meanwhile is slightly older, although it only dates back to the mid-1970s. The *Oxford English Dictionary* defines it as 'an individual's interpretation or assessment of a person, thing, or situation; a particular way of regarding or understanding something'.

Somewhere along the line this merged with the idea that everyone's opinion could be equally valid. Which then became amplified with the emergence of social media. As the journalist John Herrman noted, 'The great democratization of Take distribution tools', such as Twitter, 'coaxed previously private Takes out from bars and dining rooms and into the harsh sunlight.'[50] It's also likely that it's social media that's responsible for the common-or-garden 'take' being transformed into the 'hot take'. With ever more opinions swarming around the internet, the desire is to find a way to attract people's interest and to put forward an opinion which will stand out from the countless other opinions that are all vying for attention. So you go for speed and sensation. And try to make your own take as hot as possible.

There was a feeling a few years ago that the hot take was on its way out. That its time had come and gone. In April 2015, when Elspeth Reeve wrote an overview of the phenomenon for the *New Republic*, one of the journalists she interviewed thought it only had 'a few more months' of life in it.[51] A backlash was beginning to set in. The prediction turned out to be premature, however. Several years later and it's still going strong.

It isn't difficult to track down the reasons for its continued popularity. The first is that, in 2016, the United States elected some-one who was, in effect, a hot-take president. Donald Trump appears to have modelled much of his communications strategy on the exact same formula that drives the hot take. They are the blunt, over-the-top pronouncements, contrary and provocative, with a lack of concern for evidence or truth. And all this wrapped up in a 'telling it like it is' attitude, which offers some bracing common sense to cut through the political correctness that's supposedly stifling debate.

Then there's Brexit. Not only has this been responsible for launching a thousand hot takes, but it also shares many of the essential qualities that drive them. The vote itself was structured around a confrontational question which offered a simplistic black or white option. This is the nature of most referendums of course. But what exacerbated things in this case was that it was a decision between the status quo (which no one's ever really satisfied with) or an entirely abstract something else. This lack of detail behind the alternative allowed for an emotive rather than rational debate, drawing on sloganeering (not to mention a deluge of metaphors) rather than expertise. It created the vacuum which sucked in opinions that were designed more for the purpose of attracting attention than providing solutions.

But beyond both these factors, it's still probably the ever-growing influence that social media has in political communication that's had the biggest effect on the popularity of hot takes. That and the way the media infrastructure these days, along with its relationship with politics, is set up in such a way to encourage this sort of reporting. With money being generated by 'user engagement', a story with an extreme take can attract engagement from both those sympathetic to its content and those opposed to it. The former will celebrate its good sense; the latter will try to refute or complain about it. And it's this formula which has allowed hot-take politics to go hand-in-hand with today's other great crisis of political communication: the agitation over digital disinformation.

9

Digital disinformation

Democracy and its doppelgängers

Almost as important as the style and structure of political narratives is the way they're spread. The mass media, ever since it first evolved, has always played a crucial role in politics, and each new media technology has political actors scrabbling around to find ways of using it to their own advantage – while at the same time desperately trying to protect themselves from how the opposition are using it. With the advent of the digital revolution, and the speed of innovation in social media, these past few years have seen an ever-increasing acceleration of this process. So much so that we've reached the point where people are becoming increasingly worried that the political systems we have in the West aren't able to cope, and that modern communications technologies are being manipulated to undermine the democratic process. And how exactly are they being manipulated to undermine democracy? By flooding public discourse with a glut of evermore fanciful and fictitious narratives.

* * *

One of the many subgenres that flourishes on Twitter is what one might call 'satirical lexicography'. This involves picking up words that are being bandied around in politics, and defining them in a way that highlights the crude liberties that are being taken with their meaning. Here, for instance, is the comedian David Schneider's definition of the word 'democratic' as used by Theresa May in an article for the *Daily Telegraph*. The headline of May's article pronounced that 'there will be no second referendum on Brexit – it would be a gross betrayal of our democracy'.[1] This was all part of an interminable war of words in which, more often than not, the supposed moral implications of the referendum result were used as a rhetorical cudgel to fend off hostile political arguments. In response to May's declaration, Schneider mused that, in this context, 'democratic' seems to mean something along the lines of 'taking an extreme interpretation of a very narrow mandate on an impossibly oversimplified question with unknown consequences where the winning side broke the law, cheated and lied'. And by this logic 'un-democratic', he assumed, now means 'asking the people to have a final say now it's clear what's involved'.[2] Democracy still involves seeking a mandate from the people, but only when the terms of this mandate are swathed in the fog of confusion and the stench of deceit.

The relationship between the word 'democracy' and the internet has a long history. In the early days of online culture, there was a great deal of talk of the way the internet would lead to a democratization of the media. The word in this context was always meant metaphorically. It wasn't specifically related to electoral politics or a system of governance. It referred instead to participation in public debate. The way the internet allowed anyone with online access to publish their thoughts to a forum which, theoretically, had unlimited reach. Given these possibilities, so the optimistic logic of times went, citizens who were marginalized by traditional media outlets now had access to a forum in which they could get their voices heard. Not only that, but they could also easily create networks which would transform their lone voices into community action. It seemed to be a great opportunity for a more inclusive politics, better reflecting the breadth and diversity of society.

What soon became apparent was that participation didn't equate with actually having a voice. Patterns of power and influence very similar to those that existed in traditional media were being replicated online. On the internet, just as in the traditional media, economic and political status still drove impact. Yes, the equation had altered slightly – especially in the influence that grass-roots groups could have – but in the end, money and power won out. So much so that by the late 2010s the idea that the internet would be a champion for democracy was being replaced by assertions that digital technology, and particularly social media, was a serious threat to the very idea of democracy. Technology was in danger of destroying the system of governance that had sustained liberal democracy since the days of the Enlightenment. And the crisis was spearheaded by the controversy over the complex of issues and arguments that got bundled together under the term 'fake news'.

The roots of this 'crisis' are as follows. Put in rather basic terms, our knowledge and understanding of the world comes via two main sources. The first of these is direct experience: what happens to us personally and what we as individuals observe with our own eyes (including what we observe of the experience of people in our immediate community). We make sense of this raw data of personal experience partly due to our innate cognitive abilities (the way our brains are structured), and partly due to the cultural conventions and values we've acquired from our upbringing (many of which will be a result of education). These cultural values create a particular frame through which we view events, and are part of the apparatus we use to interpret and make sense of our experiences.

But knowledge of the world which comes directly from personal experience is only a fraction of our overall understanding of what's happening in the world. The rest of it is mediated knowledge – mediated either by people we know or by the content we read and view in newspapers, books, on television and the internet. This mediated knowledge is not raw data about the world. It's already been processed and packaged by those doing the mediating. In the current media ecosystem, this often involves several layers of processing and packaging: from PR firms and spin doctors to news organizations and commentators on social media, all selecting, shaping and simplifying the information, usually with a particular purpose in mind.

As a society, we make judgements about what counts as fair mediation, and what counts as manipulation or propaganda. But of course, the dividing line between fair and unfair – between having a particular perspective on the news (which is an inevitable part of the mediation process) and having an explicit bias – is neither clear-cut nor self-evident.

When discussing the state of democracy the nature of this dividing line becomes vital. We have two processes at work at the moment which threaten to complicate this. One is the questioning and undermining of the established sources of information that comprise the traditional media institutions. The other is the effects that new forms and processes of mediation have on the influencing of public opinion, and how this can be and is exploited by those wishing to corrupt the system. Both of these are a cause for concern. As Benkler, Faris and Roberts put it, if the electorate at large 'are subject to manipulation through ever-more-refined interventions informed by ever-improving scientifically tested social and cognitive psychology', then the idea of deliberative democracy by an informed citizenry exercising self-governance is a utopia'.[3] Democracy is a rule-based system, and when it appears that people are using new and covert ways to undermine these rules, it puts the system as a whole in jeopardy. Which is why the 'fake news' phenomenon became such a decisive issue.

Attention-hacking

As I noted at the beginning of this chapter, a good political story relies on more than just structure and content. It also relies on the way it's told and, perhaps more significantly, its ability to reach an audience. It's here, of course, where the media play a vital role. And it's for this reason that 'mediatization' – the way that media outlets frame political discourse and how the political system in general is shaped and influenced by mass media – is such an important part of modern-day politics.[4]

As a politician, how does one ensure your message gets relayed to the audience you're trying to reach? The old-fashioned way, especially for domestic politics, is to buy advertising. Advertising is a guaranteed way of narrating *your* side of the narrative to the general public. But other than this, candidates' messages are mostly narrated with the help of the news media. And the way the media go about this is, once again, very much structured according to the logic of story.

These days, journalists and commentators turn an election campaign into an ongoing series of events, many of which are focused around key decision points made by the electorate or candidate which influence the shape of the story. These decision points – the results of primary votes or caucuses, the release of opinion polls, the action of and response to debates – all provide the dramatic momentum for the plot. As soon as they've taken place they get commented upon and evaluated until the next key decision point is imminent. Thus, we get a daily serialization of the various candidates' fortunes, and a blow-by-blow account of the political and emotional vicissitudes they go through.

The sociologist Francesca Polletta argues that the power of stories comes from their complexity.[5] This complexity, she says, is rooted in the fact that stories always involve interpretation in the way that other forms of communication don't. If you present an argument, you're very explicitly stating the message you intend to convey. Whereas with stories the audience naturally expects they're going to have to interpret them, and that their meaning is larger than the specific events they describe. In other words, meaning isn't tied down is the way it is with a specific argument.

Political stories are narrated in a myriad of ways and by a host of different agents, and each act of narration is also an act of interpretation. From the slogans and symbols on the clothing people wear to the bumper stickers they sport; from the memes they create, and the hashtags they use, to the quotes they highlight and circulate. In all these cases, the original message that's been framed by a politician will be filtered through the belief system of the person sharing it. It's likely to be endorsed, amplified, re-appropriated or satirized. The audience is far from a passive element in the communication process, and it would be wrong to suppose that they simply consume politicians' messages at face value. Much of political storytelling takes places via an ongoing dialogue – between politician and the media, between politicians and other politicians and, increasingly, by politicians and their fans and critics on social media.

This relentless filtering and interpretation has been a key part of the mediatization of politics for some decades now. Both in the way the news is narrated, and the position it occupies in modern culture, reporting – just like politics – is edging up towards the entertainment industry. The business of television news underwent a significant identity shift in the 1980s, first in the United States and then in Britain. Whereas previously, news programming had been limited to a thirty-minute slot each evening on US television, in the 1980s, it began to expand into rolling coverage, with straightforward reporting propped up by commentary and debate. Economically, news shifted from being the one slot in the evening schedule which had no expectation or pressure to make money – it was a service the networks were required to provide for the public good – into something that could be highly profitable. And it achieved this by giving in-depth accounts and interpretation of the events of the day. In order to be engaging, the reporting needed to be dramatic. It needed to include opinion and conflict to attract attention to itself.

One way in which it does this is its obsession with process and people. For the most part the news is far more likely to focus on the struggles for power than the purposes to which that power is being used. It's more interested in personal politics and the drama generated by them, than by social politics and the issues which fuel them. As both Trump and the Leave campaign for Brexit have found, the greater the outrage generated by a political stunt, the more intense the coverage is. Or as Andy Wigmore from the Leave.EU campaign put it, 'I'm an agent provocateur ... my job is to provoke, it's to spin stories.'[6]

It's for this reason that technology writer Zeynep Tufekci argues that today it's the flow of attention rather than of information which matters most.[7] Social media in particular responds to people who can best exploit this, who can attract and keep an audience. As Tufekci goes on to say, digital platforms like Facebook and Twitter make their money, after all, 'by keeping people on their sites and apps; that aligns their incentives closely with those who stoke outrage, spread misinformation, and appeal to people's existing biases and preferences'. The traditional media then pick the low-hanging fruit provided by online controversy, helping turn the flow of news into a parade of sensationalist talking points. Once again, Trump is the paradigm example. The constant provocations, spectacles and controversies make it difficult for journalists *not* to write about him. He forces himself centre stage. Or as the journalist Amanda Carpenter puts it, there hasn't been a single slow news day since the moment Trump announced he was running for president.[8]

F for fake

The Ukrainian television programme StopFake News encourages its viewers to interact with each weekly episode by playing along at home with their 'StopFake Bingo!' game.[9] As the show explains, 'Over the past few years readers may have already noticed that nearly all Russian fake stories about Ukraine tend to fall into similar patterns – stories about fascists, stories about Ukraine's president drinking, etc.' Rather than simply taking these smears on their national character lying down, viewers are encouraged to print out the 'Bingo Caller's Card' from the show's website, then listen out for examples of the hackneyed disinformation that's being spread about their country. Categories include themes such as 'Ukraine will freeze without Russian gas!', 'Ukraine uses ISIS/Islamist fighters in the Donbas!' (the armed conflict in the Donetsk and Luhansk region of Ukraine) or just 'Something about Eurovision'. As the programme says, why not convert Russian propagandists' cliché-ridden lack of originality into home-grown entertainment.

The StopFake project was set up as a fact-checking organization. Disinformation has long been a problem in Ukraine, mostly due to its troubled relationship with its large eastern neighbour, and the aim was to provide a forum which would counter the false stories being circulated about the country. StopFake News is its weekly newscast. As newscasts go it's rather unusual in that all the stories it reports on are false. Fact-checkers check the facts of each of these and ensure they're in some way misleading, wrong or downright untruthful. The goal is to identify the lies, and then debunk them on the air – while the audience at home is hopefully filling up its bingo card.

StopFake was originally set up in 2014 – that is, over two years before the concept of 'fake news' began dominating political discourse in the West. It wasn't until November 2016 that the phrase really began to take hold in the Anglophone media. Around that time a number of media outlets started reporting on a trend of clearly fabricated stories that were being spread online. When referencing these they used a term that had been coined a couple of years earlier by the journalist Craig Silverman: 'fake news'.[10] It's a simple enough phrase, which seemed to sum up what was, if not a new phenomenon, one which was seeing a sudden upswing.

* * *

Raymond Williams begins his introduction to *Keywords* by recalling how he noticed that something about the English language seemed to have changed during the course of the Second World War. After the war, words that had previously had one shade of meaning now seemed to mean something slightly different. The war had had a huge impact on the culture of the country, and the shockwaves of this, he believed, could also be felt in the way people were now speaking.

As we discussed earlier in the book, words nearly always change their meaning slightly over time. There's nothing unusual about this. In Chaucer's day, for instance, 'girl' referred to a child of either sex, and 'meat' meant any food which wasn't drink. Both of these have narrowed their meaning over the centuries. Some words come to mean the opposite of what they once did. There was a time when 'terrific' was a synonym for 'frightening', referring to anything that caused terror.

But the phenomenon that Williams noticed was a little different. And based on his intuition about this, he formulated the idea for his book: to track the way that some of the fundamental terms we use to explain and understand our culture have shifted their sense over the years. In most cases the linguistic and cultural history he tracks in the book unfolds over centuries – although as his initial example shows, meanings can also change over the course of a half dozen years or so when society is shaken by an event as disruptive as war. In the case of the term 'fake news', the evolution of its meaning has been even more dramatic. In a period of just three months its meaning shifted and expanded in ways that have had a profound influence on contemporary society.

The history of the word 'fake' itself is relatively short by the standard of much English vocabulary. It doesn't appear in the language until the nineteenth century. The verb 'to fake' began as thieves' slang, before moving into more general usage. In its earliest incarnation it had a range of meanings, including to loot, wound, kill, as well as to tamper with something in order to deceive. The first known example given by the *Oxford English Dictionary* is from 1819 in a dictionary of 'flash' language written by a convict who'd been transported to Australia. In an explanation that's relevant to draft dodgers of all eras, this dictionary explains that 'to fake your *pin*, is to create a sore leg, or to cut it, as if accidentally – in hopes – to get into the doctor's list'.

But back to 2016. As I say, the evolution of the term begins with a number of news reports about the spate of fabricated stories prior to the 2016 US presidential election. In response to this, a string of political commentators and public figures began blaming 'fake news' for 'poisoning civil discourse' and corrupting democracy.[11] Attention was initially focused on websites which manufactured these sorts of stories in order to generate advertising revenue.[12] This in turn led to debate about what responsibilities tech companies such as Facebook and Google should have for dealing the problem. The definition of 'fake news' at this stage incorporated various different shades of misinformation and disinformation – from stories which were completely false to those which were based on genuine information but had been manipulated or distorted, to content which was presented in a deceptive way (via the massaging of statistics or other facts), to that which was factually correct but was presented in a misleading context (e.g. the recirculation of stories from several years ago).

This type of 'fake news' is something which can have very real and very dangerous consequences. It's also something which is now a worldwide problem. An investigation by Yemisi Adegoke and BBC Africa Eye, for example, looked at the way that the spread of false information via social media was responsible for a spate of politically motivated rioting, attacks and deaths between the Fulani and the Berom in Nigeria in 2018.[13] Graphic and violent images that were circulated online were being incorrectly attributed to different factions in society, and this was all it took to provoke an outbreak of bloody reprisals by one community on the other.

In tracking the meaning of any word, it's always important to look at the context in which it's being used – who says it, when and for what purposes. It's this which imbues a word with its cultural force. This became very apparent when, in stage two of the evolution of 'fake news', it was appropriated by the political right. In early December 2016, barely a month after his election victory, Trump tweeted that some of the reports in the media about him 'are ridiculous & untrue – FAKE NEWS!'[14] He followed this up in his first press conference as president-elect by greeting a question from a CNN reporter with a dismissive 'You are fake news!'[15]

At this stage, the term was mostly applied to specific, disputed stories: the way that opinion polls during the election had been so off the mark, or how a reporter from *Time* magazine had mistakenly written that the bust of Martin Luther King had been removed from the Oval Office when Trump moved in.[16] In the next stage of its evolution however, the term began to be used as a general excuse for any news story you wished to castigate. And by now it was being adopted across the political spectrum. Not only was Syrian president Bashar Assad invoking the term to dismiss an Amnesty International report on torture and mass killings,[17] but at almost exactly the same time the Labour Party leader Jeremy Corbyn also used it to dismiss claims he might be considering stepping down.[18]

Here again though, Donald Trump employed it with the greatest blunt force. He used it to blatantly chastise anything he disagreed with, tweeting in his relentless obsession with ratings that 'any negative polls are fake news'.[19] This use was quickly picked up by his supporters – his deputy assistant Sebastian Gorka, for example, memorably avoiding a question he didn't like from *Newsnight*'s Evan Davis by shouting back 'You've just committed fake news!'[20]

The end point for all this is the way the term ultimately began to be used to undermine the legitimacy of the press generally. The concept was co-opted into the right's long-running strategy of demonizing the 'mainstream media' for being elite, patronizing and out of touch with the concerns of ordinary people.[21] By claiming that, as Rush Limbaugh puts it, the media are 'fraudulently reporting and lying to you' and have 'lost their moral authority'[22] the assertion was that news organizations were failing at what their defining function is. Painting them with the self-contradictory notion of 'fake news' was attacking the very essence of their identity, while at the same time switching the focus away from the substance of actual reporting. And so, barely a month after Trump's inauguration, and only three months after it first appeared on the scene, the meaning of 'fake news' had lost any real relationship with identifying what was true and what was not, and instead had become all about the exercise of power, clear and simple.

Rewriting the dictionary

At the start of 2017, a couple of weeks after Donald Trump's inauguration, the UK Parliament set up an inquiry into 'fake news' and ways of combatting what it described at the time as 'the growing phenomenon of widespread dissemination ... and acceptance as fact of stories of uncertain provenance or accuracy'.[23] When they published their interim report a year and a half later, one of their recommendations was that the term itself should now be dropped. The phrase 'fake news', they wrote, is now 'bandied around with no clear idea of what it means, or agreed definition' and is therefore no longer fit for purpose.[24] As such, they recommended it should be replaced with something more descriptively appropriate: misinformation or disinformation. Similar calls have come from both journalists and academics. The journalist James Ball, for instance, wrote that putting the term 'fake news' out to pasture is something that 'we should do everything in our power to make ... a reality'.[25] While an influential report written by Claire Wardle and Hossein Derakhshan for the Shorenstein Center purposefully avoided using the term at all, and argued that we need to think 'more critically about the language we use so we can effectively capture the complexity of the phenomenon'.[26]

The trouble with this suggestion to drop the term is that this isn't quite how language works. It's extremely difficult to engineer the replacement of a word that's already in everyday use. Take, for instance, the campaign to stop using 'honour killing' – a term which, for many, includes within it a sense of moral justification for a particular type of murder.[27] Despite well-argued attempts to avoid it over the years, the phrase is still very much a part of everyday vocabulary.

As the parliamentary report and others weighing in on the topic have explained, there are several strong reasons for avoiding 'fake news'. For a start, the issue of completely fabricated stories (i.e. those which began the 'fake news' frenzy) is only a very small element of the convulsions affecting modern media. Misleading stories are also commonplace in mainstream newspapers after all, as well as on hyper-partisan blogs and extremist websites. Add to this the prevalence of memes with false information, the mainstreaming of conspiracy-theory shows and the sinister union of data misuse and propaganda, and you can see how actual fake news was only ever the tip of the iceberg. This, combined with the way that the bastardized version of the term has become a powerful propaganda tool in its own right, means that, as Craig Silverman puts it, the term is thus both ubiquitous and horribly muddled.[28] Wiping it from the word-stock and starting afresh would make for a far healthier public conversation about politics, truth and the media. But unfortunately, it's very doubtful that this is going to happen. The difficulty is that the phrase has become such a part of the culture today that attempting, from above, to shift people's patterns of use is unlikely to have much effect. Even if a few academics, journalists and policymakers decide to adopt a different term, this doesn't mean the population at large will.

One of the most potent reasons that the term is here to stay is because it's come to reference two narratives which structure much of modern politics. The first of these concerns the way that campaigns of misinformation are facilitated by online technologies. For this narrative, 'fake news' symbolizes a host of different factors, most of them centring around our relationship with technology. This is the story of democracy under threat from rampantly advancing technologies, and ultimately of humankind inadvertently surrendering its freedom to the machines (albeit, for the moment, machines exploited by ruthless political operatives and foreign powers). It's partly an unintended – although not unpredictable – by-product of the huge role that social media now plays in our lives. And it's viewed as one of the most pressing issues, alongside climate change, that humanity as a whole needs to address.

The other narrative, which is equally powerful, is that of the ordinary citizen being kept in their place by a corrupt and self-serving elite. This is the story that Donald Trump has used to great effect both in his campaigning and in his presidency, where he's cast himself as a straight-talking outsider who has taken the fight directly to the political establishment, and to their corrupt allies, the press. This narrative has been a familiar refrain throughout this book, and was already well-established before the phrase 'fake news' began trending, thus it was a simple step to appropriate the term as part of this story.

The problem, then, is that even if the British government, Facebook and media outlets all decide to drop the term in place of something a little more descriptively appropriate, this doesn't mean it will fade away. These two stories underpin a great deal of the concerns in current politics, and the term 'fake news' has become shorthand for evoking both of them. If politics was merely about identifying complications in social infrastructure and concocting policies to tackle them, then yes, a more measured term would be better. But it's also about persuasion and power struggles – about rhetoric, public opinion and propaganda. And in this respect, the term 'fake news' is itself proving as powerful a tool as all the many other strategies of misinformation and disinformation.

Part Four

Fiction and reality

10

The fabric of reality

False flags

In 1984, a former KGB agent who'd defected to Canada gave a television interview in which he exposed the workings of the propaganda strategies used by the Soviet Union. A sustained campaign of disinformation, Yuri Alexandrovich Bezmenov, explained, wasn't aimed at converting people to a particular way of thinking. Instead, the goal was that the target should be bombarded with an endless stream of confusing and contradictory information until such time that they simply became 'demoralized [from being] unable to assess true information. The facts tell nothing to him. Even if I shower him with information, with authentic proof, with documents, with pictures … he will refuse to believe it.'[1]

The 'fake news' phenomenon appears to be having precisely this effect, through a mixture of contemporary social media, the evolving nature of traditional media and the aggressive propaganda tactics of populist movements and their backers. As the journalist Max Read put it in an article for *New York* magazine, what's disappeared from the internet isn't *truth* so much as *trust*: 'The sense that the people and things we encounter are what they represent themselves to be.'[2]

But there are signs that the problem is actually deeper than this. It's not just a matter of the 'fake news' phenomenon breeding a collective cynicism. It's that for some people, surface reality is now viewed as a charade. Reality itself is now seen as an intricately designed fiction that's created and enacted by those in power to mask the real nature and purpose of modern-day politics. And in the last few years a whole vocabulary has made its way into the mainstream to document the different elements of this subterfuge.

* * *

The massacre of twenty young school children along with six adults in Sandy Hook, Connecticut, was one of the worst mass shootings in the history of the United States. Even in a culture in which gun-related killings are all too frequent, the fact that many of the victims were only six or seven years old made this incident especially shocking. The perpetrator, a twenty-year-old man named Adam Lanza, killed himself at the scene. In the official report by the Office of the Child Advocate, which was released two years after the event, it was concluded that his actions were a result of a mixture of deteriorating mental health problems, a damaging preoccupation with violence and the easy access he had to lethal weapons.[3]

The tragedy took place on 14 December 2012. As always with coverage of extreme and unexpected events, the very early reporting of the incident was occasionally confused about exactly what was happening. Almost immediately, small pockets of people were fabricating stories about the event, aimed at refuting the official reports. The way the media story unfolded, and the ways the breaking news led to occasionally muddled and conflicting reports, was seized upon by some people as proof of a cover-up. Only a month after the incident had happened, a half-hour video that was uploaded to YouTube which claimed to 'expose' the truth about the story had been viewed over 10 million times.[4] The video asserted that the whole massacre had been staged by the authorities. That it was part of a campaign by 'New World Order global elitists' who wanted to undermine the American people's basic freedoms.

There were various hypotheses about how the masterminds behind this conspiracy had engineered the incident. One suggestion was that the killer had been psychologically manipulated into carrying out the killings. The radio host and conservative political commentator Rush Limbaugh speculated that it may in fact have been a result of the approach of Armageddon. It all happened precisely a week before the world was scheduled to end with the Mayan apocalypse, after all. Lanza had somehow 'been convinced the world was gonna end Friday and he was discombobulated by it', Limburgh said on his show.[5] There was a rumour that Lanza's mother was a prepper – one of a large number of survivalists who were in constant readiness for apocalyptic emergencies. As part of this belief system, Limburgh suggested, she'd showed her son 'guns and he went in there and did what he did to either deal with the pressure of it or maybe save people from the end'.

The ideas espoused by Limburgh here are part of a larger trend of thinking in today's society: the belief that there's a fundamental schism in contemporary society, a schism not between right and left, not between conservative and liberal or traditionalist and progressive, but instead a rupture between a surface reality and the truth that lies beneath. It lies between what the media tells us and what it manages to keep hidden, between what political correctness would have us think and what human nature actually demands of us.

This idea of a rupture in the fabric of surface reality is a bizarre twist on a trend of thought that developed in the late twentieth century. According to the philosopher Paul Ricoeur, the three figures who had arguably the most influence on the intellectual life of the twentieth century, Freud, Marx and Nietzsche, all pursue in their work the idea that everyday experience is illusory.[6] For all three of them, the basic underlying idea is the same. The actual truth about our individual and social motivations, about how the world works, is hidden from sight. The way we think, and the way we understand our lives, is the result of a distorted sense of perception. To get access to the real truth we need new ways of interpreting everything from the nature of consciousness and the impact of political and economic systems to our understanding of power and morality. Ricoeur refers to this as a 'hermeneutics of suspicion' – the attempt to reveal, through processes of interpretation, meanings that are hidden from plain sight but that structure the experience we have of life. And somehow, a very crude and simplistic version of this hermeneutics of suspicion has begun to creep into the arena of modern politics.

The fabricated narratives around the Sandy Hook hoax consist of various different versions of the idea that a powerful elitist force, be it the government (who at the time was the Obama administration), gun-control groups or organizations such as the Illuminati, staged the entire massacre. The whole episode, according to this logic, is a 'false flag' operation. This term comes from the way pirate ships would fly the flag of their quarry or enemy so as to disguise their actions. Today, it's used to refer to the tactic of carrying out covert attacks against your own side in a conflict, which you then blame on an enemy in order to either provide a pretext for attacking them or – as in the usage here – create an excuse for bringing in repressive domestic legislation.

In the case of Sandy Hook, the accusation is that the tragedy was staged by government conspirators in collaboration with the media so as to provide public support for gun control and government surveillance programmes. In many of the versions of this narrative, the children who died in the tragedy are not supposed to have been real in the first place, or they've been removed to a secretive witness-protection scheme.

And the victims' families and the local residents who show up in TV report are all apparently paid extras, employed by the government as part of the subterfuge.

Crisis actors

In Shakespeare's *Julius Caesar*, Cassius devises a ploy to get the influential Brutus on his side as he formulates his conspiracy to act against Caesar's growing tyranny.

> I will this night,
> In several hands, in at his windows throw,
> As if they came from several citizens,
> Writings all tending to the great opinion
> That Rome holds of his name; wherein obscurely
> Caesar's ambition shall be glanced at:
> And after this let Caesar seat him sure;
> For we will shake him, or worse days endure.[7]

Cassius has a host of letters sent to Brutus, each made to look as if they come from a different concerned citizen, and each praising Brutus's name and character while at the same time casting oblique aspersions against Caesar.

In 2015 the *Hollywood Reporter* revealed that a company from New York named Extra Mile Casting had sent an email to people on its books looking for actors to work as extras in the crowd at one of Donald Trump's rallies.[8] The email read: 'This event is called "People for a Stronger America" … We are looking to cast people for the event to wear t-shirts and carry signs and help cheer [Trump] in support of his announcement.'

What both Cassius and Trump's campaign are doing here is what's known as astroturfing – buying outside support to create the illusion of grass-roots excitement (AstroTurf being the brand name for the artificial grass that's used on sports pitches, and which was named after the Houston Astros baseball team where it was first used). This is a way of making something look popular or credible by bolstering the apparent interest in it – but secretively paying people to create this impression. It's used in various public relations contexts, from advertising to lobbying. And recently, it's a term that's begun showing up more and more in political contexts.

There's a legitimate question of what precisely constitutes a faked spectacle here. After all, political campaigns regularly pay for services such as pollsters, direct-mail outs, social media assistance and canvassers, and none of this is considered unethical. The difference with astroturfing, however, is that the employees are pretending to be something they're not. The journalist Al Tompkins gives a good example of how the strategy works. In May 2018, he exposed the way that paid actors were used to disrupt a city council vote in New Orleans about sustainable energy.[9] 'Protesters' were paid around $60 to take part, or $200 for a 'speaking role' which involved reciting a pre-written speech. They'd been hired by a PR firm, which in turn was employed by one of the local energy companies that was concerned about the outcome of the council vote. Whenever someone made a comment criticizing sustainable energy, the 'protestors' would start applauding in the hopes that the councillors would believe there was a groundswell of opposition to any new legislation.

The crude 'hermeneutics of suspicion' that appears to be taking over the culture means that people are constantly sceptical of the way the news might have been mocked up for the camera, and knowledge that practices like this exist have simply fuelled such scepticism. There was a minor controversy in late 2018, for instance, when a woman appearing on the BBC's *Newsnight* programme as one of a panel of citizens discussing the latest Brexit developments was 'exposed' by certain online news organizations as having previously worked as an extra on various TV dramas. The programme had referred to her as a vicar, although it later turned out she was actually a pastor with a very small, fringe religious organization. This, plus her strong pro-government opinions, along with the fact that she'd occasionally worked as a background artist for television, had some people claiming she was surely an actor employed by the BBC as part of a right-wing conspiracy.[10] For a couple of days the allegation bounced around social media as proof of systematic bias in the mainstream media. But while incidents such as this are symptomatic of the fractious nature of modern political discourse, a far more sinister aspect to this whole trend is the way that it's not just political supporters who are now being accused of being fake, but victims of mass shootings well.

The journalist Jason Koebler tracks the use of the phrase 'crisis actor' to a press release from an acting studio called Visionbox in Colorado in 2012, which announced that 'a new group of actors is now available nationwide for active shooter drills and mall shooting full-scale exercises'. The press release goes on to say that all their actors are fully trained in 'victim behavior' and will 'bring intense realism to simulated mass casualty incidents in public places'.[11] Actors of this sort, who are usually known in emergency response training contexts as 'role players', are a fairly standard element of preparation for the handling of unexpected, catastrophic events. They're simply performers who've been employed to play the victims of disasters in emergency drills, thereby offering a level of realism for those who are preparing for the possibility of having to deal with real emergencies.

But in this particular case, only two months after the publication of the press release the Sandy Hook massacre took place. For those intent on viewing the tragedy as a false flag operation, this provided a perfect plot point for their narrative.

The 'evidence' for the assertion that those directly affected by the tragedy are 'crisis actors' is a mixture of circumstantial anomalies in the logic of some of the news reports, and other random coincidences. Thanks to platforms such as YouTube, it's easy to scan and search news footage, zone in on or highlight supposed discrepancies, and create an alternative narrative based on an eclectic mix of cherry-picked examples. Those advocating these theories identify supposed resemblances between people who've been featured in reports about the tragedy and those who've been spotted in the media at other events. They ask why it is that family members of the deceased are hanging around, continually putting themselves forward for interviews. They find examples of what, they say, are interviewees being trained by media experts in how to tell their story. And from all this they build a case which supposedly refutes the official version of events.

One of those who was instrumental in spreading the false rumours about government-paid 'crisis actors' in the Sandy Hook tragedy was the conspiracy theorist and radio talk show host Alex Jones. He asserted, for instance, that a television interview given by Veronique De La Rosa, the mother of the youngest victim, was conducted in a studio in front of a green screen, rather than the town hall where it actually took place. He argued that whenever the interviewer, Anderson Cooper, turns his head, a glitch in the way the technology is set up means his nose disappears.[12] Based on 'evidence' such as this, Jones repeated over and again on his radio show that the whole tragedy had been faked. As of time of writing, he's being sued by the parents of the victims for the emotional pain he's inflicted on them by relentlessly spreading these rumours.

But he's also been involved in another lawsuit – a custody battle with his ex-wife. As part of his defence for this, and in a moment of supreme irony, his lawyer has claimed that Jones shouldn't be seen as a traditional newscaster, but as a performance artist. The persona that appears on the radio show, that rants angrily against the government, that weaves and propagates elaborate 'alternative' histories of the world, is simply a character that Jones is playing for the entertainment of his audience.[13] Mistaking Jones's onscreen persona for the real person, his lawyer has said, would be like mistaking the Joker in *Batman* for the real Jack Nicholson.[14]

This would seem to be the logical end point for the convergence of the worlds of news reporting and entertainment. The onscreen Jones is merely a comic book character. An archetypal villain, riling up his audience in a fervour of moral indignation. The spectacle provokes the viewers' emotions and functions as a form of cathartic engagement. But at its root, so the justification from Jones's legal team goes, it's nothing more than an elaborate fiction. The big difference, of course, is that whereas the world of comic books dreams up imaginary outrages and flash points to drive their plots, Jones is exploiting the very real tragedies of real people as part of his showmanship.

Deep states

In June 2018, there was a huge protest in front of the government building in Bucharest.[15] The turnout, according to government figures, supposedly made it the largest public demonstration in the country since the revolution of 1989. Yet as demonstrations go, it was rather a curious affair. Whereas demonstrations usually protest against those in power, this one was organized by the party who were currently in government, the Social Democrats (PSD). Furthermore, for 'organized', one should, according to many commentators, substitute the word 'stage-managed'. People from across the country were encouraged by party officials to travel to Bucharest to join the protest, with coaches provided specifically for this purpose and extra trains being laid on. There were even reports of the coercion of local councils to ensure their citizens took part.[16]

The official slogan for the demonstration was 'We Want Prosperity, Not Security!', and the event was supposedly targeting abuse of power by the judiciary and secret service. This was the official line. A more sceptical interpretation was that it was an attempt by the governing party to claim they had strong public backing for their bid to take greater control of the state: particularly the presidency and the justice system, neither of which were under their control at the time. The leadership of the PSD refer to these branches as the 'parallel state'. In November 2017, they issued a statement condemning the way that 'under the cover of the so-called anti-corruption campaign, the parallel state aims to harass and, in the last instance, decapitate the legitimately elected political power'.[17] For the novelist Mircea Cărtărescu, the event had an almost incomprehensible logic: 'A party that dismisses two of its own governments and organises a protest meeting when it is in government – this hasn't been seen anywhere in the world … Our country branding is the Absurd.'[18]

The concept of the 'parallel state' was originally coined by the historian Robert Paxton as a way of describing institutions which are state-like in the way they're structured and organized, but which aren't actually an official part of the legislative state.[19] For the most part, they promote the same political values and actions that the state itself. As such the term has usually had a slightly different meaning from the similar concepts of the 'deep state' or the 'state within a state', both of which are used to describe factions within the institutional set-up of a country which work without the authority, and often in direct opposition, to the established state. In the Romanian case however, 'parallel state' is being used very much as a synonym for 'deep state' – a usage which has also been adopted in Turkey by President Recep Tayyip Erdoğan to describe the supposed followers of his critic Fethullah Gülen – as well as support from other assorted enemies such as the CIA and Jewish bankers – who hold various bureaucratic and judicial positions, and who, he alleges, are working to bring down his government.

Romanian and Turkish politicians aren't the only ones drawing on paranoid suspicions that target an enemy within. The 'deep state' is yet another concept symptomatic of the conviction that surface reality is not what it seems, and that politics today is a game of purposeful manipulation by sinister unelected forces. The rhetoric used by the Romanian leaders and by Erdoğan is very similar to that used by Donald Trump against members of the US government who don't automatically rubber stamp his directives. In fact, Romanian presidential hopeful Liviu Plesoianu asserted as part of his campaign against the imagined machinations of his own country's parallel state that 'we salute President Trump's fight against the American deep state. We know what forces are thrown against him.'[20]

In the US context, the term is mostly used to refer to unelected officials in the bureaucracy of government, as well as those in the technology and banking sectors. These various different groups supposedly constitute a shadow government which looks after the day-to-day operation of the state but, crucially, also works against anyone it considers to be opposed to its interests or values. And it does this all by covert means, and removed from the scrutiny of the democratic system. An *ABC News/Washington Post* poll from April 2017 found that 48 per cent of Americans – equally split between Democrat and Republican voters – believed in the existence of a deep state comprised of 'military, intelligence and government officials who try to secretly manipulate government policy'.[21]

For Trump, as with many populist politicians, the concept fits easily into the narrative that establishment forces are aligned against him. This, for example, is how Joel Pollak defined the problem in an article for the right-wing website *Breitbart*: as soon as Trump took power, '[h]oldovers from the Obama administration, and left-leaning career servants, began to work against the new administration … Members of the law enforcement and intelligence communities also leaked damaging, often classified, information to the media.'[22] The whole idea offers a way of preserving Trump's status as outsider even while in office, and gives him someone to blame if his initiatives don't work out. Although, as the journalist Dan Rather suggests, it also has more sinister implications: 'When I hear the faux outrage about the so-called "Deep State", I really think it's more raging against being confined by the rule of law and the Constitution.'[23]

A similar dynamic is at work in the UK, with parts of the judiciary and the civil service being branded as 'traitors' if their jobs bring them into conflict with the will of populist sentiment. The term 'deep state' itself may be used with much less frequency in Britain, but many of the suspicions about the workings of power are the same. One of the few people who has used the term in the context of UK politics is Steve Hilton, David Cameron's former director of strategy and now a television presenter in the United States.[24] According to Hilton, Tony Blair warned Cameron just before the 2010 general election of the way that the members of the civil service see themselves as 'the true guardians of the national interest', and believe it's their job to actually run the country.

Hilton's is an archetypal populist take on the idea. The rallying cry of the 'deep state', he says, is not '"We the People" but "You the People, ruled by We the Elite"'. In other words, while the subterfuge and collusion detected in 'false flag' operations and the use of 'crisis actors' is the work of government forces, belief in the 'deep state' goes beyond this, and identifies sinister ways of frustrating the will of the people even when the people's representatives are ostensibly in power.

Gas lights

In an article on the trend in popular culture for a particular type of psychological drama, the journalist Zoe Williams suggested that 'what we call post-truth politics would actually be better classed as gaslighting'.[25] Gaslighting is a psychological condition named after a play written by the early-twentieth-century British writer Patrick Hamilton. Hamilton had something of a fascination for narcissistic sociopaths in his work, which possibly reflected a similar strain in his own character – his brother Bruce once said he'd have made an excellent police chief in a Stalinist state.[26] His other great stage success *Rope*, based loosely on the Leopold and Loeb murder case, was the story of two university students who murder a classmate as an intellectual exercise. His final three novels, the *Gorse Trilogy*, tell of the sordid exploits of a conman in post-war Britain who sexually preys on his victims. In *Gas Light*, the central character Jack Manningham mentally tortures his young wife Bella by manipulating her into believing that she's losing her mind. And while *Gas Light* is not in any sense a political play, it obviously chimed with the sentiments of the late 1930s and early 1940s. It opened in London at the end of 1938, just a few months after the Munich Agreement, and in 1941, as the United States entered the war, began a run on Broadway which lasted for four years.

The word 'gaslighting' has been used since the 1960s to describe a form of mental persecution in which one person attempts to undermine another's sense of reality, to attack their mental stability and, thus, manipulate their behaviour. In the play, Manningham contradicts Bella's accounts of her own behaviour, making her believe her memory is failing and that her grip on reality is slipping. Over the last two decades, the term has also started being applied to politics. In his book *State of Confusion: Political Manipulation and the Assault on the American Mind*, the clinical psychologist Bryant Welch argues that political gaslighting techniques have become embedded in contemporary American politics, facilitated by the combination of traditional propaganda techniques with modern communications, advertising and marketing strategies.[27] A politician will lie about something, will be called out about the lie by the media, will dismiss the criticism and emphatically reiterate the lie, while at the same time attacking the press for being biased for making the allegation. And they'll continue doing this until, little by little, the audience watching begins to lose their bearings about what's true and what isn't.

In Hamilton's play, Manningham's assault on Bella's perception of reality is so intense that she slowly begins to believe him when he says he fears she might be losing her mind. As the campaign of psychological torture progresses, she becomes ever more dependent on him to tell her what is and what isn't real. For many political commentators, this is precisely the state of affairs that's afflicting America due to repeated exposure to Donald Trump's persistent assault on truth.[28]

The journalist Amanda Carpenter sees gaslighting as pivotal to Trump's political success, and at the very heart of the post-truth phenomenon.[29] She breaks down the Trump gaslighting technique into a five-stage process. First, he asserts something which has little or no basis in reality but is highly controversial and thus bound to attract attention – an early example was his advocacy of the idea that Barack Obama hadn't been born in the United States (and thus wasn't a 'true' American). He then spreads the rumour by citing vague or imaginary sources, while at the same time ensuring that he doesn't explicitly commit to it himself – ('Many people are saying …'; 'A very reliable source has informed me …'). He follows this by ramping up media interest by promising to reveal more about his knowledge of the issue at some indeterminate time in the future. Then uses the furore he's provoked as an opportunity to attack any of his opponents who try to criticize his pursuit of the issue. Finally, he'll declare victory in the dispute, regardless of how the facts on the ground have played out – so, for instance, claiming that it was actually Hillary Clinton who'd raised questions about Obama's place of birth, and that he, Trump, had been the one to resolve the issue by suggesting Obama should simply produce his birth certificate. And of course, every time he cycles through this formula, he provokes the press into promoting his distorted view of the world. So even if we don't believe the endless catalogue of nonsensical assertions, they still dominate the news agenda.

Once the concept of gaslighting became a popular way of criticizing the propagandist techniques of those in power, of course, it also became readily available for use by all parts of the political spectrum. Thus, at a rally in 2018, the NRA's executive vice-president Wayne LaPierre could claim that the opponents of gun control, including the survivors and relatives of tragedies like the Sandy Hook shooting, are themselves 'gaslight[ing] tragedy ... They exploit victims to advance their ultimate agenda: kill the NRA and napalm the second amendment right out of existence.'[30] The point has been reached, in other words, where one group is gaslighting another about the use of gaslighting in society.

11

Conspiracy politics

Epileptic trees

What gaslighting has in common with the other three terms we looked at in the previous chapter is that they started out referring to practices which do actually exist in the world. Examples of false flag operations punctuate the history of twentieth-century conflict; political astroturfing is becoming more commonplace; secret service organizations have often been accused of operating as a state within a state in totalitarian regimes; and gaslighting as a form of psychological manipulation is a very real form of abuse. But each of them has, over the last few years, been co-opted to describe paranoid fantasies or politically motivated distortions of the world, and from this have been used as way of corrupting or confusing political discourse. The process in each case is thus precisely the same as what happened with 'fake news'. And there's one other thing they all have in common: they all feed into a single overarching narrative – a narrative which mixes scepticism and suspicion about politics with an obsession with the processes of storytelling themselves.

* * *

Most of the time we approach fiction and reality with very different mindsets. The easiest way to explain this difference is through the emblem of 'Chekhov's gun'. This is the dramatic rule, succinctly illustrated by the writer Anton Chekhov, that if you have a gun hanging on the wall in Act One of your play, it must, without exception, be fired in Acts Two or Three. Or to put it more generally, whatever you introduce into the drama needs to be there for a purpose. This is because drama is built upon consequence, and every detail included in a story automatically becomes freighted with meaning. Every element serves a purpose – and for the audience, the expectations generated about the revelation of this meaning are one of the primary pleasures of the fictional experience. Why is that gun hanging on the wall? Who's going to fire it? And who's going to end up staring down its barrel?

The principle of 'Chekhov's gun' is so central to fiction that it's spawned a host of dramaturgical variations.[1] You can have 'Chekhov's armoury', made of multiple 'Chekhov guns', or 'Chekhov's army' made up of characters who seem marginal to the plot but turn out to be pivotal. In a film, the giveaway for this is if the status of the actor playing this marginal role seems far too famous for the part. 'Chekhov's gun' can be a boomerang if it's used multiple times. You can have 'Chekhov skills', where the hero happens to learn something early in the plot which turns out to be crucial later. Or 'Chekhov news item': a seemingly trivial piece of information that, by the end of proceedings, has changed the whole direction of the story. Then there's 'Chekhov's cough' – innocent as it may seem at the beginning, in fact a sure sign of consumption or other life-threatening illnesses. And so the list goes on.

Such is the importance of this as a premise in fiction that it becomes a focus of obsession for fan communities. In the era of social media, huge online groups congregate to try to predict the narrative of certain shows, picking out small, curious details from the plot which they then subject to intense speculation. All of which has led to the phenomenon of the epileptic trees: a type of over-the-top fan theory prompted by the logic of Chekhov's gun.[2] The specific reference here is to a speculative hypothesis for events in the first series of the television show *Lost*. For some unexplained, and thus mysterious, reason, trees on the island on which the series was set were continually shaking. Why could this be? And what significance did it have for the story as a whole? Well, one plausible, if unlikely, explanation that was that the trees were suffering from epileptic fits. As the saying goes, when you've eliminated the impossible, whatever remains, however improbable, must be the truth.

So that's fiction. Everything's connected, to paraphrase E. M. Forster. One thing invariably leads to another, and the plot steers a steady course along this line of connections. Any inadvertent rupture in the chain of causality is likely to be seen as a hole in the plot – as evidence of shoddy craftsmanship. Or, as Roland Barthes puts it, 'narrative is never made up of anything other than functions ... Even were a detail to appear irretrievably insignificant ... it would nonetheless end up with precisely the meaning of absurdity or uselessness' (think, for example, of the various red herrings that punctuate the storyline of a detective novel).[3] Or again, to cite Forster, it's causality which creates plot. A plot doesn't simply describe how things happen one after another; it describes why they happen. Why one event leads to another.[4]

Real life, on the other hand, doesn't operate with the same obvious mechanical precision. It may be the case that there's a basic underlying ideology in human thought that everything is, ultimately, explainable. That there's a cause – or reason – for all things. It's also the case that the human brain is actively looking for patterns in the world. Beliefs about causality are part of our basic cognitive machinery as humans.

We're predisposed to view the world in terms of cause and effect.[5] Research shows that our brains are already working in this way from when we're no more than six months old.[6] We use an understanding of causal relations to learn about and comprehend the world, to make predictions and build our belief systems.[7]

But – and it's a big but – the chains of causality in the real world are far from tidily arranged. Knowledge of many of them is as yet still out of reach of human understanding. So, while we may instinctively perceive things in causal terms, we learn to appreciate that the physical nature of the world is far from straightforward. Which is why, when we walk into a real-life room which happens to have a rifle hanging on the wall, we're not automatically primed to expect that someone is going to be stretchered out with a bullet-wound before the end of the evening.

This then is a basic difference in the mindsets we use to approach real life and fiction. It's a matter of degree. Causality is a feature of both. Science, after all, is predicated on causality. But we have careful expectations about causality for reality, and heightened expectations about it for fiction. That's not to say we can't get muddled between the two. Superstitions are founded on precisely this. Based on what's known as the post hoc fallacy (or to give it its full name, *post hoc ergo propter hoc*), a type of flawed reasoning which supposes that just because Event A follows Event B, Event A must have been caused by Event B. Just because I was wearing yellow socks on the two occasions that I beat Bob at tennis, it must have been the yellow socks that gave me that competitive edge. The mistake of taking correlation as causation.

Which brings us, finally, to conspiracy theories. Because in the case of conspiracy theories, this balance of expectations about causality becomes upended. The mindset usually reserved for fiction tips over to embrace reality.

An explanation for everything

Conspiracy theorists are often as obsessed with the way a story is told as they are with the story itself. The usual narrative they tell is a straightforward one. A secret plot with a malevolent purpose is being enacted by an influential network of conspirators. This plot involves illegal collusion by those wielding power in society, which is kept hidden from the public by elaborate illusions. In telling this story, conspiracy theorists often aim to directly contradict the prevailing consensus about how and why events happened. Dismissing the claims from the mainstream media lets believers argue they are avoiding the brainwashing that's deluding the majority of the population. Instead, they valorize what the political scientist Michael Barkum calls 'stigmatized knowledge – that is, knowledge claims that run counter to generally accepted beliefs'.[8] For conspiracists, the mass media are seen as part of the conspiracy itself; stooges controlled by the puppet masters pulling the strings of the conspiracy. It's in this way that *how* a story is told becomes part of the story itself.

One of the paradoxes of the present day is that the language of conspiracy theories has now become a mainstay of political culture despite the intense scepticism that conspiracy theorists have of anything that's embraced by the mainstream. From Trump's championing of the Birther movement and his paranoia about the deep state to the fear of European Union plots by hard-line Brexiters, conspiracy-theorist rhetoric is very much a regular part of modern political discourse. One plausible reason for this is the close relationship between the logic that structures conspiracies and the beliefs underpinning populism. As Alex Krasodomski-Jones has argued, conspiracy theories and populist movements are centred around antagonism towards the establishment and on alleged corruption in government institutions.[9] They see themselves as committed to the pursuit of truth, and to piercing the false consciousness that's distorting public understanding of the way the world is governed. Recent research shows that in the UK, a full 60 per cent of people believe at least one conspiracy theory.[10] As the leader of this research project, John Naughton, said in an interview with the *Guardian*, these sorts of theories are 'a way of trying to make sense of a complex and confusing world for an ordinary citizen'.[11] And in this respect, they function in precisely the same way as stories do.

The underlying archetype for the conspiracy-theory narrative is, once again, the *Overcoming the monster* story. Conspiracy thinking is based on dreams of the forces of good thwarting evil, of citizen detectives shining the light of truth into the dark recesses of government deceit. A monster (in this case the government or its agents) who's infinitely more powerful than the hero (the citizen detectives) has already enslaved a large part of the population through a mixture of brainwashing and repressive legislation. The odds are thus greatly stacked against the hero. Despite this, they doggedly track down the monster, identify a single flaw in its defences (discrepancies in the evidence, inconsistencies in the official narrative) which the monster has been too arrogant to concern itself about. At great personal risk, the hero exploits this small weakness and brings the monster/corrupt political system crashing down.

Along with this basic structure, there are two other fundamental elements of the logic behind conspiracy theories which turn them into narratives. The first is that nothing happens by accident. Correlation, in the conspiracy-theory universe, is always understood as causation. Conspiracy theorists still see themselves as working to scientific principles – collecting and scrutinizing evidence, building hypotheses based on empirical findings, testing these against new evidence. But a mixture of scepticism of mainstream explanations, confirmation bias and an absolutist faith in causality results in markedly unscientific conclusions. For instance, if there are inconsistencies in news reports about an event, this is immediately taken as significant, as proof of a deliberate cover-up. It's never simply an oversight or accident. Instead it's Chekhov's continuity error. Artefacts and events are thus transformed into symbols, imbuing them with a significance that's drawn from the overarching story.

The second fundamental element of conspiracy theories is the existence of an ending. Because events are never understood as random or coincidental, there's always an explanation for them waiting to be found. A solution out there somewhere, which can be revealed with the right detective work, and which will produce a definitive answer about what really happened. As Barkun says, one of the primary appeals of conspiracy theories is that they offer explanations for the confusion and obscurity that is actual life.[12]

Again, this matches the logic of a story. By its very nature a narrative has a beginning, a middle and an end. As we've discussed earlier, the meaning of the whole is reliant on the events which constitute the ending. Unlike real life, which is experienced as open-ended and is characterized by uncertainty of the future, stories have conclusions which help explain the significance of all the vicissitudes and reversals of fortune that have brought us to this point.

A Promethean tale of occultism

When the investigative journalist Bob Woodward published his book about the Trump White House, press secretary Sarah Huckabee Sanders dismissed it, along with the criticism it made of the administration, as a work of 'fiction'.[13] A similar excuse was made by Brett Kavanaugh in his hearings for the Supreme Court about revelations in his old friend Mark Judge's memoir, *Wasted*.[14]

Judge's book recounts his experiences as an alcoholic, and includes a character named Bart O'Kavanaugh who gets blackout-drunk one night. If this had referenced a real incident from Kavanaugh's teenage years, it would have undermined his defence against the accusations made by Christine Blasey Ford that he'd attempted to sexually assault her at a high school party one night when he was very inebriated. But Kavanaugh rejected the characterization by asserting simply that the book was a fictionalized account of Judge's life.[15]

Both these defences play on a fairly straightforward distinction between factually based narratives and fiction. Framing something as fiction implies that it's made-up, fabricated and intentionally twisting the facts of the matter. At least, that's the standard formula. In the conspiracy-theory world on the other hand, this sort of distinction between fact and fiction is very often blurred. And in many cases, the two concepts actually change place.[16]

As we've seen, conspiracy-theory thinking involves an exaggerated scepticism of knowledge that comes from establishment sources – places such as research institutes and universities. This thus rules out a great deal of the conventionally accepted 'facts' about the workings of the world. In the conspiracy-theorist logic, knowledge of this sort is merely propaganda created by the dark forces who are manipulating society. It is, in other words, fictional.

If facts are fiction, the corollary, presumably, would be that fiction is fact. Maybe unsurprisingly, there are indications that this is precisely the logic that drives many conspiracy theorists. Rob Brotherton notes, for instance, that the Oklahoma City bomber Timothy McVeigh justified killing low-level government employees by likening them to the storm troopers in *Star Wars*. Despite their being innocent on an individual level, he rationalized, they were nevertheless guilty by association simply because they worked for the evil empire.[17]

Then there are the comments made by the author of *The Handmaid's Tale*, Margaret Atwood, in an interview with Ramin Setoodeh for *Variety*, suggesting that the 9/11 terrorists were also indirectly inspired by *Star Wars*. 'Remember the first [film]?' she said to Setoodeh. 'Two guys fly a plane in the middle of something and blow that up? The only difference is, in "Star Wars," they get away. Right after 9/11, [the government] hired a bunch of Hollywood screenwriters to tell them how the story might go next. Sci-fi writers are very good at this stuff, anticipating future events.'[18]

A similar argument to this last statement is popular among flat-earthers: that the authorities actively promote science fiction which includes examples of space travel because this reinforces the ideology of a spherical globe. According to this mindset, Hollywood blockbusters are a form of government propaganda aimed at manipulating the population into unconsciously embracing the beliefs of the ruling elite. A conspiracy theorist named Isaac Weishaupt, for instance, wrote a long treatise called *The Star Wars Conspiracy: Hidden Occult and Illuminati Symbolism of Aliens & the New Age*. As the title suggests, this argues that George Lucas's film is an 'occult scripture being readily consumed by today's entertainment-obsessed masses', and its portrayal of aliens and extraterrestrial life is 'paving the way for future rigged revelations of "evolved" alien entities that are truly demons in disguise'.[19] Rather than being fiction, the film is actually laying out in detail its blueprint for the overthrow of society as we know it. A detailed reading of the film, which is what Weishaupt happily provides in his book, shows very clearly how the story is actually a fable about the occult ideas practised by the Illuminati, including the battle they're waging between the forces of light and darkness, as well as 'Adolf Hitler's belief in the Super-Man with latent internal powers, and the necessary destruction of Christianity as part of the future world religion'. If one then factors in Disney's purchase of the rights to the *Star Wars* franchise, we have a situation where the establishment are now able to programme 'the minds of the youth to accept this future world which is a deceptive lie'. As the book's blurb warns: 'Don't let the religion of Star Wars infiltrate and possess your mind without first considering the true teachings insidiously hidden within this Promethean tale of occultism.'

Absurd as this may sound, there *are* occasional examples of the plots of Hollywood films being mistaken for reality, which would lend credence to the accusation that the government is using fiction as a way of manipulating the public into supporting its actions. For instance, during the UK Chilcot Inquiry into Britain's role in the Iraq War, it was disclosed that some of the supposed intelligence collected by Britain's Secret Intelligence Service which suggested that Saddam Hussein was in possession of weapons of mass destruction was in fact lifted from the plot of the 1996 film *The Rock*.[20] The intelligence dossier that helped make the case for war referred to nerve agents being transported in a specific type of glass container – a detail which, as the writer of the film David Weisberg later explained, was 'complete fabrication ... pure invention' designed to add a bit of visual colour to what was in reality a rather mundane (albeit extremely lethal) technology.[21]

Examples such as these are few and far between. But it's worth noting that fiction is often both a response to and an influence on important events in society, and that the interplay between the two can produce chains of mutual influence, with reality shaping fiction, which in turn shapes reality, and so on. Or to put it another way, the worlds of literature and fiction are drawn upon to help us explain and express real-life events, while real-life events are then processed through culture via fiction. *The Handmaid's Tale* is a perfect example of this. It's a fictional narrative based upon behaviours and policies which have all existed in reality in parts of the world. As Atwood explains, 'One of my rules was that I would not put any events into the book that had not already happened in what James Joyce called the "nightmare" of history, nor any technology not already available.'[22] All the repressive behaviours of the totalitarian regime she invents has precedents in real-life totalitarian regimes around the globe. And just as reality influenced her fiction, so her fiction then influenced reality. The symbolism of *The Handmaid's Tale*, as discussed in earlier chapters, has gone on to become a powerful rallying strategy in protests supporting women's rights, thus influencing contemporary history.

Another similar example is the graphic novel *V for Vendetta*, written by Alan Moore and illustrated by David Lloyd. The mask worn by the protagonist in the story is modelled on the historical figure of Guy Fawkes and symbolizes renegade political action under a corrupt political regime. David Lloyd's design for this mask was then reproduced in the film of the comic, and this in turn was adopted as a symbolic costume by anti-capitalist and anti-government protesters around the world. The symbols from fiction are thus given new meaning by being used in the very real political struggles of the present.

The political scientists Joseph Uscinski and Joseph Parent have argued that the structure that underpins conspiracy theories is often not that different from many of the arguments made in normal political discourse.[23] The only real distinction, they say, is that with conspiracy theories everything becomes that much more exaggerated, stark and distrustful. But as we've seen, exaggeration, bluntness and a fearful lack of trust are becoming ever more the norm for mainstream politics these days.

12

The lie that tells the truth

The last word in truth

In approaching the topic of storytelling from the perspective of current politics, one obvious question that arises is whether there's a link between the use of narrative and the spreading of falsehoods. We often think of storytelling in terms of making things up, of invention and fiction. So, can this help explain why politicians – particularly those today – are seen as fabulists, lying their way to power, then continuing to lie with impunity throughout their spells in office? And if we really are careening towards a full-blown crisis in civilization due to the wanton disregard that our current leaders have for the concept of truth, is there anything we can do to change the narrative, and restore a sense of stability and decorum to public debate? To answer both these questions, we need to return first to the topic of what exactly constitutes the truth when it comes to the world of politics.

* * *

At the beginning of *F for Fake*, his film about forgery, fraud and artistic hoaxes, Orson Welles announces, 'Tell it by the fireside or in a marketplace or in a movie, almost any story is almost certainly some kind of lie.'[1] This is a long-standing view of storytelling – that it deals somehow in falsehoods and fabrication. As the old adage has it, even when the narrative is grounded in reality, you shouldn't let the facts get in the way of a good story. The idea that stories are antithetical to truth-telling dates back at least as far as Plato, who famously banned poets and the narrators of myths from his ideal society. In Book X of the *Republic* he chastises them for dealing in imitations of reality rather than in reality itself. 'The tragic poet', he writes, 'if his art is representation, is by nature at third remove from the throne of truth, and the same is true of all other representative artists.'[2]

About two millennia later, the Elizabethan writer Sir Philip Sydney offered a strong counterargument to this claim that poets, by the very nature of their profession, lie. 'How often, think you, do the physicians lie, when they aver things good for sicknesses, which afterwards send Charon a great number of souls drowned in a potion before they come to his ferry?' he asked. 'Now for the poet, he nothing affirms, and therefore never lies. For, as I take it, to lie is to affirm that to be true which is false.'[3] The poets and storytellers of the world don't merely imitate, they create. And in creating they can transcend the limitations of factual reality.

In trying to refute Plato's argument, Sidney puts his finger on an important point about our understanding of truth. The idea of what counts as truth is always influenced by the conventions at play in a particular context. Medical truths, philosophical truths and poetical truths aren't necessarily the same things. Or at least, the way we categorize them – the way we assert that this thing is true while that thing isn't – depends on a different set of expectations and measures in each case. This isn't to say that truth is relative. But that it takes on a slightly different shape depending on the forum in which it's being debated.

Let's look at two diverse examples. The first concerns a clash between medicine and the media. In the days running up to the first anniversary of the release of the Lockerbie bomber Abdelbaset al-Megrahi in 2009, one of the doctors who'd diagnosed his medical condition reflected on the way that this diagnosis had been used in the legal proceedings which resulted in al-Megrahi's release. There was a political storm raging at the time over whether the release had been part of a deal between the oil company BP and the Libyan government. The fact that Megrahi was still alive, despite the medical panel having apparently given him just three months to live due to prostate cancer, was causing great consternation in certain quarters. The doctor, Karol Sikora, defended his role in the proceedings by attempting to clarify what he'd actually said in his diagnosis, and how this had then been interpreted by both politicians and the media. Quoted in an article in the *Observer* he explained:

> In medicine we say 'Never say never and never say always', because funny things happen. All you can do is give a statistical opinion, and that's fraught because the media, the law, and indeed patients, don't like statistical opinion. They want to know 'Is it this or is it that?' A court is all about guilty or not guilty.[4]

The idea he's getting at here is that different domains – the law, journalism, medicine – have different criteria for establishing whether something is factually true or not. For the legal process overseeing Megrahi's release, the decision to be made was a simple yes or no – he either was or wasn't to be released. And for commentators in politics and the media, the assumption seems to have been that this simple yes or no question should also have applied to his medical condition: he was going to die within three months, or he wasn't. For Dr Sikora and those in his profession, medical 'facts' simply don't have this structure. They're a matter of probability, based on expert interpretation. Truth is a mixture of the knowledge we have available to us at any one time, and the way it's framed in what we say. Dr Sikora hadn't been lying in his diagnosis (as Philip Sidney suggests physicians so often do), nor had he necessarily been wrong. Instead, his words had been interpreted by the politicians and the media using a different set of standards for what constitutes the truth.

The second example relates directly to the debate over storytelling that's stretched from Plato through Sidney to the present day. In 2003, the writer James Frey published a memoir about his experiences of being a drug addict called *A Million Little Pieces*. Initial reaction to the book was extremely positive and turned Frey into something of an overnight literary star. But a few months into his new-found fame, reports began to emerge that he'd exaggerated, if not fabricated, parts of the content. Allegations began circulating that what was being promoted as a factual memoir of his life was, at least in places, a work of imagination. The whole thing escalated into a full-blown literary scandal, culminating in Frey and his publishers having to apologize to readers for misleading them. People who'd purchased the book were offered a refund if they agreed to sign a statement declaring that they wouldn't have bought it if they'd known at the time that the content wasn't, in the strict sense of the word, the unvarnished truth.[5]

When the paperback version was printed a little while after the furore, Frey added a disclaimer. Here he explained that he'd 'embellished' details about his experiences in order 'to serve what I felt was the greater purpose of the book'.[6] He hadn't been thinking in terms of fiction or non-fiction when he wrote it, he said. These simply weren't categories he had in mind during the composition of the book. It was only after it had been published that he began to realize the extent to which these different genres implied certain expectation about the content which shaped the way people perceived the book.[7]

His overall justification for his actions was that memoir, in his view, 'allows the writer to work from memory instead of from a strict journalistic or historical standard. It is about impression and feeling, about individual recollection.' Thus, deep down, his 'memoir is ... a subjective truth, altered by the mind of a recovering drug addict and alcoholic. Ultimately, it's a story, and one that I could not have written without having lived the life I've lived.'[8] He's making much the same argument that Picasso made when he said that 'art is a lie that makes us realize truth, at least the truth that is given us to understand.'[9] A story can be true to the spirit or feeling of an experience, even if it departs from the mundane facts of that event.

The problem Frey ran into, however, is that the publisher explicitly categorized the book as a memoir, and for most people, this created a very different set of expectations from those that Frey himself had apparently been working with. Take, for instance, this review by Sean O'Hagan in the *Observer*, part of which was still included as an endorsement on the cover even after the scandal.[10] 'Were it fiction,' O'Hagan writes, 'James Frey's big, bruising, macho, tear-stained tale of personal decline and against-all-odds redemption would be scarcely believable. As a memoir, it is almost mythic.'

Some years later, when interviewing Frey, the journalist Decca Aitkenhead gave a succinct summary of the whole incident. '*A Million Little Pieces* was ... hardly a corrupting assault on the very foundations of truth,' she wrote. 'Frey was right to point out that most memoirs take liberties with factual accuracy – but it was stretching the point to suggest that categories of fiction and non-fiction were fundamentally meaningless, and therefore irrelevant.'[11] In other words, Frey was guilty of lying because he flaunted the conventions used by contemporary non-fiction publishers. If the book hadn't been framed as factually true, he may well have got away with presenting it as a 'subjective truth'. But by calling it a memoir, he entered into a contract with the reader which was built on unembellished factual detail.

When he came to write his follow-up book, the novel *Bright Shiny Morning*, he was much more circumspect, asserting in the opening sentence that 'nothing in this book should be considered accurate or reliable'.[12]

Truthful hyperbole

So how about politics? How are the parameters that define what counts as truthfulness and what counts as lying drawn in this context? Is there a similar grey area of ambiguity surrounding factual pronouncements here as there is in both medicine and memoir?

All politicians lie, of course.[13] We know this. So much so in some cases that, for the journalist Louis Heren, the default mindset to adopt when interviewing anyone in politics is: 'Why is this lying bastard lying to me?'[14] Most politicians also try their damnedest to pretend they don't lie. And while we may decry this tendency towards deception in our elected leaders, the actual relationship we have with lying can often be confusingly ambivalent. The political scientists Thomas Cronin and Michael Genovese list a number of key paradoxes of the American presidency, one of which is that 'We want a decent, just, caring, and compassionate president, yet we admire a cunning, guileful and, on occasions that warrant it, even a ruthless, manipulative president'.[15] If this is true, the idea is straight out of Machiavelli and his assertion that those 'princes who have accomplished great deeds are those who have cared little for keeping their promises and have known how to manipulate the minds of men by shrewdness'.[16]

The 'paradoxes' that modern-day politicians like Donald Trump or Boris Johnson embody are numerous. In Trump's case they're so abundant that the *Washington Post* had to introduce a new category to their ongoing survey of political falsehoods. The 'Bottomless Pinocchio', as they call it, is awarded to those 'who repeat a false claim so many times that they are, in effect, engaging in campaigns of disinformation'.[17] As of January 2019, the only currently elected official who'd met this standard was Trump – and he'd done so on fourteen separate occasions.

For many, however, including Trump's vice-president, this sort of behaviour is all a welcome change from 'politics as usual'. 'He's entitled to express his opinion' Mike Pence said, with reference to inaccurate statements on voter fraud. 'I think the American people find it very refreshing that they have a president who will tell them what's on his mind.'[18] In other words, the authenticity that comes from speaking one's mind is a form of truthfulness which trumps evidence-based assertions of knowledge.

Despite all this, there was (and often remains) a great reluctance in the media to describe Trump's behaviour – or that of any other politician – as out-and-out lying. In political circles, accusations of lying have traditionally been a highly sensitive issue, and even in these unusual times, many people still feel uneasy about using the word. Politicians themselves, maybe unsurprisingly, have never been too keen on using it to describe their own actions. Instead we have a whole lexicon of increasingly elaborate euphemisms, from Edmund Burke's 'economical with the truth' to Winston Churchill's 'terminological inexactitude'. Trump himself is apparently keen on the idea of 'truthful hyperbole'. As Tony Schwartz, who coined the term when ghost-writing *The Art of the Deal*, said in an interview with the *New Yorker*, this is, of course, a flat-out contradiction in terms. 'A way of saying, "It's a lie, but who cares?"'[19]

Just as politicians shy away from using the word about themselves, they're also careful to avoid it when describing their colleagues.

The cynic would say this is simply an extension of the tendency for what George Orwell called the ubiquity of 'euphemism, question-begging and sheer cloudy vagueness' in political discourse.[20] Or as the comedian George Carlin put it, politicians speak with 'great caution because they must take care not to actually say anything'.[21]

But there's something more substantial to it than this. Back in 2004, during that year's first presidential debate, John Kerry objected to being accused of saying that President Bush had lied by asserting that 'I've never, ever used the harshest word as you did just then, and I try not to'.[22] His attitude is of a part with the way the word is expressly prohibited within the chamber of the House of Commons in the UK. Along with insults such as 'blackguard', 'coward', 'stoolpigeon' and 'traitor', it's deemed 'unparliamentary language'.[23] Something which 'breaks the rules of politeness' and is thus categorically forbidden.[24] In this tradition, an accusation of lying is an attack on someone's honour. And its consequences are a form of social stigma. It's for this reason that the act of being caught in a lie can often be more politically damaging than the corrupt behaviour that's being covered up in the first place.

Journalists, similarly, are often highly cautious about using the word. After a speech given by Paul Ryan to the Republican National Convention in 2012, for instance, a full fifteen different types of euphemisms were recorded by one report, as journalists attempted to avoid the term.[25] There were 'factual shortcuts', 'misleading elements' and 'heavy inaccuracies' in what Ryan had said. There was 'outright distortion' and a range of various 'inconsistencies and contradictions'. But there were no actual 'lies'.

In recent years, cable television and internet-based reporting have shown less aversion to the word, with the result that, in the opinion of the *New York Times*, 'lying, as a denunciation, has flattened into just another charge'.[26] For many, however, it still isn't used lightly.

Faced with the rhetoric flowing from the Trump camp early in his presidency, editorials by two major news organizations publicly debated the ethics and pragmatics of using the word. The *New York Times* decided in the end that they would go ahead with it.[27] Editor Dean Baquet argued that, while he appreciated the 'gravity' of its implications, 'we should be letting people know in no uncertain terms that [what Trump's team is saying is] untrue'. National Public Radio, on the other hand, opted against it. 'Our job as journalists is to report, to find facts, and establish their authenticity and share them with everybody', they reasoned.[28] 'It's really important that people understand that these aren't our opinions ... [T]he minute you start branding things with a word like "lie", you push people away from you.'

The main sticking point with the word is that it's usually interpreted as meaning there's explicit *intent* on the part of the liar. As philosopher Arnold Isenberg's definition has it, 'A lie is a statement made by one who does not believe it with the intention that someone else shall be led to believe it.'[29] This, of course, makes it very difficult to ever categorically say that someone has lied, because to do so would mean knowing what's going on inside their head.

This also allows for a lot of semantic equivocation. In the press conference following the outcry over the 'alternative facts' dispute, for example, Sean Spicer, the former White House press secretary, explained that his aim was always to be honest with the American people: 'I think sometimes we can disagree with the facts', he said, 'but our intention is never to lie to you.'[30] As a sentence, this makes very little sense. Unless you go ahead and substitute the word 'facts' with 'interpretations'.

It's not just intent though. The philosopher Don Fallis suggests there's another important element that should be part of any definition.[31] For it to be a lie you have to say something you believe is false *in a context where truthful assertions are the norm*. For example, if you're on stage and declare, 'This is I, Hamlet the Dane', that isn't a lie. The expectations of a theatrical performance are that what you see on stage specifically *isn't* literally true (this is much the argument that Sidney made when he wrote that poets never affirm anything and therefore never lie). If you're in a court of law, on the other hand, and claim you saw a Scandinavian gentleman about to stab his uncle, when you know very well that nothing of the sort actually happened, that would count as a lie. And it would involve immediate social sanction.

While the examples of stage-acting or giving sworn testimony are fairly clear-cut, there are other contexts where things aren't so straightforward. Take, for example, advertising. Most societies have regulatory bodies to ensure that advertisers are prevented from making false claims, either about their own products or about those of their competitors. In the UK, for instance, the Advertising Standards Authority is meant to ensure that adverts are 'legal, decent, honest and truthful'.[32] In the United States, the Federal Trade Commission plays much the same role. So, for example, when Rice Krispies, at the height of the swine flu scare and without adequate scientific evidence, claimed they helped 'support your child's immunity', the regulator was able to step in and have a word.[33]

This is all good and well in protecting the consumer of breakfast cereals from overt manipulation. But unfortunately, it doesn't apply to political advertising. Political adverts can make whatever claims they want to, and the regulatory bodies have no power whatsoever to sanction them. In the United States, the rationale for this is that political speech is protected by the First Amendment. As the judge ruling on a dispute in Ohio a few years ago explained, 'We do not want the government deciding what is political truth ... Instead, in a democracy, the voters should decide'.[34] In the UK the reasoning's much the same, but without the clear-cut justification that the constitution brings to bear. By Don Fallis's definition then, whatever one claims in a political advert is not really a lie – at least to the extent that it involves no social penalty.

Fallis builds his argument on Paul Grice's 'cooperation principle' in conversation – the idea that sustainable social interaction depends on people being able to rely on certain norms and expectations of behaviour.[35] Lying, in situations which depend on being truthful (i.e. most everyday interaction), is an act of non-cooperation. It's an example of the two people engaged in a conversation *not* working together to construct a meaningful dialogue.

Within these various parameters, then, is someone like Donald Trump lying? He says things which are in direct conflict with what he's said before, certainly. He also regularly asserts things based on flawed or non-existent evidence. The basic pattern behind his 'truthful hyperbole' appears to divide into two general trends: there's the way he characterizes the state of the country, summoning up the image of 'American carnage' and a *Crippled America*,[36] when much of the evidence is that growth and employment have been on the rise for the last few years.[37] Then there are the statements related to his self-image, and specifically those challenging what he perceives as attacks on his popularity or success.

Neither are straightforward lies if we take intent into account. The description of 'American carnage', while not in line with a holistic picture of the US economy, is likely the experience for large sections of the population, especially those in communities where manufacturing jobs have dwindled or vanished altogether. Meanwhile, the psychology of the narcissist, of which Trump seems to be a textbook case,[38] is self-belief in an over-inflated self-image. As the philosopher Harry Frankfurt writes, 'It is often uncertain whether Trump actually cares about the truth of what he says. Since a person does not lie unless he makes an assertion that he himself takes to be false, we cannot properly say that he is lying if he actually believes what he says.'[39] Which is perhaps why being challenged about what are clearly false statements doesn't seem to have the same effect with him as it does for other political careers.

It's this strand in political discourse – the bluster of over-confident assertion coupled with a dismissive regard for factual evidence – which is perhaps most representative of the post-truth era. The approach was summed up in a moment of self-reflexive confession by the conservative writer James Delingpole. Following an embarrassing television interview in which he repeatedly failed to answer a string of simple factual questions to back up his assertions about the implications of a no-deal Brexit, Delingpole attempted to explain away his performance by describing himself as 'one of those chancers who prefers to leave everything to the last minute in the hope you can wing it using a mixture of charm, impish humour, and nuggets of vaguely relevant info snatched on the hoof from the recesses of your memory.'[40] This is a definition that could apply to many of the more high-profile politicians of today. And it's a state of affairs in which truth, as a guiding principle for political debate, becomes almost an irrelevance.

Strategic catachresis

There's one other telling aspect to the way that Trump and politicians of his ilk stretch the truth, however. This is to do with the way they manipulate the words and concepts they use. The way they exploit the flexibility of language to create the specious logic which underpins the central narrative they're pushing.

At the heart of this is a rhetorical technique which is particularly popular with conspiracy theorists. This involves appropriating certain key words for purposes which appear to be almost the precise opposite of what these words conventionally mean. Take, for instance, the way that the conspiracy-theorist website *InfoWars*, run by Alex Jones, uses the word 'truth' itself. 'Our team risks threats from the globalists and works hard every day to bring you the truth the Main Stream Media and Globalist forces don't want you to hear.'[41] As we've seen, among the 'truths' they've been working so hard to promote is the idea that the Sandy Hook massacre was entirely fabricated by the government. Then there's the way that groups such as the 9/11 Truth Movement, who dispute the established account of the 11 September attacks, attempt to annex the same word.[42] Or how the campaign group 'Swift Boat Veterans for Truth' tried to undermine the image of John Kerry as a war hero during the 2004 presidential campaign (so much so that the term 'swiftboating' came to describe a specious or untruthful political attack).[43] In each case the organizations are resolutely using the word 'truth' in ways which run counter to received opinion about the workings of the world, and are thus staking claim to that term for themselves. George Orwell once again provides a satirical example of this in *Nineteen Eighty-Four* with the 'Ministry of Truth' – the department that actually looks after propaganda, and which 'curates' the historical records to ensure they present the government-approved version of events.

Of course, as we've seen throughout the book, language is always being manipulated for persuasive purposes. And as part of this, individual words often have their meaning stretched or twisted. From a purely technical point of view, it would be wrong to categorize this as a 'misuse' of language, because it's precisely this flexibility which makes language such a powerful means of communication.

From a moral perspective, on the other hand, this sort of manipulation can often be very questionable. At its most extreme it can lead to doublespeak: language that purposefully distorts or obscures the straightforward meaning of words so as to disguise the actual facts of the matter. This is something that's particularly prevalent in military discourse, which is rife with terms such as 'enhanced interrogation' (torture) and 'ethnic cleansing' (racially motivated genocide). The National Council of Teachers of English in the United States runs an annual Doublespeak Award for those who've 'perpetuated language that is grossly deceptive, evasive, euphemistic, confusing, or self-centered'.[44] Past winners include the US State Department for their (aptly Orwellian) 1984 announcement that they'd ceased using the word 'killing' in official reports about overseas human rights abuses, and instead were using the phrase 'unlawful or arbitrary deprivation of life'.[45]

But the technique underpinning *InfoWars*'s use of the word 'truth', or Trump's appropriation of 'fake news' is rather different. For most of the time they're not simply trying to obscure events through the use of confusing or euphemistic language. Instead, it's what might technically be called 'strategic catachresis'. Catachresis is a rhetorical term which refers to the use of a word or phrase in a way that significantly departs from its conventional usage. Or, as Dr Johnson put it, it's when 'words are too far wrested from their native signification'.[46] So the word 'truth' when applied to hypotheses about elaborate government cover-ups is being well and truly wrested from its native signification. In fact, it's being strategically annexed by a group with a very different world view from the mainstream. For those who believe in this world view, this isn't doublespeak because it isn't actually deceitful. Instead, it's an attempt to recalibrate the language.

Importantly, the reason it works (when it does) is less to do with the word itself than with the wider narrative of which it's a part. In cases such as these, 'truth' becomes less about observable facts, and instead refers to an extreme form of anti-establishment scepticism. It becomes part of the populist narrative of the common people versus the secretive, corrupt elite. Part of a world view structured around subjectivity and scepticism.

The irony of this modern-day crisis over belief in verifiable evidence is that we live in an age where information is so readily accessible. Statements made by a politician aren't lost to the ether once spoken, or reliant on hearsay. They endure on the internet. Likewise, scientific consensus and empirical data isn't hidden away in reference libraries or academic silos. It can be called up by anyone, anywhere, instantaneously. Yet still false information thrives. And one of the key reasons for this is because the prevailing narratives that have taken hold in parts of the collective imagination override a categorical insistence on established truths.

A fitting ending, or the paradox of anti-politics

I began this book with a brisk outline of one of the most ubiquitous plots in drama. It's a plot that's used time and again by politicians running for office:

> Something is rotten in the state of Denmark (or Washington, or Westminster). To stop the rot – or drain the swamp – an outsider needs to step up. Someone untainted by the cronyism of the halls of power, and armed with unconventional methods. Someone who can take the fight to the complacent, self-serving political establishment – and in doing so, bring about a change both in the system itself and the lives of the millions of everyday people who look to him or her as their champion.

Over and again we see this narrative being drawn upon by candidates as they delineate their political personas. And over and again it's those who best frame their message according to this template who are mostly likely to succeed in capturing the imagination of the electorate.

For aspiring candidates, sticking to a few basic storytelling principles can be a great first step on the road to power. Appreciating the way that stories are structured around character; how they rely on conflict, which is provided by the persona of the antagonist. That this conflict needs to provoke a sense of moral outrage by appealing to the value-systems of the audience. That these values are symbolized by a clearly defined goal which the politician commits to deliver. That when it comes to character, consistency equals authenticity – and that actions produce character, and character enacts story. To remember that attention is all important in today's media environment, and that the language used to frame issues is a vital part of the storytelling process. Yes, the political message is important. But it's how this message is communicated which makes the difference between triumph and obscurity.

The aim throughout this book has been to examine the fundamental role that storytelling of this sort plays in politics, and how this can help us better understand the current political environment, especially as it's shaped by populism and post-truth. But as I've hopefully shown, storytelling isn't restricted to persuasion. It can be found across all quarters of political life. It's a powerful tool for explaining and mapping out issues; a highly effective vehicle for the dissemination of disinformation. Such are the uses it can be put to that it's not just those running successful campaigns who draw on narrative but also those trying to undermine the system through deception and deceit.

There's a middle ground though between outright deception and the ethically virtuous campaign looking for an effective way to articulate its message. And arguably, it's this middle ground which best represents the crisis in politics today. A middle ground in which the particular use of narrative *does* compromise ideas of truth and reality, and drifts towards make-believe.

In their book on *Network Propaganda*, Benkler, Faris and Roberts point to two ways in which political storytelling that tends towards the fictional rather that the factual can be of great harm to society. Not only does it destabilize the concept of democracy and provide a space in which propaganda can thrive, but it also 'makes actual governance difficult'.[47] The latter point is well illustrated by the quagmire that's engulfed the practical business of Britain planning its withdrawal from the EU. Throughout the referendum and through into the negotiations, Brexit was conceptualized as a simple story about control, sovereignty and national identity. The allusions and metaphors that people used to argue their side of the case drifted off into the realms of fiction, conjuring up either idealistic or dystopian scenarios meant to rouse the emotions of their followers. Yet the actual policy implications for the process are anything but simple. From a prudent legislative perspective, it's one of the most intricate scenarios the UK has been involved in over the last several decades. This mismatch resulted in those negotiating policy struggling vainly to map this complexity onto the simple populist narrative.

This basic pattern – the use of a simple story for persuasion, which ignores the nuance and complexity of the reality of things – can be found in the rhetoric of contemporary politicians across the globe. And at its heart is a striking paradox. Politics as a spectator sport has rarely been more popular. Its mixture of entertainment value with real consequences produces massive audience engagement. Yet at the same time, we're living in an era in which politicians, parliaments and whole political systems are being vilified in ways they haven't been for decades. Their actions are *a betrayal of the will of the people*. The institutions which comprise them *aren't fit for purpose*. The result is that the most prominent actors on the political stage today are those who cast themselves as non-politician-politicians. The era we're living through isn't characterized simply by post-truth and populism. It's also, increasingly, an era of anti-politics. Or at least, of the rhetoric of anti-politics.

The consequence of all this is that the political story that's in the ascendency at the moment is an increasingly simplistic one, built on a scepticism of expertise, evidence and experience. And while political narrative is a highly effective form of persuasion and can be a helpful matrix for policy-making and problem-solving, it can also lead astray. When it relies too heavily on broad generalizations, when it devolves into a one-dimensional plot that ties everything up in a neat and straightforward way, it betrays the real-life struggles of the very people it's meant to be empowering.

Afterword: The narcissism of the present

Unprecedented times

Towards the end of 2020, Oxford Dictionaries announced that it wasn't choosing a single 'word of the year' that year.[1] The events of the previous twelve months had been too self-consciously dramatic to be neatly summed up in a solitary word. Pandemics, lockdowns, global protests, debates about racial justice, and the fall-out from a 'contested' US presidential election all vied for primacy. Instead, the dictionary opted to announce a list of notable words which reflected what had, in their opinion, been 'an "unprecedented" year'.

In some ways this reflected the rise and fall of the 'word-of-the-year' phenomenon as a popular internet fad – something which perfectly suited the way online culture revels in easily consumable talking points until interest becomes saturated and the focus shifts to other quirks in the culture. It was also symptomatic of the way that 2020 marked something of a zenith in the way culture fetishizes particular years, imbuing them with a specific narrative symbolism. The year '2020' became a byword for an excess of historic experiences, for one crisis piling upon another to create an almost apocalyptic intensity.

It's part of the narcissism of the present – probably an inevitable part – that we tend to think that the events we're dealing with today are unprecedented; that things have never been this bad, severe or note-worthy. There's also a tendency to be somewhat blinkered in our focus on our direct surroundings or those which are most prominently featured in the media – viewing local events as unique, and failing to appreciate the ways in which similar trends are or have been developing in other parts of the world, with similar patterns of evolution and similar tactics of promotion and resistance. Over the past few years, this exceptionalism of the present day has often also been accompanied by a propensity for reaching for extreme analogies to describe or denounce what's going on. A form of 'concept creep' clouds the rhetoric that people use to talk about what's happening, which in turn can often frustrate the possibility for clear analysis. As we've seen over these last few years, this has had the effect of boosting the profile of extremist groups and their ideas, with media representation thriving on conflict and drama and thus favouring precisely the style of politics that fanatical movements embody.

As noted throughout the book, however, many of the issues highlighted in commentaries on contemporary politics have been a feature of most historical periods in some form or other. The second half of the 2010s may have been characterized as an era of 'post-truth', but politicians have always taken a creative attitude to what they communicate. In the United States, for instance, despite the much-publicized First Amendment ('Congress shall make no law . . . abridging the freedom of speech, or of the press'), the relationship between the government and the press began experiencing difficulties from the very beginning of the republic. Only a year after George Washington retired, his successor, John Adams, brought in laws that criminalized the publishing of opinions critical to the government, thus attacking head-on the freedom of the press. For all his talk of the 'fake news media' being 'enemies of the people', Donald Trump never went quite this far.

Having said that, the years of the Trump presidency, from his running for election in 2015–16 to the disputed transition in 2020–21, have proved to be an excellent case study in the power of political storytelling and its relation to the workings of power. It began with a flurry of pronouncements and events which signalled the dawning of a 'post-truth' era and ended with the distorted narratives encapsulated in a series of increasingly unhinged conspiracy theories. The 'Stop the Steal' campaign – the idea that Trump was the true winner of the election – that was championed by the then president and his supporters in the aftermath of his 2020 election loss attempted to build on the narrative he'd nurtured throughout his political career. 'Stop the Steal' was premised on the idea that a corrupt and self-serving elite was manipulating the institutions of power in order to disenfranchise the people at large. Its storyline matched the archetypal populist narrative almost precisely, and it gave Donald Trump one final chance to play his preferred role of outsider politician doing battle against a crooked and unscrupulous machine.

The mainstreaming of conspiracy theories represented by the 'Stop the Steal' story repositioned them from being the delusional product of a fragile mind to a powerful form of political propaganda. Despite the 'election fraud' story being wholly invented, with no notable evidence to back it up, it still operated as a forceful means of persuasion. It didn't quite undermine the results of the poll – one of the great laws of life is that what's done is done – but it gave a notable jolt to the media narrative for several weeks. It also had a profound effect on social order in the dying days of the Trump administration, culminating in the attack on the Capitol on 6 January 2021. This was political storytelling in its purest form, untethered entirely from facts or reality, and yet still able to have a profound impact on public opinion.

The story of history

In the final few weeks of the Trump administration, there was a great deal of talk about the legacy of his presidency and particularly about how his actions and behaviours in those last few weeks were likely to shape the way history would remember him. The role that narrative plays in how we represent – and thus how we understand – history is the subject of an influential argument put forward by the historian Hayden White.[2] White contends that all written histories have a narrative structure to them and that the choices the historian makes in organizing this structure represent their ideological perspective on the events and processes they're analysing. To put it in rather more basic terms, the historian chooses the facts they wish to present, draws links between them (Event A happened because of Event B) and decides the details of the order in which they're represented. The motivation for these choices comes from the overall world view the historian has – for instance, viewing the unfolding of world events as a meaningful progression of human civilization rather than a chaotic pile-up of arbitrary crises. Because of this, our understanding of history – and all this entails about our sense of identity and shared culture – is fundamentally structured by narrative.

The French writer Christian Salmon takes this one step further, suggesting that a belief in the power of storytelling is itself integral to the American national psyche. The traditional idea of America was of a country where anything was possible, and everyone could 'write their story on a blank page and start a new life. It was both nation and narration.'[3] It is perhaps for this reason that the example of the United States becomes such a compelling focus for spectators around the world. It's not only the fact that the United States has a central position in geopolitics, and thus political decisions that are taken there can be consequential around the world. The character-driven nature of its political system – the voting for a president rather than a party, for example – along with the media ecosystem that covers political contests makes the United States a stand-out example of the use and effects of political storytelling.

The new normal

Following Joe Biden's inauguration in January 2021, there were several headlines about how the news media were likely to react to politics returning to its everyday, 'boring' self.[4] What would the new politics look like without the daily staging of conflict and outrage by those in and around power? To put these sorts of comments in perspective, it's worth rewinding the clock by half a year to the early summer of 2020, when the streets of America were starting to fill with people protesting against the killing of George Floyd by a police officer in Minneapolis. The events prompted by George Floyd's murder happened at a time when the majority of countries around the world were battling the Coronavirus pandemic, when populations were having to deal with the first phase of extended periods of lockdown, and many were speculating about how this experience might change long-term priorities in society. There was a sense that the severity of the pandemic crisis might, just possibly, bring about a period of self-reflection for society, which would, in turn, lead to a more caring, just and equitable approach to politics.

But while protesters began taking to the streets to demand racial justice, Donald Trump started tweeting threats to the demonstrators, telling them that 'when the looting starts, the shooting starts' – a phrase with a racially charged history which Twitter felt violated its rules on glorifying violence and thus hid from its main timeline.[5] That same day a CNN news crew was arrested by riot police on live television for trying to cover the demonstrations. What was starkly apparent in all this – and in the way events unfolded over the next few days and months – was that, despite the way the Coronavirus pandemic had upended so much of the everyday experience of society, the underlying trends in modern politics still persisted. And not simply that, but one of the most worrying aspects of the 'new normal' of the early twenty-first century was the way that ideas and actions from the far-right had penetrated the mainstream in Western politics – so much so that state-sanctioned violence, white supremacism and press intimidation could all play out on the streets and screens while populations around the world felt powerless to do anything to prevent them. Even with the world in the midst of a severe health crisis, the same stark political divisions could be mobilized to further inflame emotions.

It's naïve to think that a change in the occupancy of the White House will mollify these trends completely. To an extent, the Trump years brought ideological conflicts of this sort into clear relief. In doing so, it almost certainly also exacerbated tensions. But the conflicts remain embedded in widely differing narratives about the state of society, which are then given voice by high-profile actors in the public realm. Many of the most pressing debates about politics today are not about policy but about the power that rhetoric, disinformation and propaganda is having in society. They're about how the narratives told by agitators and extremists are spread throughout society; if and how these people are held to account by institutions and public bodies; and about the extent of the effects they have on the world. As we've seen throughout the book, storytelling is an essential part of the way we make sense of our experience and understanding of the world, but it's also central to how we shape the type of society in which we want to live.

Notes

Chapter 1

1 A Guarantee: The World Will Not End on Friday, http://www.npr.org/sections/13.7/2012/12/19/167530202/a-guarantee-the-world-will-not-end-on-friday

2 Beyond 2012: Why the World Didn't End, https://www.nasa.gov/topics/earth/features/2012.html

3 In Panicky Russia, It's Official: End of World Is Not Near, http://www.nytimes.com/2012/12/02/world/europe/mayan-end-of-world-stirs-panic-in-russia-and-elsewhere.html

4 End of the World – As It Didn't Happen, https://www.theguardian.com/science/2012/dec/21/end-world-live-blog

5 Ford Tells GM, NBC to Pull Apocalypse-Themed Chevy Super Bowl Ad, http://jalopnik.com/5882408/chevy-claims-ford-begged-them-nbc-to-pull-apocalypse-themed-super-bowl-ad

6 Brands Capitalize on the 'Impending Apocalypse', https://www.bloomberg.com/news/articles/2012-12-19/brands-capitalize-on-the-impending-apocalypse

7 Is 2016 Really One of the Worst Years in History? http://www.telegraph.co.uk/men/thinking-man/is-2016-really-one-of-the-worst-years-in-history/

8 http://utopia2016.com

9 Jeremy Deller Flies Flag for Thomas More's Utopia, 500 Years Later, https://www.theguardian.com/artanddesign/2016/jan/25/jeremy-deller-flies-flag-thomas-more-utopia-500-years-later

10 I Am an Essex Girl – Reclaim 'Essex girl' and Remove It from the Dictionary, https://www.change.org/p/i-am-an-essex-girl-reclaim-essex-girl-and-remove-it-from-the-dictionary

11 'Essex Girls' Will Not Be Removed from Oxford English Dictionary Despite Campaign, http://www.standard.co.uk/news/uk/essex-girls-oxford-english-dictionary-insists-it-wont-remove-term-despite-campaign-a3378331.html

12 'Paranoid' Announced as the Cambridge Dictionary Word of the Year, http://www.cambridgenetwork.co.uk/news/paranoid-announced-as-the-cambridge-dictionary-word-of-the-year/

13 Dictionary.com's 2016 Word of the Year: Xenophobia, http://blog.dictionary.com/xenophobia/

14 Stop 'Fascism' Becoming Word of the Year, Urges US Dictionary, https://www.theguardian.com/books/2016/dec/01/stop-fascism-becoming-word-of-the-year-urges-us-dictionary

15 Why 'Surreal', Not 'Fascism', Is Merriam-Webster's Word of the Year, http://www.vox.com/culture/2016/12/20/14008046/word-of-the-year-surreal-fascism

16 Top 10 Collins Words of the Year 2016, https://www.collinsdictionary.com/word-lovers-blog/new/top-10-collins-words-of-the-year-2016,323,HCB.html

17 Brexit Named Word of the Year, Ahead of Trumpism and Hygge, https://www.theguardian.com/books/2016/nov/03/brexit-named-word-of-the-year-ahead-of-trumpism-and-hygge

18 Democracy Sausage Snags Word of the Year as Smashed Avo, Shoey Lose Out, http://www.abc.net.au/news/2016-12-14/democracy-sausage-snags-word-of-the-year/8117684

19 Le Festival du mot, http://www.festivaldumot.fr/article/le-mot-de-l-annee

20 'Filterblase' ist das Wort des Jahres, http://www.20min.ch/community/stories/story/-Filterblase--ist-das-Wort-des-Jahres-13588184

21 Trump Chosen as 'Sign of the Year' by Swiss Deaf Society, http://www.swissinfo.ch/eng/sign-of-the-times_trump-chosen-as--sign-of--the-year--by-swiss-deaf-organisation/42766640

22 'Gold' Named 2016 Kanji of the Year, http://en.rocketnews24.com/2016/12/12/gold-named-2016-kanji-of-the-year/

23 Austrian Academics' Word of the Year Is 51 Letters Long and Almost Impossible to Say, http://www.independent.co.uk/news/world/europe/austrian-academics-choose-bundespraesidentenstichwahlwiederholungsverschiebung-word-of-year-election-a7466176.html

24 Oxford Dictionaries Word of the Year 2016 Is ... https://www.oxforddiction
     aries.com/press/news/2016/11/17/WOTY-16

25 Wort des Jahres, http://gfds.de/aktionen/wort-des-jahres/

26 2016 Word of the Year Is Dumpster Fire, as Voted by American Dialect
     Society, http://www.americandialect.org/wp-content/uploads/2016-
     Word-of-the-Year-PRESS-RELEASE.pdf

27 Unwort des Jahres, http://www.unwortdesjahres.net

28 'Traitor of the People' Is Germany's Worst Word of 2016: Here's Why,
     https://www.thelocal.de/20170110/traitor-of-the-people-is-germanys-
     worst-word-of-2016-heres-why

29 2016 Has Been One of the Greatest Years Ever for Humanity, http://blogs.
     spectator.co.uk/2016/12/2016-one-greatest-years-ever-humanity/

30 Welcome to Dystopia – George Orwell Experts on Donald Trump,
     https://www.theguardian.com/commentisfree/2017/jan/25/george-orwell-
     donald-trump-kellyanne-conway-1984

Chapter 2

1 Oxford Dictionaries Word of the Year 2016 Is ... https://www.oxforddiction
    aries.com/press/news/2016/11/17/WOTY-16

2 Williams, R. (2014 [1976]) *Keywords: A Vocabulary of Culture and Society*,
    Fourth Estate.

3 Britain Has Had Enough of Experts, says Gove, https://www.ft.com/content/
    3be49734-29cb-11e6-83e4-abc22d5d108c

4 Donald Trump Inspired Brexit Campaign Because Facts Don't Work, Says
    Leave Founder Aaron Banks, http://www.independent.co.uk/news/uk/home-
    news/brexit-news-donald-trump-leave-eu-campaign-facts-dont-work-arron-
    banks-lies-referendum-a7111001.html

5 Revealed: Trump's Election Consultants Filmed Saying They Use Bribes
    and Sex Workers to Entrap Politicians, https://www.channel4.com/news/
    cambridge-analytica-revealed-trumps-election-consultants-filmed-saying-
    they-use-bribes-and-sex-workers-to-entrap-politicians-investigation

6 Welcome to Trumplandia, Where Feelings Trump Facts, http://theweek.
    com/articles/656455/welcome-trumplandia-where-feelings-trump-facts

7 Davies, W. (2018) *Nervous States*, London: Jonathan Cape, p. xvi.

8 Amateurs in the Oval Office, https://www.theatlantic.com/magazine/archive/2015/11/amateurs-in-the-oval-office/407830/

9 Trump Calls Fact Checkers 'Bad People', https://www.washingtonpost.com/video/politics/trump-calls-fact-checkers-bad-people/2018/08/13/af7147a8-9f47-11e8-a3dd-2a1991f075d5_video.html

10 Partisan Trolls Are Attacking Facebook's Latest Fact-Checking Partners, https://www.poynter.org/news/partisan-trolls-are-attacking-facebooks-latest-fact-checking-partners

11 Nichols, T. (2017) *The Death of Expertise*, Oxford University Press, p. ix.

12 McIntyre, L. (2018) *Post-truth*, MIT Press.

13 Kakutani, M. (2018) *The Death of Truth*, New York: HarperCollins.

14 *Meet the Press* 01/22/17, https://www.nbcnews.com/meet-the-press/meet-press-01-22-17-n710491

15 'Alternative Facts' Named Worst Word of the Year, https://www.plainenglishfoundation.com/documents/10179/54323/PEF%20Worst%20Words%20of%20the%20Year%20media%20release%202017.pdf

16 Taxi Driver Argument, https://www.youtube.com/watch?v=4n-UGQcG3Jw

17 Our job as scientists is to find the truth. But we must also be storytellers, https://www.theguardian.com/commentisfree/2018/jul/20/our-job-as-scientists-is-to-find-the-truth-but-we-must-also-be-storytellers

18 Latour, B. and Woolgar, S. (1979) *Laboratory Life: The Construction of Scientific Facts*, Sage, p. 88.

19 https://twitter.com/MerriamWebster/status/823221915171061760

20 Conway: 'Alternative Facts', https://www.merriam-webster.com/news-trend-watch/conway-alternative-facts-20170122

21 Living in Fear of Muprhy's Law, http://www.writestuff.fi/blog/living-in-fear-of-muprhys-law.

22 https://twitter.com/realdonaldtrump/status/1014286054805987330?lang=en

23 https://twitter.com/MerriamWebster/status/1014270254049087488

24 Jackson, H. (2002) *Lexicography: An Introduction*, London: Routledge.

25 Williams, R. (2014 [1976]) *Keywords: A Vocabulary of Culture and Society*, Fourth Estate, p. 11.

26 'Just a Theory': 7 Misused Science Words, https://www.scientificamerican. com/article/just-a-theory-7-misused-science-words/

27 In Praise of Urban Dictionaries, www.guardian.co.uk/books/2011/apr/21/ in-praise-urban-dictionaries

28 Obamacare, http://www.urbandictionary.com/define.php?term=ObamaCare &page=3

29 Kellyanne Conway Is a Star, http://nymag.com/daily/intelligencer/2017/03/ kellyanne-conway-trumps-first-lady.html

30 Academics Use New Dictionary to Aid Students in Era of Fake News, https://www.timeshighereducation.com/news/academics-use-new-dictionary-aid-students-era-fake-news

31 Facts, http://www.allsides.com/dictionary/facts

32 Facebook Touts Video Metrics, Outlines More Scrutiny for Show Funding, https://www.axios.com/facebook-touts-video-watch-platform-metrics-17385ab1-2861-4e12-a9ca-1866e1faddd8.html

33 'Truth Isn't Truth': Giuliani Trumps 'Alternative Facts' with New Orwellian Outburst, https://www.theguardian.com/us-news/2018/aug/19/truth-isnt-truth-rudy-giuliani-trump-alternative-facts-orwellian

34 A Trump Surrogate Drops the Mic: 'There's No Such Thing as Facts', http://www.esquire.com/news-politics/videos/a51152/trump-surrogate-no-such-thing-as-facts/

35 Nietzsche, F. (2003) *Writings from the Late Notebooks*, Cambridge University Press, p. 139.

36 Thucydides (2009) *The Peloponnesian War*, trans. M. Hammond, Oxford University Press, pp. 170–1.

37 Aristotle (1991) *The Art of Rhetoric*, trans. H. Lawson-Tancred, Penguin, pp. 140–1.

38 Hume, D. (1985 [1738]) *A Treatise on Human Nature*, Penguin, Book 2, Part 3 Section 3.

39 Huxley, A. (1958) *Brave New World Revisited*, Harper & Brothers.

40 Kahneman, D. (2011) *Thinking, Fast and Slow*, Penguin, p. 12.

41 Hugo Mercier, H. and Sperber, D. (2017) *The Enigma of Reason*, Harvard University Press.

Chapter 3

1   Revealed: One in Four Europeans Vote Populist, https://www.theguardian.
    com/world/ng-interactive/2018/nov/20/revealed-one-in-four-europeans-
    vote-populist

2   How Populism Became the Concept That Defines Our Age, https://www.the
    guardian.com/commentisfree/2018/nov/22/populism-concept-defines-
    our-age

3   Taking on the Times, https://www.nratv.com/episodes/commentators-
    season-7-episode-1-taking-on-the-times

4   Hawkins, K. A. and Rovira Kaltwasser, C. (2017) 'The Ideational Approach
    to Populism', *Latin American Research Review*, 52: 4, pp. 513–28.

5   Cummings – Why Leave Won the Referendum, Nudgestock 2017,
    https://youtu.be/CDbRxH9Kiy4

6   Eatwell, R. and Goodwin, M. (2018) *National Populism: The Revolt Against
    Liberal Democracy*, London: Pelican, p. 48.

7   Liberals Must Learn the Politics of Emotion to Beat Rightwing Populists,
    https://www.theguardian.com/commentisfree/2018/nov/26/liberals-
    politics-emotion-right-wing-populists

8   Edward Snowden Reconsidered, https://www.nybooks.com/daily/2018/
    09/13/edward-snowden-reconsidered/

9   Laclau, E. (2005) *On Populist Reason*, Verso.

10 Anderson, B. (1983) *Imagined Communities: Reflections on the Origin and
    Spread of Nationalism*, Verso.

11 THE SUN SAYS Here's Our Message to MPs Ahead of Historic Brexit
    Vote — Great Britain Trusted You, Now You Trust Britain, https://www.the
    sun.co.uk/news/6505185/the-sun-says-great-britain-brexit-vote-betrayal-
    leave-remain/

12 Brexit: MPs from Four Parties Jointly Launch Push for People's Vote
    Campaign, https://www.theguardian.com/uk-news/2018/apr/15/brexit-
    mps-from-four-parties-jointly-launch-push-for-peoples-vote

13 Muller, J.-M. (2016) *What Is Populism?* Penguin.

14 The phenomenon bears some resemblance to Alexandra Georgakopoulou's
    concept of the use of 'reference' stories among groups of friends with a

closely shared history. Georgakopoulou, A. (2005) 'Same Old Story? On the Interactional Dynamics of Shared Narratives', in U. Quasthoff and T. Becker (eds), *Narrative Interaction*, Benjamins, pp. 223–41.

15 Meltdown in Duluth: Trump Yells at Protesters and 'Elites' at Rally, https://www.yahoo.com/news/meltdown-duluth-trump-yells-protesters-elites-rally-130345147.html

16 Williams, R. (2014 [1976]) *Keywords: A Vocabulary of Culture and Society*, Fourth Estate, p. 112.

17 From Trump to Boris Johnson: How the Wealthy Tell Us What 'Real Folk' Want, https://amp.theguardian.com/commentisfree/2018/nov/23/trump-boris-johnson-rightwing-populists

18 What Donald Trump Owes George Wallace, https://www.nytimes.com/2016/01/10/opinion/campaign-stops/what-donald-trump-owes-george-wallace.html

19 https://twitter.com/LeaveMnsLeave/status/1053181556704112640

20 https://twitter.com/nhsvbrexit/status/1053209505985675264?s=21

21 Davies, W. (2018) *Nervous States*, Jonathan Cape, p. 26. Ruth Wodak makes much the same point in Wodak, R. (2017) 'The "Establishment", the "Élites", and the "People": Who's Who?' *Journal of Language and Politics*, 16: 4, p. 557.

22 A Youth Revolt in France Boosts the Far Right, https://www.washingtonpost.com/sf/world/2017/04/19/a-youth-revolt-in-france-boosts-the-far-right/

23 Trump: Our Campaign Is About Giving Voice to the Voiceless, https://grabien.com/story.php?id=64409; Donald Trump accepts nomination, says he's voice for the voiceless, http://www.dispatch.com/content/stories/local/2016/07/21/0721-GOP-main-story.html

24 'It's Called VOICE': Trump Announces Immigration Crime Program, http://uk.businessinsider.com/its-called-voice-trump-announces-immigration-crime-program-immigration-crime-2017-2

25 Spivak, G. (1988) 'Can the Subaltern Speak?' in C. Nelson and L. Grossberg (eds), *Marxism and the Interpretation of Culture*, University of Illinois Press, pp. 271–313.

26 http://americasvoice.org/about-us/

27 Trump's Office on Immigrant Crime Is Dramatic Overhaul, https://uk.news.
    yahoo.com/trumps-office-immigrant-crime-dramatic-overhaul-190652046.
    html

28 WH Official: Objections to Undocumented Immigrant Crime Office Are 'Un-
    American', http://edition.cnn.com/2017/03/02/politics/kfile-gorka-on-voice/

Chapter 4

1   When You Treat Politics as Entertainment, You Get Sean Spicer at the Emmys,
    https://www.washingtonpost.com/news/wonk/wp/2017/09/18/when-you-
    treat-politics-as-entertainment-you-get-sean-spicer-at-the-emmys/

2   'Just Like Show Business': Why Celebrities Are Taking over Politics,
    https://www.smh.com.au/opinion/just-like-show-business-why-celebrities-
    are-taking-over-politics-20180115-h0ibp5.html

3   Evans, R. (1994) *The Kid Stays in the Picture*, Faber and Faber, p. 217.

4   Kalder, D. (2018) *Dictator Literature: A History of Despots through Their
    Writing*, Oneworld.

5   Dictator Literature by Daniel Kalder Review – The Deathly Prose of Dic-Lit,
    https://www.theguardian.com/books/2018/apr/25/dictator-literature-
    daniel-kalder-review

6   Raza: The Strange Story of Franco's 'Lost' Film, http://www.bbc.com/culture/
    story/20180921-raza-the-strange-film-that-franco-left-behind

7   'Saddam Novel' on Sale in Tokyo, http://news.bbc.co.uk/1/hi/world/mi
    ddle_east/4996116.stm

8   Erdoğan, What Have You Done?, https://www.pastemagazine.com/articles/
    2017/04/erdogan-what-have-you-done.html

9   The Hornet's Nest, https://www.kirkusreviews.com/book-reviews/jimmy-
    carter/the-hornets-nest/

10 In Political Fiction the EU Is Either Non-existent or Portrayed as Corrupt
    and Dystopian, http://blogs.lse.ac.uk/europpblog/2013/03/13/political-
    fiction-european-union-eu-steven-fielding-corruption-dystopian/

11 Donald Trump Is the First True Reality TV President, http://time.com/
    4596770/donald-trump-reality-tv/

12 Inside Donald Trump's 'Atrocious', Razzie-Winning Ghost-Sex Rom-Com, https://www.thedailybeast.com/inside-donald-trumps-atrocious-razzie-winning-ghost-sex-rom-com

13 Donald Trump Appeared in a Playboy Softcore Porn Video, https://www.huffingtonpost.co.uk/entry/donald-trump-playboy-porn_us_57eee2fbe4b0c2407cde0fd2

14 How Hollywood Remembers Steve Bannon, https://www.newyorker.com/magazine/2017/05/01/how-hollywood-remembers-steve-bannon

15 How Donald Trump's Top Guy Steve Bannon Wrote a Hollywood Sex Scene Set in Outer Space, https://www.thedailybeast.com/how-donald-trumps-top-guy-steve-bannon-wrote-a-hollywood-sex-scene-set-in-outer-space

16 Steve Bannon, Donald Trump's Campaign CEO, Once Wrote a Rap Musical, https://www.thedailybeast.com/steve-bannon-donald-trumps-campaign-ceo-once-wrote-a-rap-musical

17 Sarah Palin, Movie Star? https://blogs.wsj.com/speakeasy/2011/07/13/the-undefeated-sarah-palin-movie-star/

18 What Can We Learn from Dictators' Literature? https://quillette.com/2018/12/14/what-can-we-learn-from-dictators-literature/

19 For example, Harari, Y. N. (2011) *Sapiens: A Brief History of Humankind*, Harper.

20 White, H. (1980) 'The Value of Narrativity in the Representation of Reality', *Critical Inquiry*, 7: 1, p. 5.

21 Press Release: PwC's Entertainment & Media Outlook Forecasts U.S. Industry Spending to Reach $759 Billion by 2021, https://www.pubexec.com/article/press-release-pwcs-entertainment-media-outlook-forecasts-u-s-industry-spending-reach-759-billion-2021/

22 Polletta, F. (2006) *It Was Like a Fever: Storytelling in Protest and Politics*, University of Chicago Press.

23 Salmon, C. (2010) *Storytelling: Bewitching the Modern Mind*, Verso.

24 Kahneman, D. (2011) *Thinking, Fast and Slow*, Penguin, pp. 24, 29.

25 Trump Is a Great Storyteller. We Need to Be Better, https://www.nytimes.com/2016/12/10/opinion/sunday/trump-is-a-great-storyteller-we-need-to-be-better.html

26   Obama: My Biggest Failure Was Not Telling a Story, https://m.youtube.com/watch?v=QXI-rIX0Usk

27   Cornog, E. (2004) *The Power and the Story: How the Crafted Presidential Narrative Has Determined Political Success from George Washington to George W. Bush*, Penguin.

28   Gore, Bush Clash over Tax Cuts, http://www.washingtonpost.com/wp-srv/aponline/20001003/aponline230544_000.htm

29   How to Win an Election, https://www.nytimes.com/video/opinion/100000004216589/how-to-win-an-election.html

30   It's Storytelling, Stupid: What Made Donald Trump Smarter Than Hillary Clinton, https://www.thedailybeast.com/its-storytelling-stupid-what-made-donald-trump-smarter-than-hillary-clinton

31   The Fable of the Master Storyteller, http://chinamediaproject.org/2017/09/29/the-fable-of-the-master-storyteller/

32   Narrative, https://www.nytimes.com/2004/12/05/magazine/narrative.html

33   Democratic Victory Task Force, Final Report and Action Plan, https://uploads.democrats.org/Downloads/DVTF_FinalReport.pdf

34   Paul Ricoeur: The Philosopher Behind Emmanuel Macron, https://www.irishtimes.com/culture/paul-ricoeur-the-philosopher-behind-emmanuel-macron-1.3094792

35   Ricoeur, P. (1988) *Time and Narrative, Volume 3*, trans. K. Blamey and D. Pellauer, University of Chicago Press.

36   Inside Macron's Mind: A Tint of Paul Ricœur, https://www.institutmontaigne.org/en/blog/inside-macrons-mind-tint-paul-ricoeur

37   NATO Comprehensive Operations Planning Directive, https://publicintelligence.net/nato-copd/

38   NATO Military Concept for Strategic Communications, https://publicintelligence.net/nato-stratcom-concept/

39   Laity, M. (2015) 'Nato and the Power of Narrative', in J. Jackson, T. Thomas, M. Laity and B. Nimmo (eds), *Information at War: From China's Three Warfares to NATO's Narratives*, Legatum Institute, pp. 22–9.

40   Aldous Huxley Is Hired at Eton, http://www.history.com/this-day-in-history/aldous-huxley-is-hired-at-eton

41 1984 v. Brave New World, http://www.lettersofnote.com/2012/03/1984-v-brave-new-world.html

42 Williams, R. (1979) *Politics and Letters: Interviews with New Left Review*, Rowman & Littlefield, p. 384.

43 The last time sales of *Nineteen Eighty-Four* had surged like this was in the wake of the revelations from Edward Snowdon about the United States's mass surveillance systems.

44 The Traditional Way of Reporting on a President Is Dead. And Trump's Press Secretary Killed It, https://www.washingtonpost.com/lifestyle/style/the-traditional-way-of-reporting-on-a-president-is-dead-and-trumps-press-secretary-killed-it/2017/01/22/75403a00-e0bf-11e6-a453-19ec4b3d09ba_story.html

45 Susskind, J. (2018) *Future Politics*, Oxford University Press, p. 12.

46 Arendt, H. (1970) *Men in Dark Times*, Jonathan Cape, p. 105.

47 Sidney, P. (1973 [1595]) *An Apology for Poetry: Or, The Defence of Poesy*, ed. G. Shepherd, Manchester University Press, p. 107.

48 Elisabeth Moss on the Handmaid's Tale: 'This Is Happening in Real Life. Wake Up People', https://www.theguardian.com/tv-and-radio/2018/may/05/elisabeth-moss-handmaids-tale-this-is-happening-in-real-life-wake-up-people

49 Margaret Atwood on What 'The Handmaid's Tale' Means in the Age of Trump', https://www.nytimes.com/2017/03/10/books/review/margaret-atwood-handmaids-tale-age-of-trump.html

50 Website Removes Sexy 'Handmaid's Tale' Halloween Costume After Backlash, https://etcanada.com/news/369844/website-removes-sexy-handmaids-tale-halloween-costume-after-backlash/

51 Cosplay Won't Solve the Meme Gap Dooming the #Resistance, https://www.wired.com/story/politics-meme-gap/

52 The United States and Iran: It's Like '50 First Dates', https://www.newyorker.com/news/news-desk/the-united-states-and-iran-its-like-50-first-dates

53 Princess Leia Gave the Women's March a New Hope, https://www.wired.com/2017/01/princess-leia-womens-march/

54 What Is Political Resistance? An Exploration of the Word and Its Political Connotations, http://www.publicseminar.org/2017/02/what-is-political-resistance/

55 This sort of co-option is by no means a new phenomenon. Orwell was embraced by some on the right directly after the publication of *Animal Farm*, with his condemnation of Soviet totalitarianism being seen also as an attack on the socialist ideals which first prompted the Russian Revolution.

56 Disturbingly Orwellian ... a witch hunt ... and no, Boris ISN'T racist, https://www.pressreader.com/uk/daily-mail/20180810/281479277241902

57 Reagan Presses Call for Antimissile Plan Before Space Group, https://www.nytimes.com/1985/03/30/us/reagan-presses-call-for-antimissile-plan-before-space-group.html

58 Cheney: Being Darth Vader Not so Bad, http://www.nbcnews.com/id/2157 5478/ns/politics-white_house/t/cheney-being-darth-vader-not-so-bad/

59 To Darth Vader's Theme Music, Dick Cheney Wows GOP Crowd, https://www.politico.com/states/florida/story/2015/11/to-darth-vaders-theme-music-dick-cheney-wows-gop-crowd-027930

60 George Lucas Wrote 'Star Wars' as a Liberal Warning. Then Conservatives Struck Back, http://time.com/4975813/star-wars-politics-watergate-george-lucas/

61 https://www.empireonline.com/movies/features/star-wars-archive-george-lucas-1999-interview/

62 Trump Keeps Saying 'Enemy of the People' – But the Phrase Has a Very Ugly History, https://www.businessinsider.com/history-of-president-trumps-phrase-an-enemy-of-the-people-2017-2

63 Departing Dacre Lashes Out for Final Time, https://www.theguardian.com/media/2018/nov/04/paul-dacre-ex-daily-mail-liberal-brexit-hating-media-speech

Chapter 5

1 MacCabe, C. and Yanacek, Y. (2018) *Keywords for Today: A 21st Century Vocabulary*, Oxford University Press, pp. 241–2.

2 Lyotard, J.-F. (1984) *The Postmodern Condition: A Report on Knowledge*, trans. G. Bennington and B. Massumi, University of Minnesota Press.

3 De Fina, A. (2017) 'Narrative Analysis', in R. Wodak and B. Forchtner (eds), *The Routledge Handbook of Language and Politics*, Routledge, pp. 233–46.

4 Atkins, J. and Finlayson, A. (2013) "'... A 40-Year-Old Black Man Made the Point to Me": Everyday Knowledge and the Performance of Leadership in Contemporary British Politics', *Political Studies*, 61, p. 173.

5 Green, M. C. and Brock, T. C. (2000) 'The Role of Transportation in the Persuasiveness of Public Narratives', *Journal of Personality and Social Psychology*, 79: 5, p. 719.

6 Silbert, L. J., Honey, C. J., Simony, E., Poeppel, D. and Hasson, U. (2014) 'Coupled Neural Systems Underlie the Production and Comprehension of Naturalistic Narrative Speech', *Proceedings of the National Academy of Sciences of the United States of America*, 111: 43.

7 The Cinderella Man – Damon Runyon – The New York American – 6/14/1935, https://deadlineartists.com/contributor-samples/the-cinderel la-man-damon-runyon-the-new-york-american/

8 Why the Story of Cinderella Endures and Resonates, https://www.smithson ianmag.com/smithsonian-institution/does-world-need-yet-another-cindere lla-180954549/

9 'Cinderella Man' James Braddock Gets Statue Treatment in Hometown, https://www.ringtv.com/539280-cinderella-man-james-braddock-gets-statue-treatment-in-hometown/

10 Goldschmied, N. and Vandello, J. A. (2009) 'The Advantage of Disadvantage: Underdogs in the Political Arena', *Basic and Applied Social Psychology*, 31: 1, pp. 24–31.

11 Propp, V. (1968 [1927]) *Morphology of the Folktale*, trans. L. Scott, University of Texas Press.

12 Hogan, P. C. (2016) 'Story', *Literary Universals Project*, https://literary-universals.uconn.edu/2016/11/20/story/

13 Vonnegut, K. (2005) *A Man Without a Country*, Seven Stories Press.

14 Del Vecchio, M., Kharlamov, A., Parry, G. and Pogrebna, G. (2018) 'The Data Science of Hollywood: Using Emotional Arcs of Movies to Drive Business Model Innovation in Entertainment Industries', https://arxiv.org/abs/1807.02221

15 Tobias, R. B. (2003) *20 Master Plots: And How to Build Them*, Writer's Digest Books.

16 Snyder, B. (2005) *Save the Cat! The Last Book on Screenwriting You'll Ever Need*, Michael Wiese Productions.

17 Reagan, A. J., Mitchell, L., Danforth, C. M. and Sheridan Dodds, P. (2016) 'The Emotional Arcs of Stories are Dominated by Six Basic Shapes', *EPJ Data Science*, 5: 31.

18 Booker, C. (2004) *The Seven Basic Plots*, Bloomsbury.

19 Hogan, P. C. (2009) *Understanding Nationalism: On Narrative, Identity, and Cognitive Science*, Ohio State University Press.

20 Hogan, P. C. (2003) *The Mind and Its Stories: Narrative Universals and Human Emotion*, Cambridge University Press.

21 Tracing a Meme from the Internet's Fringe to a Republican Slogan, https://www.nytimes.com/interactive/2018/11/04/technology/jobs-not-mobs.html

22 Donald Trump Tells a Fake American Story. We Must Tell the Real One, https://www.theguardian.com/commentisfree/2019/mar/04/donald-trump-american-story-robert-reich

23 High Noon's Secret Backstory, https://www.vanityfair.com/hollywood/2017/02/high-noons-secret-backstory

24 Star Wars Is More Political Than You Think, https://www.huffingtonpost.com/entry/star-wars-is-more-political-than-you-think_us_590b663de4b056aa2363d298

25 Rinzler, J. W. (1983) *The Making of Star Wars: Return of the Jedi*, Ballantine Books.

26 The Aura of Arugulance, https://www.nytimes.com/2009/04/19/opinion/19dowd.html

27 This is something he'd also done in his debut feature, *THX 1138*, which included excerpts from speeches by Richard Nixon as part of the dialogue (*THX 1138*, the George Lucas Director's Cut Two-Disc Special Edition, Warner Brothers).

28 The Danger of a Single Story, https://www.nytimes.com/2016/04/19/opinion/the-danger-of-a-single-story.html

29 Clinton, Blair, Renzi: Why We Lost, and How to Fight Back, https://www.theguardian.com/world/2018/nov/22/clinton-blair-renzi-why-we-lost-populists-how-fight-back-rightwing-populism-centrist

30 The Paranoid Fantasy Behind Brexit, https://www.theguardian.com/politics/2018/nov/16/brexit-paranoid-fantasy-fintan-otoole

31 Six Words Gets to the Point, https://www.sixwordmemoirs.com/about/
#story-of-six-words.

32 John McDonnell Calls Winston Churchill a 'Villain', http://www.bbc.co.uk/
news/uk-politics-47233605

33 https://twitter.com/bbclaurak/status/1095803128123920385

34 The Danger of a Single Story, https://youtu.be/D9Ihs241zeg

Chapter 6

1 Here's Every Word of Kanye West's Bizarre Meeting with President Trump,
https://eu.usatoday.com/story/life/people/2018/10/12/heres-every-word-
kanye-wests-bizarre-meeting-president-trump/1609230002/

2 John Yorke: 'Into the Woods', Talks at Google, https://www.youtube.com/
watch?v=P0UZHUnB5pQ

3 Todorov, T. (1969) 'Structural Analysis of Narrative', *NOVEL: A Forum on
Fiction*, 3: 1, pp. 70–6.

4 Polletta, F. (2006) *It Was Like a Fever: Storytelling in Protest and Politics*,
Chicago University Press, p. 10.

5 Campbell, J. (1949) *The Hero with a Thousand Faces*, Princeton University
Press, p. 23.

6 Yorke, J. (2013) *Into the Woods: A Five-Act Journey into Story*, Penguin.

7 Hogan, P. C. (2003) *The Mind and Its Stories: Narrative Universals and
Human Emotion*, Cambridge University Press.

8 Field, S. (1979) *Screenplay: The Foundations of Screenwriting*, Dell
Publishing Company, p. 25.

9 Snyder, B. (2005) *Save the Cat! The Last Book on Screenwriting You'll Ever
Need*, Michael Wiese Productions, p. 55.

10 Vonnegut, K. (2005) *A Man Without a Country*, Seven Stories Press, p. 37.

11 *Hamlet*, Act 2, Scene 2, line 541.

12 Kozintsev, G. (1966) *Shakespeare, Time and Conscience*, trans. J. Vining, Hill
and Wang.

13 Trump Says Second Amendment Rights Are 'Under Siege'. But He Vowed to Defend Them in Defiant NRA Speech, http://time.com/5265969/donald-trump-nra-convention-speech/.

14 Personal interview.

15 Intelligence Report: On Putin's Orders, Russia Sought to Influence Presidential Election, https://www.usnews.com/news/world/articles/2017-01-06/intelligence-report-on-vladimir-putins-orders-russia-sought-to-influence-presidential-election

16 Johnson, B. (2014) *The Churchill Factor*, Hodder and Stoughton, p. 8.

17 Fisher, W. R. (1987) *Human Communication as Narration: Towards a Philosophy of Reason, Value, and Action*, University of South Carolina, pp. 146–7.

18 https://twitter.com/realDonaldTrump/status/1068442531887632384

19 The Courage to Change – Alexandria Ocasio-Cortez, https://m.youtube.com/watch?v=rq3QXIVR0bs

20 Testimony of Michael D. Cohen Committee on Oversight and Reform U.S. House of Representatives, 27 February 2019, https://int.nyt.com/data/documenthelper/636-michael-cohens-congressional-t/3a1530b333230e775df5/optimized/full.pdf

21 Wodak, R. and Krzyżanowski, M. (2017) 'Right-Wing Populism in Europe & USA: Contesting Politics & Discourse Beyond "Orbanism" and "Trumpism"', *Journal of Language and Politics*, 16: 4, pp. 475.

22 Lempert, M. and Silverstein, M. (2012) *Creatures of Politics Media, Message, and the American Presidency*, University of Indiana Press.

23 In the UK, a number of Boris Johnson's supporters made precisely the same predictions prior to his becoming prime minister in 2019 (I Was Boris Johnson's Boss: He Is Utterly Unfit to Be Prime Minister, https://www.theguardian.com/commentisfree/2019/jun/24/boris-johnson-prime-minister-tory-party-britain).

24 Lempert, M. and Silverstein, M. (2012) *Creatures of Politics Media, Message, and the American Presidency*, University of Indiana Press, p. 16.

25 Stonor Saunders, F. (2001) *Who Paid the Piper? The CIA and the Cultural Cold War*, Granta.

26 Leab, D. J. (2007) *Orwell Subverted: The CIA and the Filming of Animal Farm*, Penn State University Press.

27 There's some speculation about whether this is a truthful or apocryphal account of the ending. The original film was taken out of circulation by Orwell's estate. Keeping It All in the (Nuclear) Family: Big Brother, Auntie BBC, Uncle Sam and George Orwell's Nineteen Eighty-Four, http://frames cinemajournal.com/article/keeping-it-all-in-the-nuclear-family-big-brother-auntie-bbc-uncle-sam-and-george-orwells-nineteen-eighty-four/

28 Goldman, W. (1983) *Adventures in the Screen Trade*, Abacus.

29 Booker, C. (2004) *The Seven Basic Plots*, Bloomsbury, p. 18.

30 Brooks, P. (1984) *Reading for the Plot: Design and Intention in Narrative*, Knopf.

31 Labov, W. and Waletzky, J. (1997) 'Narrative Analysis: Oral Versions of Personal Experience', *Journal of Narrative and Life History*, 7: 1–4, pp. 3–38.

32 A Second Referendum on Brexit Could Actually Happen, https://www.gq-magazine.co.uk/article/second-brexit-referendum-could-happen

33 'You Whitewashed the Corruption': James Graham and Carole Cadwalladr on Brexit: The Uncivil War, https://www.theguardian.com/tv-and-radio/2019/jan/07/you-whitewashed-the-corruption-james-graham-and-carole-cadwalladr-on-brexit-the-uncivil-war

34 Conduct of Mr Dominic Cummings, https://publications.parliament.uk/pa/cm201719/cmselect/cmprivi/1490/149003.htm

Chapter 7

1 How to Win an Election, https://www.nytimes.com/video/opinion/100000004216589/how-to-win-an-election.html

2 The 2018 film *Vice*, made about Bush's vice-president, Dick Chaney, on the other hand is a much more explicitly political film, dealing with specific policy issues, as well as the business and consequences of political practices more generally.

3 Keynote Address, 2004 Democratic National Convention, http://p2004.org/demconv04/obama072704spt.html

4 Morreale, J. (1993) *The Presidential Campaign Film: A Critical History*, Praeger.

5 Albertazzi, D. (2007) 'Addressing "the People" – A Comparative Study of the Lega Nord's and Lega dei Ticinesi's Political Rhetoric and Style of Propaganda', *Modern Italy*, 12: 3, p. 335.

6 Little Know Ye Who's Coming (John Quincy Adams), https://folkways.si.edu/oscar-brand/little-know-ye-whos-coming-john-quincy-adams/childrens-historical-song/music/track/smithsonian

7 'High Hopes' (John F. Kennedy Presidential Campaign Song), https://www.jfklibrary.org/learn/about-jfk/life-of-john-f-kennedy/fast-facts-john-f-kennedy/high-hopes

8 Republican Campaign Song: Click with Dick, https://archive.org/details/calasus_000061

9 Malcolm Turnbull's 'Continuity and Change' Slogan Straight Out of Veep, https://www.theguardian.com/australia-news/2016/mar/23/malcolm-turnbulls-continuity-and-change-slogan-straight-out-of-veep

10 When Hillary Clinton Tested New Slogans – 85 of Them, https://www.nytimes.com/2016/10/20/us/politics/hillary-clinton-campaign-slogans.html

11 If the Remain Campaign Makes the Same Mistakes Again, It Will Lose Again, https://www.theguardian.com/commentisfree/2018/dec/13/remain-mistakes-brexit-leavers

12 Cummings – Why Leave Won the Referendum, Nudgestock 2017, https://youtu.be/CDbRxH9Kiy4

13 'Illegal Immigrant' No More, https://blog.ap.org/announcements/illegal-immigrant-no-more

14 Justice Department: Use 'Illegal Aliens', Not 'Undocumented', https://edition.cnn.com/2018/07/24/politics/justice-department-illegal-aliens-undocumented/index.html

15 Ten Presidents Say the US Is a 'Nation of Immigrants'. A Government Agency No Longer Agrees, https://qz.com/1213959/uscis-deleted-nation-of-immigrants-from-its-official-mission-statement/

16 https://twitter.com/the_tpa/status/1070372258785443843?s=21

17 Both figures are for 2016, the year in which the National Living Wage first came into effect. The Living Wage Foundation: The Calculation, https://www.livingwage.org.uk/calculation

18 Westen, D. (2007) *The Political Brain*, PublicAffairs, p. 369.

19 Hasher, L., Goldstein, D. and Toppino, T. (1977) 'Frequency and the Conference of Referential Validity', *Journal of Verbal Learning and Verbal Behavior*, 16: 1, pp. 107–12.

20 Understanding Trump, https://georgelakoff.com/2016/07/23/understanding-trump-2/

21 Karen Handel's 'I Am Not a Crook Moment': 'I Do Not Support a Livable Wage!', https://georgelakoff.com/2017/06/07/karen-handels-i-am-not-a-crook-moment-i-do-not-support-a-livable-wage/

22 Brexit – The Triumph of a Word, https://www.spectator.co.uk/2016/09/brexit-the-triumph-of-a-word/

23 Lakoff, G. (2014) *The ALL NEW Don't Think of an Elephant!* Chelsea Green.

Chapter 8

1 Kitsch museum.

2 Thom, F. (1987) *La Langue de Bois*, Julliard.

3 Decoding North Korea's Fish and Mushroom Slogans, https://www.bbc.com/news/blogs-magazine-monitor-31446387

4 Bad Language: The Use and Abuse of Official Language – Public Administration Committee, https://publications.parliament.uk/pa/cm200910/cmselect/cmpubadm/17/1705.htm#a1

5 Scruton R. (2006) *A Political Philosophy: Arguments for Conservatism*, Continuum.

6 Kakutani, M. (2018) *The Death of Truth*, HarperCollins.

7 MPs Burst Out Laughing as Theresa May Says Brexit Talks Are in Their 'Final Stages', https://www.mirror.co.uk/news/politics/mps-burst-out-laughing-theresa-13420619

8 https://twitter.com/BBCPolitics/status/1019540436044603393

9 What Does 'Brexit Means Brexit' Mean? https://www.bbc.co.uk/news/uk-politics-36782922.

10 https://twitter.com/jacob_rees_mogg/status/1017697423865589760?s=21

11 Lakoff, G. and Johnson, M. (1999) *Philosophy in the Flesh: The Embodied Mind and Its Challenge to Western Thought*, Basic Books, p. 128.

12 Boris Johnson, Donald Trump and the Rise of Radical Incompetence, https://www.nytimes.com/2018/07/13/opinion/brexit-conservatives-boris-trump.html

13 'Red, White and Blue Brexit': Explaining May's Bunting-Draped Vision, https://www.theguardian.com/politics/2016/dec/06/red-white-blue-brexit-explaining-theresa-mays-bunting-draped-vision

14 Boris Johnson Calls for 'Full British Brexit' on Anniversary of Leave Vote, https://inews.co.uk/news/boris-johnson-full-british-brexit/

15 SOFT BOILED BREXIT Jacob Rees-Mogg Says Theresa May's 'Soft' Brexit Agreement Could Be Worse Than a 'No Deal' after Chequers Summit, https://www.thesun.co.uk/news/6719294/jacob-rees-mogg-brexit-theresa-may-chequers-summit/

16 Brexit: May Won't Rule Out Special Rights for EU Citizens, https://www.bbc.co.uk/news/uk-politics-44752273

17 UK Faces 'Train Crash Brexit' If It Falls Back on WTO Rules, https://www.politico.eu/article/uk-faces-train-crash-brexit-if-it-falls-back-on-wto-rules/

18 The People Want Us to Deliver a Full British Brexit and We MUST Bust Out of the Corsets of EU Regulation, Says Foreign Secretary Boris Johnson, https://www.thesun.co.uk/news/6604089/boris-johnson-full-british-brexit-eu-regulation/

19 David Davis: Brexit Will Not Plunge Britain into 'Mad Max Dystopia', https://www.theguardian.com/politics/2018/feb/19/david-davis-brexit-britain-mad-max

20 Brexit Will Be Titanic Success, Says Boris Johnson, https://www.theguardian.com/politics/2016/nov/03/brexit-will-be-titanic-success-says-boris-johnson

21 Schrödinger's Brexit, https://www.economist.com/buttonwoods-notebook/2016/11/30/schrodingers-brexit

22 'Hotel California': Brexiteer Accuses Labour of Trying to 'TRAP the UK in EU by Stealth', https://www.express.co.uk/news/politics/851424/eu-brexit-hotel-california-labour-conservatives-bbc-newsnight-britain-single-market

23   https://twitter.com/BorisJohnson/status/1019586379771203584

24   'Perverse!' Rees-Mogg Attacks Soft Brexiteers for Pushing 'Lie' Making UK
     Look 'WEAK', https://www.express.co.uk/news/uk/910817/jacob-rees-mogg-
     brexit-chancellor-philip-hammond-prime-minister-theresa-may-brino

25   Brexit 'Meaningful Vote': May Wins after Rebels Accept Compromise,
     https://www.theguardian.com/politics/2018/jun/20/lead-tory-rebel-
     dominic-grieve-accepts-brexit-meaningful-vote-compromise

26   Steve Doocy: Cages That Minors Are Being Held in Aren't Really Cages,
     http://nymag.com/daily/intelligencer/2018/06/steve-doocy-cages-minors-
     being-held-in-arent-really-cages.html

27   Laura Ingraham Compares Child Immigrant Detention Centers to Summer
     Camps, https://www.huffingtonpost.co.uk/entry/laura-ingraham-immigrant-
     summer-camp_us_5b28b769e4b0f0b9e9a4840c

28   Trump's Tent City for Children Is a Concentration Camp, https://www.sf
     chronicle.com/opinion/article/Trump-s-tent-city-for-children-is-a-13016
     150.php

29   The 'Concentration Camp' Language Debate Is the Wrong Fight,
     https://qz.com/1663546/the-concentration-camp-language-debate-is-the-
     wrong-fight/

30   Babies and Toddlers Sent to 'Tender Age' Shelters Under Trump
     Separations, https://www.theguardian.com/us-news/2018/jun/20/babies-
     and-toddlers-sent-to-tender-age-shelters-under-trump-separations

31   'Tender' Smells of Baby Powder and Strained Pears, but Not When It's
     Masking a Cruel Detention System, https://edition.cnn.com/2018/06/20/
     opinions/tender-trump-euphemisms-are-ineptly-orwellian-mcwhorter-
     opinion/index.html

32   3.8million EU Migrants Are Allowed to Stay Here after Brexit: That's
     600,000 More Than Estimated – And They Can Bring Their Families,
     http://www.dailymail.co.uk/news/article-5871947/3-8million-EU-migrants-
     allowed-stay-Brexit-bring-families.html

33   4m EU Migrants Can Apply to Stay in UK, https://www.express.co.uk/news/
     politics/977887/Brexit-news-4m-EU-migrants-can-apply-to-stay-in-UK

34   Four Million EU Nationals Will Get Right to Stay in the UK after – BREXIT
     And Violent Criminals Could Be Among Them, https://www.telegraph.co.
     uk/politics/2018/06/21/nearly-4-million-eu-nationals-will-get-right-stay-
     uk-forever/

35 https://twitter.com/StephGrisham45/status/1009881721012150272

36 https://twitter.com/realdonaldtrump/status/1009916650622251009?s=21

37 https://twitter.com/pacecase/status/1009895553356845056?s=21

38 https://twitter.com/parkermolloy/status/1009894851792515072?s=21

39 Melania Trump Jacket: Five Things 'I Don't Care' Could Mean, https://www.bbc.co.uk/news/world-us-canada-44574499

40 What We Know About How Melania Trump Decides What to Wear, https://www.thecut.com/2018/06/how-melania-trump-gets-clothes-fashion.html

41 https://twitter.com/ambiej/status/1010924872787083265

42 A Brief (Fascist) History of 'I Don't Care', https://overland.org.au/2018/06/a-brief-fascist-history-of-i-dont-care/

43 Interrogating Melania Trump's Statement Jacket and Its Fast-Fashion Fascism, https://www.newyorker.com/culture/annals-of-appearances/interrogating-melania-trumps-statement-jacket-and-its-fast-fashion-fascism

44 Melania Trump Says 'Don't Care' Jacket Was a Message, https://www.bbc.co.uk/news/world-us-canada-45853364

45 Denmark Has Got It Wrong. Yes, the Burka Is Oppressive and Ridiculous – But That's Still No Reason to Ban It, https://www.telegraph.co.uk/news/2018/08/05/denmark-has-got-wrong-yes-burka-oppressive-ridiculous-still/

46 'It is a humiliation. We look like a seven-stone weakling being comically bent out of shape by a 500 lb gorilla' BORIS JOHNSON'S blistering denunciation of our Brexit strategy..., https://www.dailymail.co.uk/news/article-6146853/BORIS-JOHNSON-JEREMY-HUNT-debate-Chequers-deal.html

47 Leave Voters Are Happy for Family Members to Lose Their Jobs over Brexit, http://uk.businessinsider.com/yougov-poll-leave-voters-happy-for-relatives-to-lose-jobs-over-brexit-2017-8

48 https://twitter.com/spikedonline/status/893019152503500800

49 Where Do 'Hot Takes' Come From? https://www.merriam-webster.com/words-at-play/origin-and-meaning-of-hot-take

50 Take Time, https://theawl.com/take-time-479afa9b3245

51 A History of the Hot Take, https://newrepublic.com/article/121501/history-hot-take

Chapter 9

1 There Will Be No Second Referendum on Brexit – It Would Be a Gross Betrayal of Our Democracy, https://www.telegraph.co.uk/politics/2018/09/01/will-no-second-referendum-brexit-would-gross-betrayal-democracy/

2 https://twitter.com/davidschneider/status/1036156280023535616

3 Benkler, Y., Faris, R. and Roberts, H. (2018) *Network Propaganda: Manipulation, Disinformation, and Radicalization in American Politics*, Oxford University Press, p. 27.

4 Flew, T. (2017) 'The "Theory" in Media Theory', *Media Theory*, 1: 1, pp. 43–56.

5 Polletta, F. (2006) *It Was Like a Fever: Storytelling in Protest and Politics*, Chicago University Press.

6 Arron Banks and Andy Wigmore Face MPs' Questions – live, https://www.theguardian.com/uk-news/live/2018/jun/12/arron-banks-and-andy-wigmore-face-mps-leave-eu-brexit-russia-live

7 How Social Media Took Us from Tahrir Square to Donald Trump, https://www.technologyreview.com/s/611806/how-social-media-took-us-from-tahrir-square-to-donald-trump/

8 Carpenter, A. B. (2018) *Gaslighting America*, HarperCollins.

9 https://www.stopfake.org/en/tag/ukraine/

10 *New York Times* Column Used Quote from fake News Site 'Without Attribution', https://www.poynter.org/reporting-editing/2014/new-york-times-column-used-quote-from-fake-news-site-without-attribution/

11 Sky Views: Facebook's Fake News Threatens Democracy, http://news.sky.com/story/sky-views-democracy-burns-as-facebook-lets-fake-news-thrive-10652711

12 How Teens in the Balkans Are Duping Trump Supporters with Fake News, https://www.buzzfeed.com/craigsilverman/how-macedonia-became-a-global-hub-for-pro-trump-misinfo

13 Like. Share. Kill, https://www.bbc.co.uk/news/resources/idt-sh/nigeria_fake_news

14 https://twitter.com/realDonaldTrump/status/807588632877998081

15 Donald Trump's Press Conference, Annotated, http://www.npr.org/2017/
    01/11/509137239/watch-live-trump-holds-first-press-conference-as-
    president-elect

16 A Note to Our Readers, http://time.com/4645541/donald-trump-white-
    house-oval-office/.

17 Assad: Torture Report Part of the 'Fake News Era', http://www.washington
    examiner.com/assad-torture-report-part-of-the-fake-news-era/article/
    2614479

18 Jeremy Corbyn Accuses BBC of Reporting 'Fake News' When Challenged
    on Resignation Rumours, http://www.independent.co.uk/news/uk/politics/
    jeremy-corbyn-bbc-fake-news-trump-reignation-rumours-labour-party-
    leader-clive-lewis-brexit-bill-a7570721.html

19 'Any Negative Polls Are Fake News' Claims Donald Trump, http://www.tele
    graph.co.uk/news/2017/02/06/negative-polls-fake-news-claims-trump/

20 Donald Trump's Press Conference Defended By Sebastian Gorka in Crazy
    Newsnight Interview, http://www.huffingtonpost.co.uk/entry/donald-
    trumps-press-conference_uk_58a6a02ee4b037d17d26854e

21 Defining the Elite Media, http://www.foxnews.com/story/2004/03/08/
    defining-elite-media.html

22 Mainstream Media IS Fake News! http://www.rushlimbaugh.com/daily/
    2016/12/09/mainstream_media_is_fake_news

23 'Fake News' Inquiry Launched, https://www.parliament.uk/business/
    committees/committees-a-z/commons-select/culture-media-and-sport-
    committee/news-parliament-2015/fake-news-launch-16-17/

24 Disinformation and 'Fake News': Interim Report, https://publications.
    parliament.uk/pa/cm201719/cmselect/cmcumeds/363/36302.htm

25 It's Time to Ditch the Term 'Fake News', http://politics.co.uk/comment-
    analysis/2018/07/29/it-s-time-to-ditch-the-term-fake-news

26 Information Disorder: Toward an Interdisciplinary Framework for
    Research and Policymaking, https://shorensteincenter.org/information-
    disorder-framework-for-research-and-policymaking/

27 Let's Stop Talking About 'Honour Killing'. There Is No Honour in Murder,
    https://www.theguardian.com/commentisfree/2014/jun/23/stop-honour-
    killing-murder-women-oppresive-patriarchy

28 I Helped Popularize the Term 'Fake News' and Now I Cringe Every Time
    I Hear It, https://www.buzzfeednews.com/article/craigsilverman/i-helped-
    popularize-the-term-fake-news-and-now-i-cringe#.yaKaGpd9V

Chapter 10

1 34 Years Ago, a KGB Defector Chillingly Predicted Modern America,
   https://bigthink.com/paul-ratner/34-years-ago-a-kgb-defector-described-
   america-today

2 How Much of the Internet Is Fake? Turns Out, a Lot of It, Actually, http://
   nymag.com/intelligencer/2018/12/how-much-of-the-internet-is-fake.html

3 Shooting at Sandy Hook Elementary School, Report of the Office of the
   Child Advocate, http://www.ct.gov/oca/lib/oca/sandyhook11212014.pdf

4 The Sandy Hook Hoax, http://nymag.com/daily/intelligencer/2016/09/the-
   sandy-hook-hoax.html

5 Limbaugh: Maybe the Mayan Apocalypse Made Adam Lanza Do It,
   https://www.salon.com/2012/12/20/limbaugh_maybe_the_mayan_
   apocalypse_made_adam_lanza_do_it/

6 Ricoeur, P. (1977) *Freud and Philosophy: An Essay on Interpretation*, trans.
   D. Savage, Yale University Press.

7 *Julius Caesar*, Act 1, Scene 2, lines 411–18.

8 Donald Trump Campaign Offered Actors $50 to Cheer for Him at
   Presidential Announcement, https://www.hollywoodreporter.com/news/
   donald-trump-campaign-offered-actors-803161

9 The 'Hire a Crowd' Business Operates Openly and Makes Journalism
   Even More, https://www.poynter.org/news/hire-crowd-business-operates-
   openly-and-makes-journalism-even-more-difficult

10 Remember the Newsnight 'Vicar' Who Supported Theresa May's Brexit
    Deal? She's a BBC ACTOR, https://evolvepolitics.com/remember-the-news
    night-vicar-who-supported-theresa-mays-brexit-deal-shes-a-bbc-actor/

11 Where the 'Crisis Actor' Conspiracy Theory Comes From, https://mother
    board.vice.com/en_us/article/pammy8/what-is-a-crisis-actor-conspiracy-
    theory-explanation-parkland-shooting-sandy-hook

12 Alex Jones, Pursued Over Infowars Falsehoods, Faces a Legal Crossroads, https://www.nytimes.com/2018/07/31/us/politics/alex-jones-defamation-suit-sandy-hook.html

13 President Trump's Favorite Conspiracy Theorist Is Just 'Playing a Character', His Lawyer Says, http://time.com/4743025/alex-jones-infowars-divorce-donald-trump/

14 In Travis County Custody Case, Jury Will Search for Real Alex Jones, https://www.statesman.com/news/20170418/exclusive-in-travis-county-custody-case-jury-will-search-for-real-alex-jones

15 Romanian Absurd: A Ruling Party That Calls a Protest Meeting, https://www.euractiv.com/section/justice-home-affairs/news/romanian-absurd-a-ruling-party-that-calls-a-protest-meeting/

16 Romania's Counterfeit Protest, https://emerging-europe.com/from-the-editor/romanias-counterfeit-protest/

17 The Romanian 'Parallel State': The Political Phantasies of Feeble Populism, http://www.criticatac.ro/lefteast/the-romanian-parallel-state-the-political-phantasies-of-feeble-populism/

18 Cited in: Romanian Absurd: A Ruling Party That Calls a Protest Meeting, https://www.euractiv.com/section/justice-home-affairs/news/romanian-absurd-a-ruling-party-that-calls-a-protest-meeting/

19 Paxton, R. (2004) *The Anatomy of Fascism*, Alfred A. Knopf.

20 Claiming 'Parallel State' Cabal, Romania's Leaders Target Anti-corruption Prosecutor, https://www.nytimes.com/2018/06/17/world/europe/romania-corruption-prosecutors.html

21 Nearly Half of Americans Think There's a 'Deep State': Poll, https://abcnews.go.com/Politics/lies-damn-lies-deep-state-plenty-americans-poll/story?id=47032061

22 2017: The Year in Resistance, http://www.breitbart.com/big-government/2017/12/24/hold-2017-the-year-in-resistance/

23 https://twitter.com/DanRather/status/1020336734553292801

24 Steve Hilton: Yes There Is a Deep State – And Tony Blair Warned Me About It, http://www.foxnews.com/opinion/2018/02/03/steve-hilton-yes-there-is-deep-state-and-tony-blair-warned-me-about-it.html

25 From Westworld to Homeland: Pop Culture's Obsession with Gaslighting, https://www.theguardian.com/tv-and-radio/2017/jan/21/gaslighting-westworld-archers-jessica-jones-homeland

26 Jones, N. (1991) *Through a Glass Darkly: The Life of Patrick Hamilton*, Scribners, p. 211.

27 Welch, B. (2008) *State of Confusion: Political Manipulation and the Assault on the American Mind*, Thomas Dunne Books.

28 Donald Trump Is Gaslighting America, https://www.teenvogue.com/story/donald-trump-is-gaslighting-america

29 Carpenter, A. B. (2018) *Gaslighting America*, HarperCollins.

30 Donald Trump Brags of Achievements and Promises NRA: I'll Defend Gun Rights, https://www.theguardian.com/us-news/2018/may/04/trump-nra-convention-dallas-gun-control

Chapter 11

1 Chekhov's Gun, https://tvtropes.org/pmwiki/pmwiki.php/Main/ChekhovsGun

2 Epileptic Trees, https://tvtropes.org/pmwiki/pmwiki.php/Main/EpilepticTrees

3 Barthes, R. (1977) *Image Music Text*, trans. S. Heath, Fontana, p. 89.

4 Forster, E. M. (1927) *Aspects of the Novel*, Edward Arnold.

5 Sloman, S. A. (2005) *Causal Models: How People Think About the World and Its Alternatives*, Oxford University Press.

6 Leslie, A. M. (1982) 'The Perception of Causality in Infants', *Perception*, 11, pp. 173–86.

7 Danks, D. (2009) 'The Psychology of Causal Perception and Reasoning', in H. Beebee, C. Hitchcock and P. Menzies (eds), *Oxford Handbook of Causation*, Oxford University Press, pp. 447–70.

8 Barkun, M. (2013) *A Culture of Conspiracy: Apocalyptic Visions in Contemporary America*, University of California Press, p. 8.

9 Suspicious Minds: Conspiracy Theories in the Age of Populism, https://www.martenscentre.eu/sites/default/files/publication-files/conspiracy-theories-populism-europe_0.pdf

10 Conspiracy and Democracy: History, Political Theory and Internet Research, http://www.conspiracyanddemocracy.org/about/

11 Study Shows 60% of Britons Believe in Conspiracy Theories, https://www.theguardian.com/society/2018/nov/23/study-shows-60-of-britons-believe-in-conspiracy-theories

12 Barkun, M. (2013) *A Culture of Conspiracy: Apocalyptic Visions in Contemporary America*, University of California Press.

13 Sarah Huckabee Sanders, Trump's Battering Ram, https://www.newyorker.com/magazine/2018/09/24/sarah-huckabee-sanders-trumps-battering-ram/

14 What a Book Critic Finds in Mark Judge's 'Wasted' 21 Years Later, https://www.nytimes.com/2018/10/02/books/wasted-mark-judge-memoir.html

15 This was despite a note at the beginning of the book saying that it was 'based on actual experiences' but that some of the names had been altered to protect the privacy of those involved. https://twitter.com/maassp/status/1045411516353302529

16 Barkun, M. (2003) *A Culture of Conspiracy: Apocalyptic Visions in Contemporary America*, University of California Press.

17 Brotherton, R. (2016) *Suspicious Minds: Why We Believe Conspiracy Theories*, Bloomsbury Sigma.

18 Margaret Atwood on How Donald Trump Helped 'The Handmaid's Tale', http://variety.com/2018/tv/news/margaret-atwood-handmaids-tale-trump-feminism-1202748535/

19 Weishaupt, I. (2016) *The Star Wars Conspiracy: Hidden Occult and Illuminati Symbolism of Aliens & the New Age*, CreateSpace Independent Publishing Platform.

20 The Rock Movie Plot 'May Have Inspired MI6 Source's Iraqi Weapons Claim', https://www.theguardian.com/uk-news/2016/jul/06/movie-plot-the-rock-inspired-mi6-sources-iraqi-weapons-claim-chilcot-report

21 'It Was Such Obvious Bullshit': The Rock Writer Shocked Film May Have Inspired False WMD Intelligence, https://www.theguardian.com/film/2016/jul/08/it-was-such-obvious-bullshit-the-rock-writer-shocked-film-may-have-inspired-false-wmd-intelligence

22 Margaret Atwood on What 'The Handmaid's Tale' Means in the Age of Trump', https://www.nytimes.com/2017/03/10/books/review/margaret-atwood-handmaids-tale-age-of-trump.html

23 Uscinski, J. E. and Parent, J. M. (2014) *American Conspiracy Theories*, Oxford University Press.

Chapter 12

1 *F for Fake*, dir. Orson Welles, 1973.

2 Plato (1987) *The Republic*, trans. D. Lee, Penguin, p. 363.

3 Sidney, P. (1973 [1595]) *An Apology for Poetry: Or, the Defence of Poesy*, ed. G. Shepherd, Manchester University Press, p. 123–4.

4 Megrahi's Doctor: 'I Just Provided an Opinion. Someone Else Let Him Go Free', https://www.theguardian.com/world/2010/aug/15/al-megrahi-karol-sikora-lockerbie

5 James Frey and His Publisher Settle Suit Over Lies, https://www.nytimes.com/2006/09/07/arts/07frey.html

6 Frey, J. (2003) *A Million Little Pieces*, John Murray, p. v.

7 Genette, G. (1997) *Paratexts: Thresholds of Interpretation*, Cambridge University Press.

8 Frey, J. (2003) *A Million Little Pieces*, John Murray, p. vii.

9 Picasso, P. (1968) 'Statement', in H. B. Chipp (ed.), *Theories of Modern Art: A Sourcebook by Artists and Critics*, University of California Press, p. 264.

10 Junk Male, https://www.theguardian.com/books/2003/may/18/biography.features

11 James Frey: 'I Always Wanted to Be the Outlaw', www.guardian.co.uk/books/2011/apr/19/james-frey-final-testament-bible

12 Frey, J. (2008) *Bright Shiny Morning*, John Murray, p. 1.

13 All Politicians Lie. Some Lie More Than Others, https://www.nytimes.com/2015/12/13/opinion/campaign-stops/all-politicians-lie-some-lie-more-than-others.html

14 Why Is This Lying Bastard Lying to Me? http://blogs.bl.uk/thenewsroom/2014/07/why-is-this-lying-bastard-lying-to-me.html

15 Cronin, T. and Genovese, E. (1998) *The Paradoxes of the American Presidency*, Oxford University Press, p. 4.

16 Machiavelli, N. (1984 [1532]) *The Prince*, trans. P. Bondanella and M. Musa, Oxford University Press, p. 58.

17 Meet the Bottomless Pinocchio, A New Rating for a False Claim Repeated Over and Over Again, https://www.washingtonpost.com/politics/2018/12/10/meet-bottomless-pinocchio-new-rating-false-claim-repeated-over-over-again/

18 Trump Allies Defend His Election Lie as 'Refreshing', http://www.msnbc.com/rachel-maddow-show/trump-allies-defend-his-election-lie-refreshing

19 Donald Trump's Ghostwriter Tells All, http://www.newyorker.com/magazine/2016/07/25/donald-trumps-ghostwriter-tells-all

20 Orwell, G. (2013 [1946]) *Politics and the English Language*, Penguin, p. 14.

21 Lying Politicians and Words, https://www.youtube.com/watch?v=SKftRlzh2RM

22 Let's Call a Lie a Lie … Finally, http://www.nytimes.com/2008/09/21/weekinreview/21healy.html

23 9 Absurd Rules About What You Can't Do in Parliament, http://www.independent.co.uk/news/uk/politics/9-absurd-things-youre-not-allowed-to-do-in-parliament-10250704.html

24 Unparliamentary Language, http://www.parliament.uk/site-information/glossary/unparliamentary-language/

25 The Media Coverage of Paul Ryan's Speech: 15 Euphemisms for 'Lying', http://theweek.com/articles/472744/media-coverage-paul-ryans-speech-15-euphemisms-lying

26 Let's Call a Lie a Lie … Finally, http://www.nytimes.com/2008/09/21/weekinreview/21healy.html

27 In a Swirl of 'Untruths' and 'Falsehoods', Calling a Lie a Lie, https://www.nytimes.com/2017/01/25/business/media/donald-trump-lie-media.html

28 NPR and the Word 'Liar': Intent Is Key, http://www.npr.org/sections/thetwo-way/2017/01/25/511503605/npr-and-the-l-word-intent-is-key

29 Isenberg, A. (1973) *Aesthetics and Theory of Criticism: Selected Essays of Arnold Isenberg*, University of Chicago Press, p. 248.

30 Spicer: 'Our Intention Is Never to Lie to You', http://www.politico.com/story/2017/01/sean-spicer-press-conference-no-intention-lie-234054

31 Fallis, D. (2010) 'Lying and Deception', *Philosophers' Imprint*, 10: 11.

32 The ASA Can't Regulate Political Advertisements. Here's Why, https://www.theguardian.com/commentisfree/2016/jul/06/advertising-standards-authority-political-advertisements

33 FTC Investigation of Ad Claims that Rice Krispies Benefits Children's Immunity Leads to Stronger Order Against Kellogg, https://www.ftc.gov/news-events/press-releases/2010/06/ftc-investigation-ad-claims-rice-krispies-benefits-childrens

34 Federal Judge Rejects Ohio Law Requiring Truth in Political Advertising, http://www.washingtontimes.com/news/2014/sep/11/federal-judge-rejects-ohio-law-requiring-truth-in-/

35 Grice, P. (1989) *Studies in the Way of Words*, Harvard University Press.

36 Trump, D. J. (2016) *Crippled America: How to Make America Great Again*, Simon & Schuster.

37 Grading the Obama Economy, by the Numbers, http://www.cnbc.com/
    2016/07/15/grading-the-obama-economy-by-the-numbers.html.

38 The Mind of Donald Trump, http://www.theatlantic.com/magazine/
    archive/2016/06/the-mind-of-donald-trump/480771/

39 Donald Trump Is BS, Says Expert in BS, http://time.com/4321036/donald-
    trump-bs/.

40 Delingpole: What It's Like to Die Horribly on a BBC Politics Show,
    https://www.breitbart.com/europe/2019/01/25/my-car-crash-interview-
    bbc-andrew-neil/

41 InfoWars Store, https://www.infowarsstore.com/infowars-media.html.

42 http://911truth.org/mission/

43 Veterans Long to Reclaim the Name 'Swift Boat', https://www.nytimes.
    com/2008/06/30/us/politics/30swift.html

44 The Doublespeak Award, http://www2.ncte.org/awards/doublespeak-award/

45 Past Recipients of the NCTE Doublespeak Award, http://www.ncte.org/
    library/NCTEFiles/Involved/Volunteer/Appointed_Groups/Past_
    Recipients_Doublespeak_Award.pdf

46 Catachresis, https://johnsonsdictionaryonline.com/catachresis/

47 Benkler, Y., Faris, R. and Roberts, H. (2018) *Network Propaganda:
    Manipulation, Disinformation, and Radicalization in American Politics*,
    Oxford University Press, p. 16.

Afterword

1 Word of the Year 2020, https://languages.oup.com/word-of-the-year/2020/.

2 White, H. (1973) *Metahistory: The Historical Imagination in Nineteenth-
   century Europe*, John Hopkins University.

3 Salmon, C. (2010) *Storytelling: Bewitching the Modern Mind*, Verso, p. 5.

4 For example Joe Biden's first @POTUS tweet is refreshingly boring,
   https://mashable.com/article/biden-first-potus-tweet; Boring Is Better,
   https://www.theatlantic.com/ideas/archive/2021/01/biden-should-build-
   back-boring/617740/.

5 The History Behind 'When The Looting Starts, The Shooting Starts',
   https://www.npr.org/2020/05/29/864818368/the-history-behind-when-the-
   looting-starts-the-shooting-starts.

Index